AF395562

Chiharu Shiota

Chiharu Shiota

THREADS OF LIFE

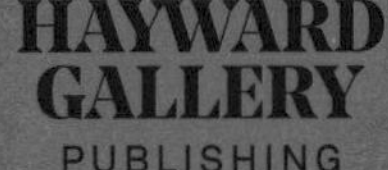

HAYWARD
GALLERY
PUBLISHING

In Chiharu Shiota's remarkable artworks, the boundaries between memory, space and emotion intertwine in unexpectedly powerful ways. Combining immersive, web-like thread structures and everyday objects, her deeply atmospheric installations explore themes of absence, presence and the intricate matrix of connections that define our lives. As they envelop viewers in a tactile embrace, these poignant installations potently conjure a sense of recollection and loss, and challenge us to reflect on both our own personal narratives and the shared stories that shape our collective consciousness.

In addition to her celebrated installations and sculptures, *Chiharu Shiota: Threads of Life* also features a selection of works on paper and videos and photographs of the artist's performances, offering an expanded understanding of her artistic preoccupations. Shiota's drawings, often characterised by delicate lines and organic patterns, evoke intimate networks of thought and emotion, whilst her performances – which emerged from her early interest in painting – often present her physical body as a canvas interacting with elements from different environments, reflecting on the inseparable character of individuality from the larger contexts that shape it. Spanning a career of three decades, all of Shiota's art compels us to reconsider our relationships with the spaces we inhabit and the memories we cherish.

This publication serves not only as a guide through her artistic journey but also as an invitation to engage with Shiota's art on a deeper level. Hayward Gallery Senior Curator Yung Ma's illuminating essay on the artist's work is complemented by her interview with the distinguished Japanese novelist Yoko Tawada. Featuring a generous array of images, this book has been vividly realised by the design studio In the shade of a tree, and in all its aspects has been creatively supervised by Hayward Publisher Mary Richards.

Chiharu Shiota: Threads of Life was realised with generous support provided by the Huo Family Foundation and Hiroyuki Maki. We are also grateful for key support from Max and Monique Burger and the TOY family, and Nicola Chu. Thanks also go to Hayward Senior Curator Yung Ma who has worked with the artist to fashion this highly compelling presentation of her work. Assistant Curator Suzanna Petot skilfully supported the organisation of this exhibition, with Curatorial Assistant Ananya Jain providing crucial additional support and Assistant Curator Katie Guggenheim carrying out important early organisation and research. Installation Manager Chris Spear planned and supervised the installation with consummate professionalism, whilst Registrar Sophie Ridsdale-Smith meticulously organised the transport and conservation arrangements for the works in the exhibition. We are all extremely appreciative of the outstanding work done by Chiharu's wonderful studio team in realising her exhibition, with particular thanks going to Julia Strebelow and Rosalie Pfleger, and above all, of course, our deepest thanks go to Chiharu Shiota herself, for creating artworks that touch our most profound emotions and inspire our imagination.

As always, I am grateful for the enthusiastic support of Southbank Centre Chief Executive Elaine Bedell, Artistic Director Mark Ball and Southbank Centre's Board of Governors. Finally, it would not have been possible to realise this exhibition without the ongoing support of Arts Council England.

Ralph Rugoff
Director, Hayward Gallery

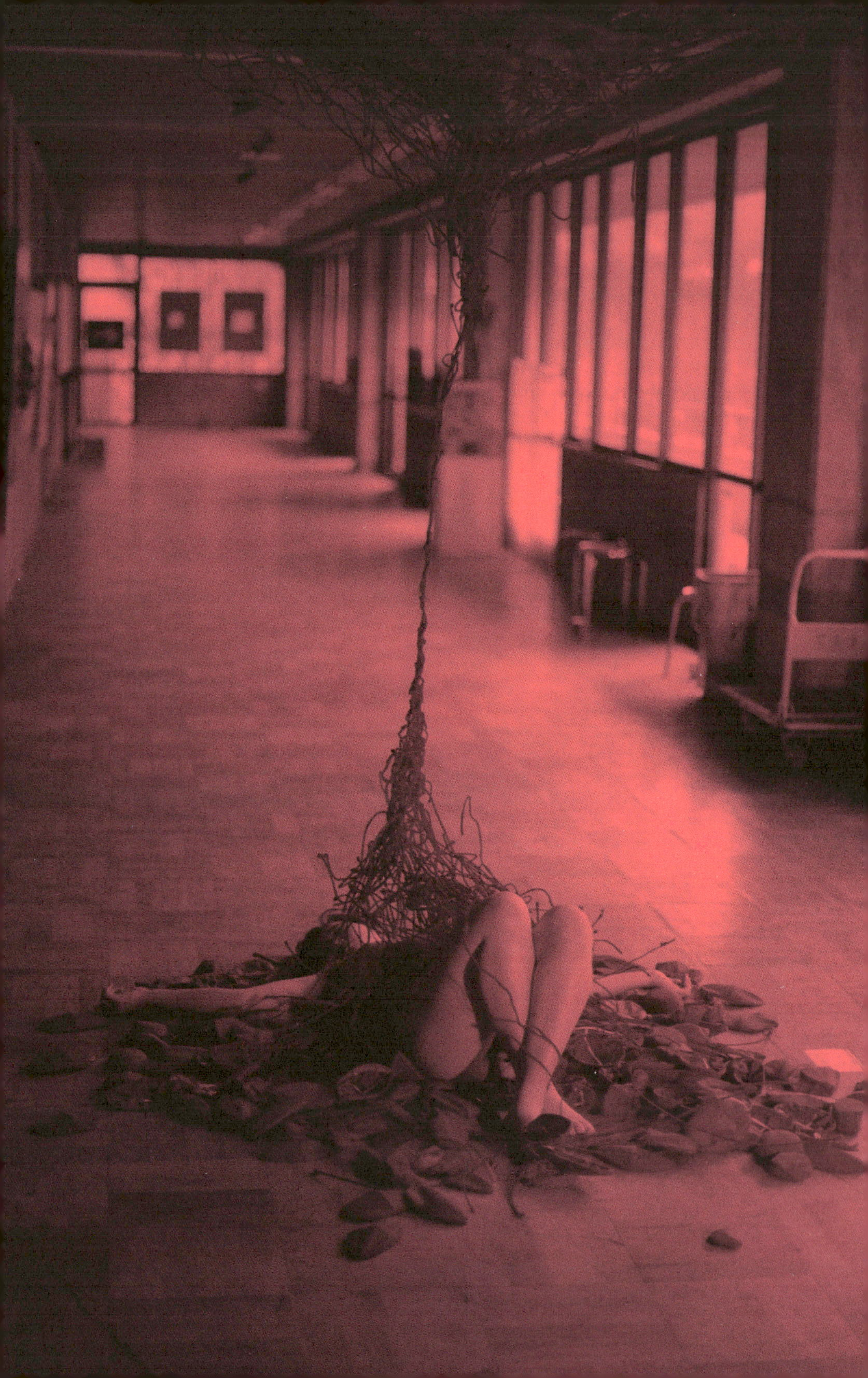

YUNG MA

Ten Thousand Layers of Connections: The Art of Chiharu Shiota

The Japanese myth says that when a child is born, a red thread is tied around their finger. It's an extension of a blood vessel from their heart to their little finger. This thread will be tied to another person. They are destined to meet and to be in each other's lives.[1]

Chiharu Shiota has spoken about how her art is linked to *Unmei no Akai Ito*, often referred to in non-Japanese-speaking parts of the world as the Red Thread of Fate or, more recently in popular culture, the Invisible String Theory, a centuries-old and widely known Japanese legend about how two people are destined to be connected by an invisible red thread. This thematic connection is especially evident in pieces such as *Connected to the Universe* (p. 128), a group of drawings Shiota began in 2019 in which threads connect small lone figures to much larger, cloud-like circular structures or organic, almost amoeba-like masses.

While this legend of a couple bound by fate is largely a romantic one, other readings have applied *Unmei no Akai Ito* to all forms of human connections and relationships. Just as many other ancient myths and lores transcend modern-day geopolitical borders, variations on this central idea concerning fate and destiny can be found in other East Asian traditions. For instance, in Chinese mythology the story of the red thread is known as *Yīnyuán*; unlike its Japanese counterpart, however, this version is solely devoted to the prospect of finding one's partner in love and life.

In Korean culture, meanwhile, this concept of providence is called *Inyeon*. This term, and the philosophy it describes, has been passed down for generations in Korea, but has in recent years garnered noticeable popularity online beyond the peninsula, thanks to Celine Song's 2023 film *Past Lives*, which embraces *Inyeon* as a core device to shape a narrative of fate, longing and missed opportunities. As described by the film's female protagonist, *Inyeon* is specifically about relationships between people, and is believed to be rooted in the Buddhist ideology of reincarnation. As she explains in the script: 'It's an "*Inyeon*" if two strangers even walk by each other in the street and their clothes accidentally brush. Because ... it means there must have been something between them in their past lives. If two people get married, they say it's because there have been eight thousand layers of "*Inyeon*", over eight thousand lifetimes.'[2]

Although *Past Lives* is categorised as a romantic drama, and the central story itself takes the form of a loose love triangle, the idea of *Inyeon* carries a much broader connotation than merely romantic love. And while the fact goes unmentioned in Song's film, *Inyeon*, too, is often symbolised as two souls being tied together across different lifetimes by a red thread woven by an ancestral spirit.

With this in mind, I would argue that the image of multiple layers of red threads conjured up by the concept of *Inyeon* is the clearest analogue for Chiharu Shiota's large-scale, immersive, often room-sized installations, which intricately weave together layers and layers of red, black or white threads to create web-like structures and arches enclosing ordinary household and utilitarian objects – doors, windows, chairs, suitcases, keys and shoes. Shiota sources many of these items from flea markets and thrift stores; sometimes, she even salvages them from the streets. Her love of 'rescuing' these objects and giving them new lives by turning them into elements of her artworks can be considered a form of reincarnation – a further echo of the Buddhist roots of *Inyeon*. Additionally, this act of incorporating objects, of tying and linking them with threads in her installations, speaks to Shiota's interest in making visible the hidden connections that surround us, beyond human relationships. She makes use of our familiarity with these commonplace objects and their inherent material memories to suggest a much wider and more expansive view of how we, collectively and as individuals, situate and relate to one another in the world. More significantly still, the process of creating these installations is no doubt labour-intensive; it is therefore unsurprising that, even though the body is absent from these fixed and static environments, one can nonetheless sense and feel the traces, even the presence, of human handiwork. In this case, Shiota herself is that invisible force. She is the unseen hands that continuously weave these objects and relationships together, as if she has dissolved into them to become the threads that connect.

*

One of the central components that allows Shiota to connect her own experiences with others' is the muddling of any sense of time and place in her works, a quality that has been consistently in evidence since her earliest ventures into artmaking. In the 1994 photographic performance *Becoming Painting*, now presented as a series of six photographs (see pp. 13, 33, 35), Shiota is seen standing in a nondescript, studio-like white space, dressed in an oversized piece of white cloth and gradually being drenched in red enamel paint. Here, any temporal or spatial contexts are decidedly irrelevant. Made during a time when Shiota was studying painting in Australia, the work is rooted in a dream – more aptly, a nightmare – she had about making self-portraits, in which she found herself trapped and suffocated inside an oil painting. To 'exorcise' those demons, Shiota proceeded to 'enact' the dream by pouring red paint over all herself, making her own body a canvas and effectively transforming herself into a painting. This act of alteration, of turning the concrete and the familiar into something abstract, even lyrical, is a further crucial element in enabling the artist to connect with others. By embracing and implementing this notion of transformation, be it of her own body or a mundane (gallery) space, Shiota has created something 'otherworldly'. Her world is a universe, an environment in which all locational signifiers are removed, leaving us to engage directly with the visual, bodily and tactile sensations and emotions embedded within it.

This sense of open-endedness, of temporal and spatial ambiguity, is also apparent in Shiota's *Try and Go Home* (1997, pp. 36–37). The work, presented as six black-and-white photographic prints, is the result of an intense five-day workshop in a castle in northern France organised by Marina Abramović, Shiota's tutor at the University of Fine Arts, Hamburg.[3] The photographs – which one might describe as a photographic performance – capture a naked Shiota, covered in dirt, climbing, rolling, sliding and crawling on a muddy slope as she tries (and fails) to get herself into a cave-like hole. In its use of the artist's own body as the predominant medium within the natural landscape, the work is, formally speaking, reminiscent of the earth body artworks made by Cuban American artist Ana Mendieta in the 1970s. Instead of focusing on the relationship between the body and the earth, however, Shiota's central idea here is 'home', represented in this work by the cave (or hole); her repeated and failed effort to fit into this supposedly comforting space is a physical manifestation of her experience of moving and living abroad. Yet the work also speaks to a more universal feeling of the diaspora experience – the feeling of wanting to go back home but being unsure how or whether one can still fit in. The ambiguous sense of existing somewhere in-between, a growing sensation of being this one thing yet also something else, never entirely sure where one stands. Of this work, Shiota has said: 'The morning after a gruelling five-day class ... the word that came to my mind was "Japan". I want to return to Japan. I want to go back there, but when I do, I don't feel at home ...'[4]

In the video performance piece *Wall* (2010, pp. 40–41), Shiota is seen lying or kneeling naked on the floor of a brightly lit, clinical white space, draped beneath piles of entangled coils of thin and transparent plastic tubes. Her fingers twitch and her chest heaves rapidly, yet the rest of her body moves only slightly. Bright red liquid runs and circulates hurriedly through the tubes, filling them with a blood-like substance, and the viewer quickly notices that time is altered, or perhaps condensed, in this space. The video is accompanied by the sound of mechanical thumping, hinting at the idea of blood being pumped through blood vessels. As the video plays on, more tubes appear atop and around the artist, tangling up and trapping Shiota's apparently sleeping (or at least motionless) body underneath. This can certainly be read as the externalisation of her internal 'red threads' of connections, exposed for the world to see. Yet, this should also be seen as Shiota's attempt to visualise the outpouring of her life force, her identity, the DNA that makes her who she is. These tubes, these blood vessels, are walls that protect her as well as confine her, giving her life while draining it away all at once.

Shiota's art is concrete, sensual, emotional, evocative – even intuitive. Rather than being guided by a set of rational ideas or principles, she chooses to react to materials and spaces with her instincts and feelings. Her works excite and overwhelm; they are at once joyful and melancholic. And beneath the act of weaving together webs of human connections with each other and the wider world, her drawings, sculptures and large thread installations enclose her personal feelings, memories and experiences: the passing of loved ones, the birth of her child, her recurring illness and her search for belonging. Her works turn the personal into the universal, creating art that explores the meaning of life, of being alive and how our bonds can go beyond the physical bounds of our material world.

In *During Sleep*, a room-sized woven installation first shown in 2002 (pp. 70–73), metal-framed single beds made up with white linens are engulfed in webs of black threads. Preceded by Shiota's earlier bed and thread installation *Breathing from Earth* (2000), *During Sleep* was also somewhat akin to *Becoming Painting*, in which the idea of dreaming was also the cornerstone. The 2002 work was largely influenced by the artist's own lack of restful sleep at the time, owing to her constant need to move apartments over a period of three years

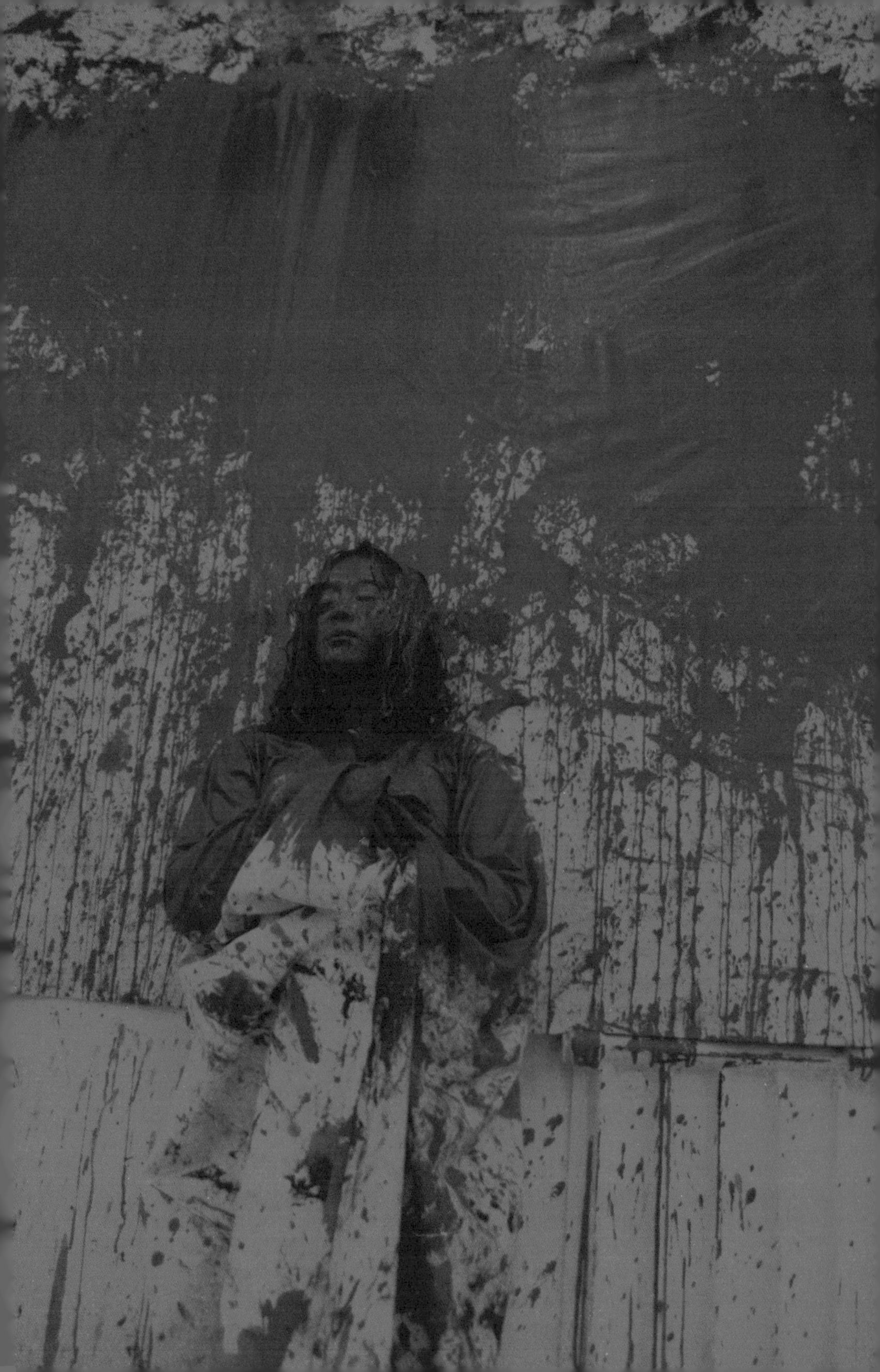

in Germany. Sleeplessness led to Shiota developing a growing feeling of losing her sense of place in a foreign land: 'I would wake up in the morning, uncertain where I was. I was desperate to create a space of my own. While I was sitting in bed, I picked up some yarn and started weaving it around my body. It was like painting in the air.'[5]

During Sleep was, on the one hand, Shiota's attempt to explore an ambiguous state that oscillates between falling asleep and being awake – a gestural manifestation of creating as well as blurring the potential space between dreaming and reality. The dense layers of black threads also cast a sense of darkness, both literal and metaphorical, over the gallery space, no doubt a visual representation of night-time and an emotional response to Shiota's sense of dislocation. Yet I suspect that in enveloping and cocooning each bed in these threads, Shiota was seeking also to create and convey a feeling of lasting peacefulness, of lying quietly and restfully in the embrace of an eternal nightfall.

It is worth noting that *During Sleep* unequivocally cemented Shiota's departure from traditional painting, even as it reaffirmed her connection to the medium in another form: the threads may be viewed as lines in a painting, and the act of weaving them becomes a way of creating a painting in space. Like many of her works, *During Sleep* – or variations of the work, with different titles – has been restaged in various scales and forms across countries since its inception, including a 2004 version at the Église Sainte-Marie-Madeleine in Lille and a 2016 iteration entitled *Conscious Sleep* (2016, p. 79) installed in a former penal establishment on Cockatoo Island for the 20th Biennale of Sydney. In some presentations *During Sleep* is populated by performers, including Shiota herself, recumbent in a dreamlike state in the beds. Given the site-specific nature of Shiota's installations, that the work should change in each iteration is inevitable. Her works can therefore be viewed as living entities that shift, evolve and grow organically through a practical lens. Moreover, this malleability suggests, intriguingly, a connectedness across Shiota's entire oeuvre – that she has been weaving a web from work to work, loosely linking them in a metaphysical manner across time and space.

Within this network, further connections can be traced. Shiota's ongoing series of 'webbed' sculptures, presented under the umbrella title *State of Being*, all contain various daily (used) items. In *State of Being (Dress)* (2025, p. 51), a white dress is suspended floating inside a black metal box, enveloped by scores of black threads. Dresses are one of the recurring 'motifs' in Shiota's practice. *Memory of Skin* (2001, pp. 38–39) is an early example, featuring five exceedingly large hanging dresses covered in dirt and soil. In the 2009 group exhibition *Walking in My Mind* at the Hayward Gallery, her first exhibition in the UK, Shiota presented *After the Dream* (pp. 48–49): occupying an entire room in the gallery, the work featured three monumental white dresses suspended within a thick, almost impregnable, web of black yarn. Playing on the idea that clothing serves as our 'second skin', the dress featured in the 2025 work is a particularly poignant illustration of Shiota's belief that objects are embodiments of human experiences, while the deliberate absence of a body paradoxically further amplifies the supposed presence of its wearer. This strategy of extracting herself (or any other bodies) from the work, leaving only a matrix of threads that hints at some sort of presence, brings forth the possibility of knitting together a lingering and haunting tapestry of unknowable memories from the past.

Letters of Thanks (2013) and its subsequent evolutions (pp. 44–47, 83–97) likewise grows organically from location to location. Comprising a number of thank-you letters woven into a ceiling-mounted, web-like structure of black threads, the work was first installed as a solo exhibition at the Museum of Art, Kochi in Japan. Shiota initially conceived the installation to explore emotional connections between its participants, but during its creation she found that it carried a profound personal resonance. Kochi is her parents' hometown, and as the piece unfolded, she realised that the letters – and the work as a whole – embodied the words and feelings she had been unable to express while her father was still alive. *Letters of Thanks* has since been exhibited in Austria, Brazil, Denmark and Germany, with Shiota incorporating fresh thank-you letters collected from each location. While previous versions have utilised black threads, Hayward's iteration is presented as a red 'rope' installation in which letters of thanks, including those Shiota has collected in London, are attached to thicker threads hanging from a net stretched across the top of the gallery's walls.

Threads of Life (2025), Shiota's latest room-sized woven installation, is produced specifically for this exhibition. The work is a reincarnation of her 2016 installation *The Locked Room* (pp. 59–65), in which seven single doors stand amid a dense network of red threads strung with numerous keys. At the centre of the physically and viscerally striking *Threads of Life* is one single set of old wooden double doors. Resembling a portal, they at once command our attention and arouse our curiosity. These doors are consumed by a series of twisted arches of red threads that link together hundreds of old keys, one of which may unlock the secret of what lies on the other side of them. Shiota's new work transforms the gallery space into an otherworldly environment that sits outside of our reality – yet, rather than obscuring the boundaries between the real and the illusory, this interstitial space is a decidedly tangible one. It invites us to explore and experience the familiar in an ethereal setting, under an anatomy of webs that suggest connections transcending self, body and humanity.

The thousand layers of threads Shiota creates reflect her sincere belief in our interconnectedness. Whether inspired by her own memories, dreams, feelings and experiences or those of others, her art puts forward the simple but vital idea that our shared human condition contains multitudes of universality. Just as an ancestral spirit weaves the red thread that connects two souls together in *Inyeon*, the hands of Shiota are omnipresent. They repeatedly and continuously draw and paint in space with her red, black and white threads, reminding us of all the connections that bind us together.

1   Denise Wendel-Poray (ed.), *Chiharu Shiota* (Paris: Editions Skira, 2024), p. 38

2   Celine Song, *Past Lives: Screenplay Book* (New York: A24, 2025)

3   In 1996, Shiota went to study at the University of Fine Arts in Hamburg under the mentorship of Marina Abramović. It was a curious case of mistaken identity as Shiota thought she was applying to study under Polish artist Magdalena Abakanowicz, whose exhibition she had seen in Japan at the age of 19. For the workshop in France, organised as part of Abramović's class, students were asked to fast and refrain from speaking for four days.

4   *Chiharu Shiota I to EYE*, exh. cat., Nakanoshima Museum of Art, Osaka, 2024, p. 90

5   Wendel-Poray (ed.), 2024, p. 77

During Sleep, 2002

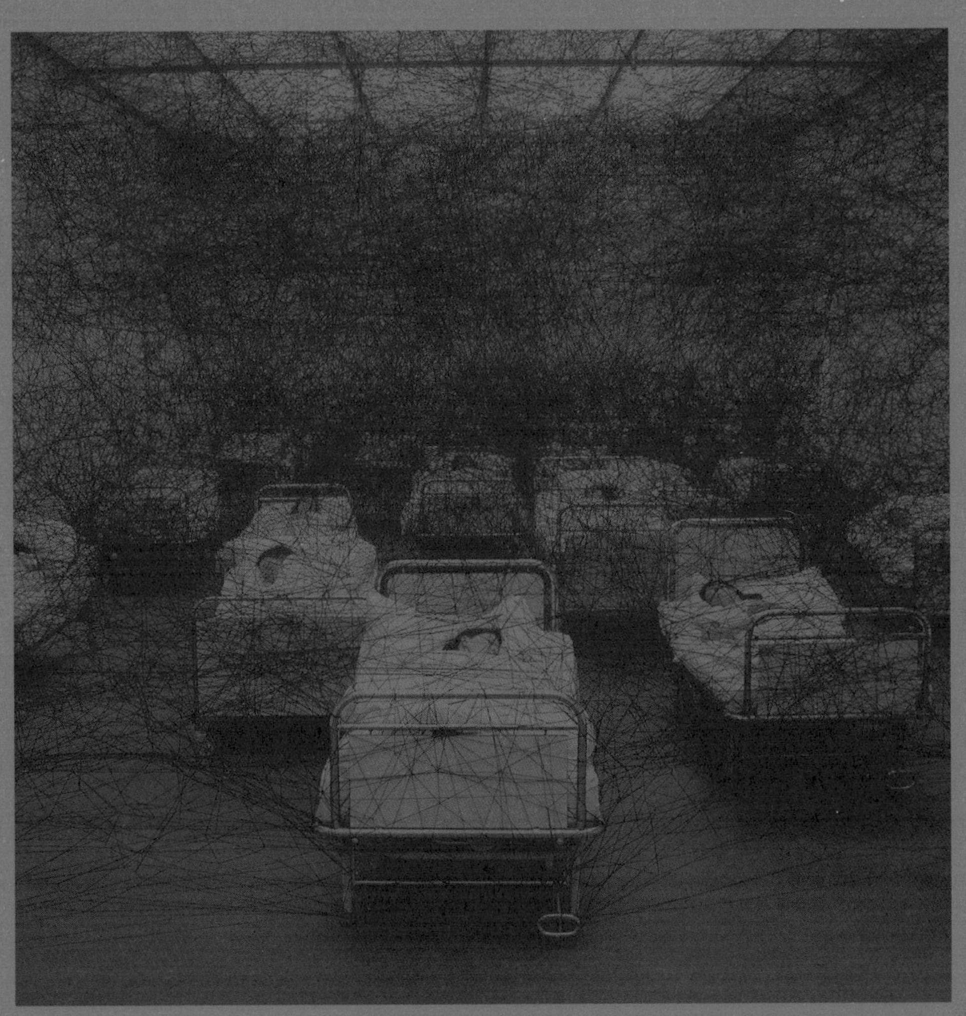

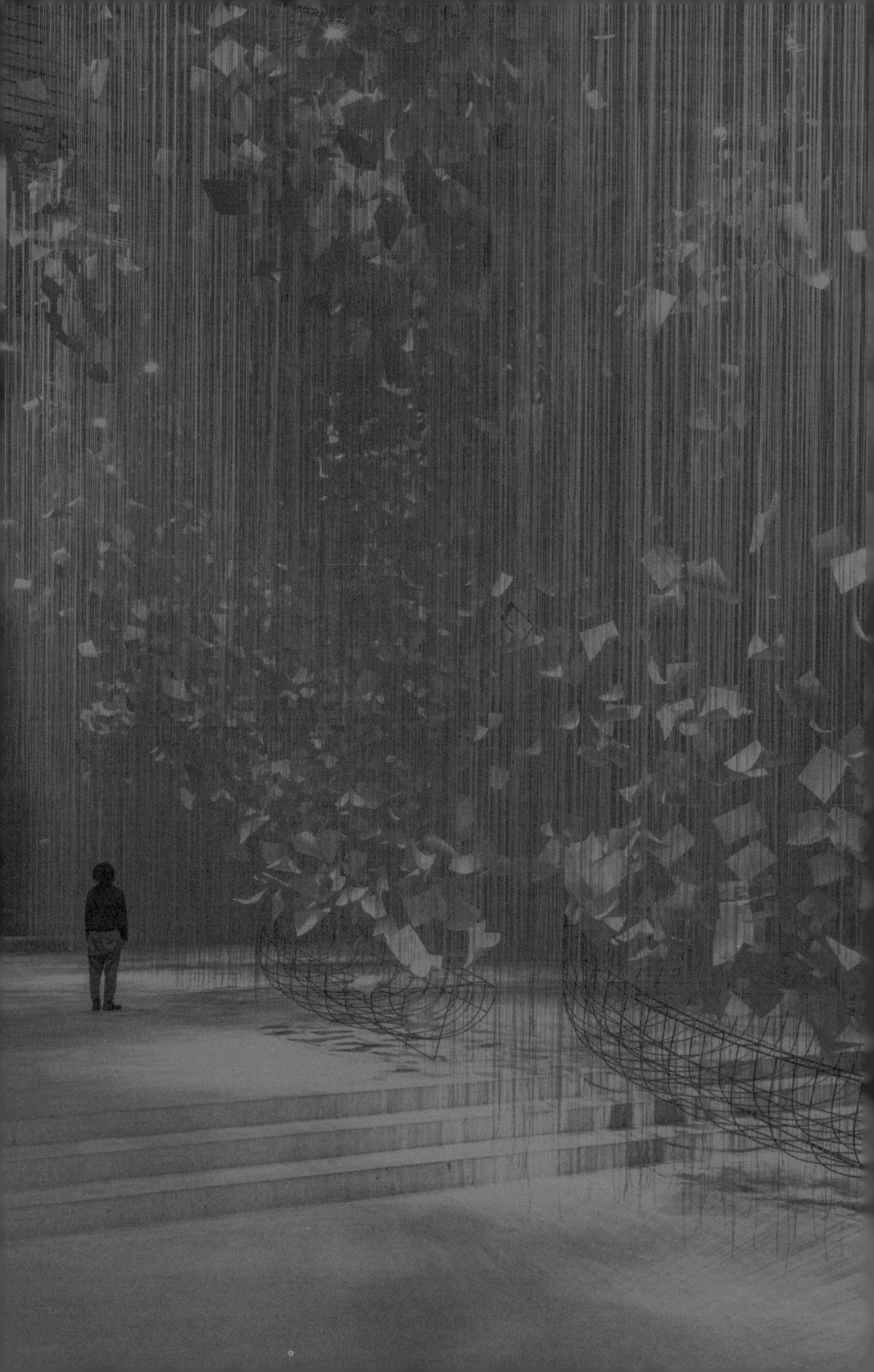

In
Conversation

YOKO TAWADA   Recently, I've been feeling annoyed when reading texts written by AI. If you give AI a task – 'Yoko Tawada interviewing Chiharu Shiota', for example – the results at first seem impressive. The fact that a machine can process such a task is truly amazing, and I do think the technology is incredible – but when I look more closely at the content, I think it still doesn't work. For example, the AI came up with this question: 'Your work doesn't use words, but it still tells a personal story. Do you think the threads you use are a kind of language?'

The question 'Is thread a language?' may not be meaningless to an interviewer who believes that language connects people, but it's meaningless to an artist. To begin with, I don't think you're even thinking about what thread is when you're using thread. I can't help but feel that you're using your brain for something else entirely – if that weren't the case, you wouldn't be able to create such wonderful works. If possible, please tell me what you're thinking as you string the threads of your installation together – a task that must take days.

CHIHARU SHIOTA　　　Yes, it can take about two weeks to install it in a museum. It's true that thread, for me, is neither a language nor just a material. Just as a painting is not just a canvas and oil paint, thread is much more than that. I paint with thread, I paint with thread all over the space. Every time the thread gets tangled, I feel that tangle in my own heart, and if I can't untangle it, I cut the thread. By repeating this movement of the heart and the movement of the thread, I want to convey something more than just the thread – something like a solid truth that lies deeper. Keeping that in mind lets me weave space to the fullest. And it's when the thread that fills the space no longer looks like thread to anyone that I feel the work is complete.

YT　　　I see – so, I need to imagine painting in three-dimensional space, rather than on two-dimensional paper. And as I do so, the threads that make up my handwriting become more and more tangled.

As a novelist, I'm interested in whether, when you touch the thread and feel the tangle in your heart, the Japanese (or other) words for 'tangled' or 'entangled' come to mind. Or are you directly connecting your state of mind with the state of the thread, without language?

CS　　　When I touch the thread and feel the tangle in my heart, it is certainly not put into words. Similarly, when I create a work, I don't do it with any particular meaning or concept in mind, but simply with the emotions I have at the time. At first, I don't even know why I want to create this kind of work, but as I get closer to completion, I begin to understand the reason. There is something that appeals to the eyes and is conveyed to the heart. I always hope to discover something there.

I remember learning about Marcel Duchamp's concept of 'delay', which meant that the meaning of a work is not put into words before it is created. Rather, language comes afterwards.

YT　　　I myself always use words to see and think about things. When I look at works using thread, I initially feel a sense of 'restraint', but then I realise that it is not restraint, but its opposite – not necessarily 'liberation', but rather a feeling of being tied together, connected. When I look at your work, Chiharu, I think that the way things are tied together, but not tangled or knotty, is a beautiful way to connect things.

CS　　　I'm really glad to hear you say that, Yoko, that you feel those two different things.

YT　　　Interviews with artists are very common these days, so I imagine you have many opportunities to put your work into words, but do you think language would be necessary for creativity if there were no journalists?

CS	Because words contain strong meanings, if I describe the red thread as 'blood-like rain', the viewer's imagination won't expand beyond blood-like rain. So, even if the final result looks like blood-like rain, while I'm creating it I'm having a much broader conversation with the red thread.

Ultimately, I believe that contemporary art is visual art, and I try not to create works that require the viewer to delve into a text or concept before experiencing them.

CS	When we used AI to generate this conversation, it suggested that here I would ask you the following question: 'Yoko, you write in both Japanese and German. Do you think each language expresses a different side of you?' But I believe that translating Japanese into German is translating the culture, and that each language does not simply express a different side of Yoko. The words contain the person, their smell, the space of their life. I believe that the two languages express not just one side, but a larger, three-dimensional space. So instead of the AI suggestion, I'd like to ask you how you create that three-dimensional space when writing in a language other than your native language, and how you interact with people.

YT	I once heard someone say that immigrant writers who write in two languages are actually writing in a third language. I can't remember who said that – I think it was a German-speaking writer from a Muslim or Southern European country. While you could put it that way, I personally think of something heavenly and sacred when I hear 'third language'. Instead, I imagine my work as being grounded, with a concrete German language meeting a concrete Japanese language and their bodies vibrating against each other. There are many different parts that vibrate – things that were previously fixed tremble and soften. But in this image, both languages are two-dimensional, and both are firmly planted on the ground, so to speak. Perhaps this is what Duchamp was suggesting, and the third dimension emerges when the element of time is added – when scenes from a novel become images in the reader's mind, or when it's translated into another language by the translator.

By the way, on the subject of translation, if a novel is written in Japanese, unless it is translated then it can only be read by people who can read Japanese. Art, on the other hand, can be taken as is and exhibited in various countries. To me, this seems like a natural thing, yet it's also a very mysterious phenomenon.

CS	I've been exhibiting in Korea and Japan for the past two weeks, and I've been thinking about translation. It's true that artworks can be exhibited all over the world without translation. I believe they have the power to appeal to people visually. However, even in art, there are certainly borders that cannot be crossed.

Speaking of translation, in preparation for my upcoming exhibition in New York, I visited Donald Keene's former home in Tokyo just three days ago. In 1943, before the end of the war, while he was assigned to the Naval Intelligence Office in Hawaii, he was translating the diary of a Japanese soldier, and was deeply moved by a note written in English on the last page: 'I want this diary to be delivered to my family when the war is over'. Indeed, he was inspired to actually return the diary to the soldier's family himself. He went on to not only translate a number of books from Japanese to English but to write several in Japanese himself. In his autobiography, Keene wrote that reading this diary was one of the catalysts that drew him even more deeply to Japanese literature, stating: 'My job is to prove that Japanese literature is world literature.'

Last year I received an invitation from the Japan Society Gallery in New York to create a work commemorating the eightieth anniversary of the end of the Second World War. They were asking me to create a connection between Japan and the US, and I remembered Keene's work and his notion of belonging to two home countries. After rereading his book, this passage especially inspired me to create a work from these soldiers' diaries. After further research I discovered that some of the wartime diaries of Japanese soldiers are kept at the National Archives outside Washington, DC – some of them are riddled with bullet holes and bloodstains. I contacted the Donald Keene Memorial Foundation, who were very kind and helpful, and so I'm presenting a work in which I tie copies of these diaries together with red thread. The exhibition is titled *Two Home Countries*. You don't have to have just one home country, do you? Perhaps if we had two or even three, wars would stop happening. That's the feeling I had as I approached this work. I felt that these diaries conveyed the feelings of soldiers not as enemies or allies, but as human beings. Many of my works are created from a single word that moves me in this way.

YT   I've also been thinking more about translation lately, because I was also in Japan recently, to see the opera *Natasha*, for which I wrote the libretto – the first time I've done this. It's a multilingual opera, with two German-speaking characters and one Japanese-speaking character, and many other languages heard. At first, the two main characters can't understand each other's language, but as they travel through hell together, they begin to understand each other on a level that transcends language.

Writing a libretto was quite different from the process of writing a novel on my own. I incorporated the composer's wishes from the writing stage and rewrote the work several times. Also, when I saw it performed on stage, I was surprised at how much of an impression the stage design made on the audience. In any case, I learned a lot through this 'collaboration'. Literary works are written so that the reader is prompted to visualise the words in their mind, but in film or theatrical art, the actual images are presented to the audience in a visible form from the start, so it's no longer necessary to use words spoken on the spot to evoke the images. If there is an image first and you are allowed to write words about it, I think the words can have a variety of effects, such as deconstructing the first impression the image gives, or suggesting a new interpretation that makes the same image appear different. I know you have also had experience of producing opera productions or collaborating with music and dance, Chiharu.

CS   Is Natasha Russian? Or is it a Ukrainian woman's name? Isn't it amazing that people who don't understand each other's languages can understand each other after experiencing hell? We all started out in a place where we couldn't understand each other, and as we go through this interview, I've started to think that perhaps it is we artists who are translating this incomprehensible world.

YT   I did indeed write Natasha as Ukrainian, although that fact does not appear in the libretto itself. I've been to Ukraine about four times, and I wrote the first draft of this libretto before Russia's military invasion. I began writing from the premise that a young man named Arato from Fukushima and a young woman named Natasha from Chernobyl meet on the shores of the Baltic Sea. Various languages can be heard in the opera – Natasha sings in Ukrainian and German, while Arato sings in Japanese, and these two voices, which should not be able to understand each other, become a dialogue through the music. *Natasha* is a story of human beings, but it begins with the sound of the sea, into which various languages can be heard mixed. These 'voices' in the opening scene may sound more like the atmosphere that remains after humans have disappeared, rather than a message from humans.

CS   Even just that line, 'a young man named Arato from Fukushima and a young woman named Natasha from Chernobyl meet on the shores of the Baltic Sea', made me think of how many nationalities and native languages intersect. And when the words are obscured by the sound of the lapping waves, is there a murmur or silence, left to the power of nature, that spreads out? Here's an interesting thing – the opera *Natasha* was composed by Toshio Hosokawa, and in 2011 I also did the set design for *Matsukaze*, another piece by Hosokawa. It was staged in Halle in Germany, the director was Sasha Waltz, and it was a collaboration between contemporary dance and contemporary art, set in the classical art of Noh. Hosokawa apparently wanted a Japanese person who understood the world of Noh to design the stage design, so he offered it to me, a person living in Berlin. However, I wasn't sure how well I did understand the world of Noh, and the costume and makeup artists – who felt the need to make it look Japanese – ended up making up the characters to look like Baka Tono, for some reason, and it all had to be redone.[1] That made me realise that just because a work is set in Japan or the world of Noh, stereotypes and biased aesthetics can sometimes ruin a stage performance.

For me, stage design is the polar opposite of the work I usually do. In my work, I create rooms where there is no one, yet there is the feeling that someone is there. There is no one in a room that only contains memories, but there are traces of someone who once lived there. Similarly, I create installations with the theme of 'presence in absence', so that when a dancer or opera singer enters, it becomes a space where someone is present, not absent.

That's very different from the collaborative way I've worked when I've done stage design, when I am only a part of creating the stage. For instance, I always decide how to light an art piece, but there is a lighting technician on stage, and during *Matsukaze* we had disagreements. He wanted the moonlit night scene to be dark, but I wanted it to be bright, to feel like a full moon. We argued about this until the very end. Then, when I saw the whole stage and the costumes for the first time during rehearsals, I was moved by the enormous amount of work that so many people had been involved in. If you only ever work by yourself, you won't get this kind of excitement.

I've done stage art for operas and plays several times in the past. How it works is that I first receive the libretto and then expand on my imagination from there. I love reading the first line of a text, especially the very first line of a novel, as I feel like I can understand the novelist's enthusiasm for their work from that first line. So, my question is, Yoko, how do you find that first line? And what were your thoughts when you wrote the first line of your novel *The Trainee*? I'd love to know.

YT   'Rooms that only contains memories ... rooms where there is no one, yet there is the feeling that someone is there.' That's a very interesting description, Chiharu. It's difficult to depict an empty space in a novel, although it may be possible in poetry. In fact, in the novel I wrote in German, you can see from the title – *Eine Affäre ohne Menschen* (An Affair without People) – that I aimed to write a book that didn't feature any humans at all. Humans can speak, so they are quick to start explaining this and that, which ends up obscuring what is really happening in the situation – or the sadness.

With *The Trainee*, I started with the unfamiliar term 'daylight saving time'. Japan does not have a system of daylight

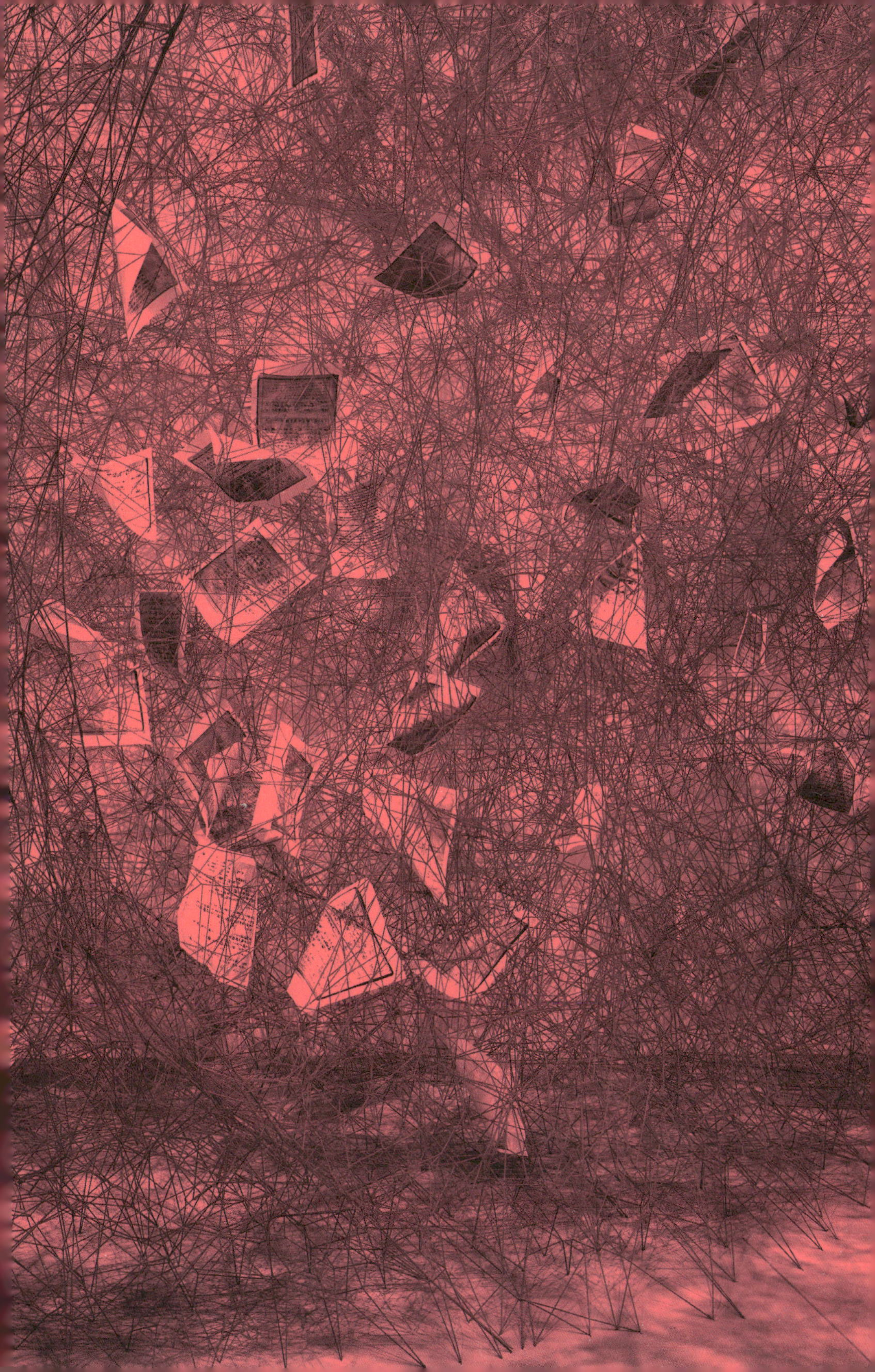

saving time, so my starting point for writing this novel was my surprise at the fact that a 'gap' already exists within a culture, even before a cultural gap is even felt.

What was your starting point, then, for the illustrations?

CS   In a way it was simple: I simply underlined the words and transformed them into pictures (see pp. 115–27). For example, if the phrase 'The clock in Dalí's painting' came up, I would draw a Dalí clock, or if the text described someone 'In the morning, lying in bed, arms stretched out toward the ceiling', I would illustrate that figure as it was.

However, it wasn't easy to turn the 900 characters of text that make up one serialised chapter into illustrations. I could only paint books, people, food – I couldn't paint what I felt was *conveyed* in your writing. I found it difficult to directly portray, for instance, the feelings of the protagonist when she was laughed at and insulted for her poor German pronunciation. When I read of her experience, I understood this feeling exactly because I had similar experiences as well, but it was too difficult to paint this feeling.

Yoko, you write while travelling to various countries, but for *The Trainee* you chose Germany in 1980. Why did you pick that time and place as the setting? And have your feelings about your adopted hometown changed since you turned sixty a few years ago?

YT   Sixty is an important birthday. The 'kan' in 'kanreki', which is celebrated at the age of 60, means 'to go around in a circle and return to the way things were'. That's why we celebrate by wearing the red chanchanko that babies wear, and five years ago, when I turned 60 myself, I was able to celebrate wearing the chanchanko that my friends, including you, Chiharu, had sewn for me. Thank you so much for all that you did.

I was born in 1960, and 22 years later, when I came to Germany in 1982, I felt like I was reborn and starting a second life. Everything was new to me for a few years after I came to Hamburg. It wasn't just that Japanese culture is completely different from European culture; it was also that, while people basically do the same things in every country in terms of food, work, romance, music and so on, there are big and small differences, which gave me the opportunity to rethink what it means to live.

Twenty-two is a young age, but in Japan it's the age at which many people graduate from university and get a job at a company, and it is also a time when one's place in society is largely determined from the outside. I now think it was a good thing that I was placed in a precarious position – in a good way – as a 'trainee', which let me immerse myself in the culture of a distant country.

Compared to the Germany of today, the Germany I came to in the 1980s also now seems like a distant country. There was no internet or mobile phones back then, so it was impossible to survive without building direct relationships with the people around me. So, conversely, I never felt lonely. I also think that Germany was at the time notably less of a visual culture. People spent their time reading books and listening to the radio. Unlike in Japan, many of my German friends didn't watch TV or read manga.

My memories of that time are full of emotional turmoil, pain and excitement – language-centred experiences, feelings which don't immediately translate into images. This is a world that is almost impossible to illustrate, so to me, the fact that you were able to produce so many pictures, Chiharu, is like a miracle.

CS   I wanted to express my images for *The Trainee* more as 'paintings' than just illustrations. I knew the fear of not being able to draw anything if I stopped, so I just kept turning the words from the novel into pictures and drawing until I decided on my own style of illustration. Drawing the first ten pictures was the hardest. In order to complete those ten, I asked you if I could read the rest of the novel, and as I did so I spread out thin paper all over the room and continued to draw sketches, ignoring the predetermined dimensions the newspaper had said the images needed to be . Finally, I was able to see the size and direction I needed to draw, and I thought I knew what I was doing. After that, however, the emotions I felt in the words and the emotions I felt when drawing didn't quite line up, and I faced a new struggle.

At this point, I decided to read the entire Yoko Tawada back catalogue, and through reading everything, I began to see how you write: the atmosphere you create, your habits, your rhythm. I wanted to understand your words more fully, to see the whole picture. To read your work means to understand your world.

Eventually, newspaper serialisation of *The Trainee* began, but when I saw my illustrations in the pages, I was again troubled: I felt they were too 'dark'. I wanted to capture the freshness I'd seen in *The Trainee*, so I tried to draw more colourful illustrations, but I struggled because I wasn't able to use colour – I find it difficult to find meaning in colour in my own work, so I was not sure how to add it to these drawings, and even if I had painted in more colours I believed the details would get lost because of the size of the image in the newspaper.

I then discovered a method of erasing my lines and illustrations, pasting coloured paper on them – wrapping paper and origami paper – and then layering the lines again. This technique finally allowed me to move forward.

YT   I find your explanation of the process that led to the creation of the illustrations very interesting, especially your concern that they were too 'dark', because I've been thinking a lot about the concepts of darkness and light – in your work generally, but especially in some of the work we have done together.

    The first time you and I worked together was on an event where the composer and musician Aki Takase played piano and I recited poetry, at the exhibition venue for your installation *From in Silence*. The installation consisted of two pianos, one burned and one intact, and my initial impression was that it was a very, very dark work. But as I looked at it, I felt as if I was being transported past the darkness and into a room deep within my heart that was normally inaccessible. Entering that room is quite frightening.

    Since then, whenever I see your work which evokes images of sick people or those who have already died and are no longer present, I've felt the same way. In contrast, when I first glimpsed *I hope...*, I felt as if a series of lamps I hadn't even known existed suddenly lit up in my heart. However, while *I hope...* was bright, it also felt frightening – like blood was falling from the sky. Your work elicits extreme darkness, extreme light, or both at the same time.

CS   It was interesting coming back to drawing for this project. I actually began my career wanting to be a painter, but although I enjoyed drawing and illustrating, I stopped painting because I couldn't stand the 'restrictions' on painting. The oil paintings I produced looked like I was imitating someone else's work. I couldn't find my own style. So, I gave up that path and instead started working on larger canvases and drawing lines in space. This was the beginning of my installations.

    When I came to illustrating *The Trainee*, I thought, 'I want to draw better', and wondered what the difference is between improving my technique and drawing a good picture. How far do I have to push myself to paint a good picture? How much do I have to destroy myself, deny my existence, think about myself as someone who will never amount to anything, in order to create a good work? Is it that the more I look into the darkness in the human heart, the deeper I dig into it, the better my work will be? Facing such negative feelings has always been essential to my creations. I wonder if this is something that exists among novelists as well.

    In the end, I decided to paint over the main character's face and hide it with her hair. By erasing the details, I wanted to show the whole person. And reading your text reminded me, Yoko, that I have sometimes wondered whether a person's back reflects their life.

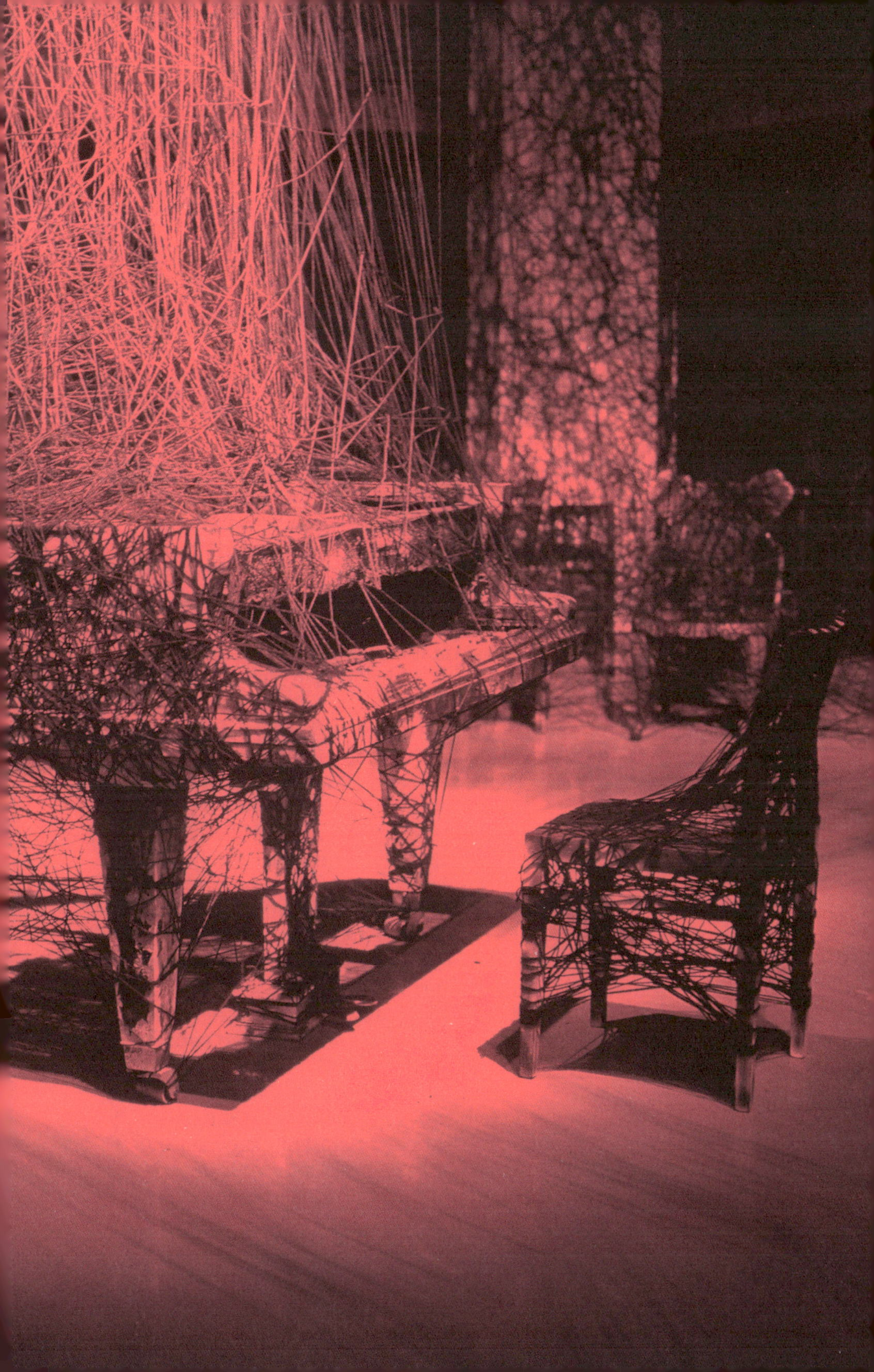

YT   I think that may be true. When the war was still going on in
the former Yugoslavia, I met a young woman who had fled
to Germany. One day I went to her house. Her facial expres-
sion and the words she spoke were positive and optimistic,
but the moment she turned her back to me as she headed
to the sink to wash the dishes, I remember a terrifying darkness and sadness coming from her back. When I honestly
told her, 'I just looked at your back and felt sad', she immediately replied: 'That's war.'
          Similarly, my father passed away last fall at the age of 91,
and what really sticks in my memory is his back.

CS   That's interesting. I wanted to carefully depict the scenes
in which your father – who came from Japan to Hamburg – appears
in this novel, and wondered how I should portray him. What kind of
person was your father, who gave you the opportunity to work at a
publishing company in Hamburg? And what kind of figure is the man
you call 'my father' in *The Trainee*? Could you tell me about the image
I tried to portray but couldn't quite get? Why is his back so important
to your impression of him?

YT   After working part-time at printing and publishing com-
panies, my father worked for a company that imported
American books to Japan. When I was in high school, he
started a bookstore that imported specialised books on
education, sociology and philosophy from Germany and
sold them to university libraries and researchers in Japan.
Through this connection, I ended up working as an intern
at a German company that did business with us – an experience which became the basis for *The Trainee*. My father
often played with me on Sundays when I was a child, but
what I remember most vividly is his back as he sat at his
desk in his small study, reading or translating. While his
face was always turned toward his family when he was
talking or playing with us, his back was perhaps the way
he returned to himself. In our social lives and relationships,
we tend to value only the eyes and face. But perhaps it's
also important to paint in the eyes and face and see the
whole person, as in your paintings.

CS   But also, when you talk about being reborn at the age of
60, and your father's final moments, I can't help but associate the
image of you sitting at your desk writing a novel with your description of your father with his back to you, 'returning to himself'.

YT	And your father is also an important figure within your work, as in the *Letters of Thanks* series (see pp. 83–97) that you'll be showing at the Hayward Gallery alongside your drawings from *The Trainee*.

CS	Yes. My father was from Kochi Prefecture and moved to Osaka to run a small factory. My mother also worked there, so I grew up watching my parents work hard during Japan's period of rapid economic growth. When I went to Germany, gained some recognition and was booked to have a solo exhibition at the Kochi Museum of Art in 2017, my father was very happy. However, he had become paralysed in an accident and was unable to get out of his hospital bed to come to the exhibition. I called that exhibition *Letters of Thanks* because I wanted to convey my gratitude to my father, who had worked so hard for his family and waited so long for his daughter to return to Japan.

Now the cover of *The Trainee* has been chosen, this story will soon be published as a book. There were many birth pains, but I now feel the sense of happiness I always have when a work is completed and goes out into the world. I learned so much from working on this illustration job, in this collaboration between us as writer and artist. And, likewise, I think this conversation was deeper and more human than an AI conversation could ever be. Thank you very much.

YT	Thank you, Chiharu.

1	The term 'Baka Tono' is not a standardised theatrical definition, but rather a combination of two Japanese terms: 'Baka' (馬鹿, meaning 'fool' or 'idiot'), and 'Tono' (殿 a formal term for lord or master). When 'Baka Tono' is used together, it refers to a foolish or silly lord who plays a role in the theatre.

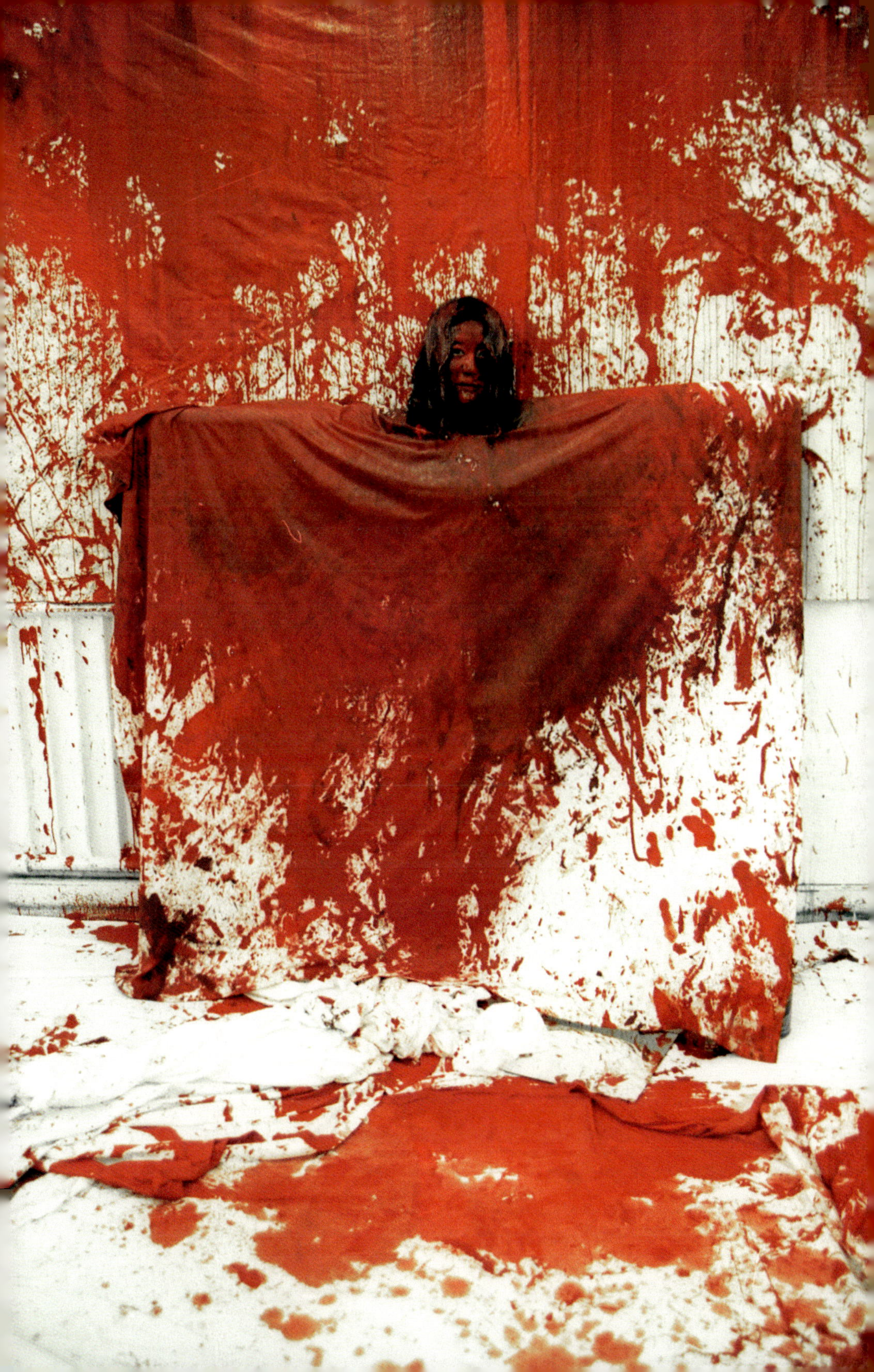

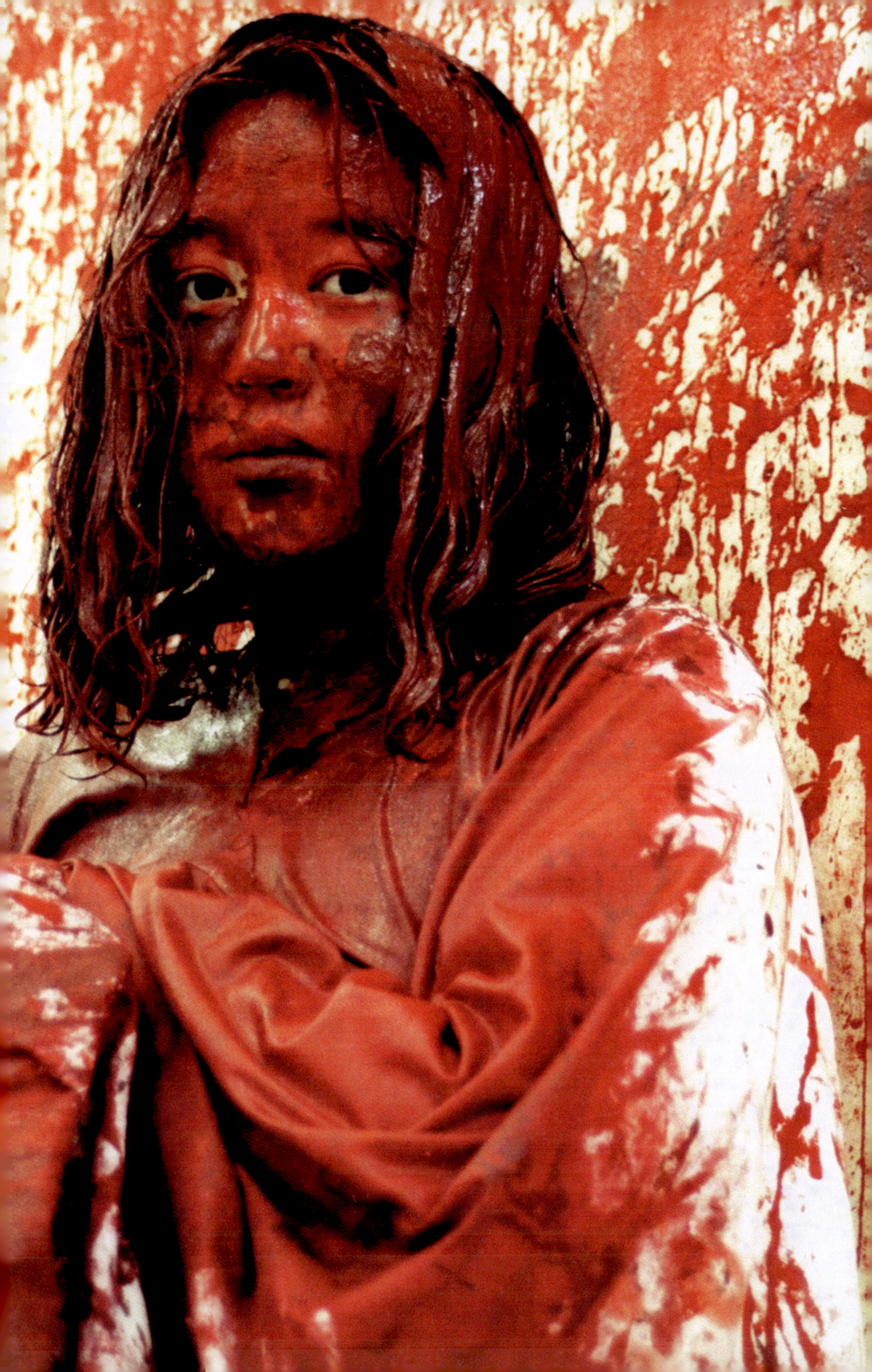

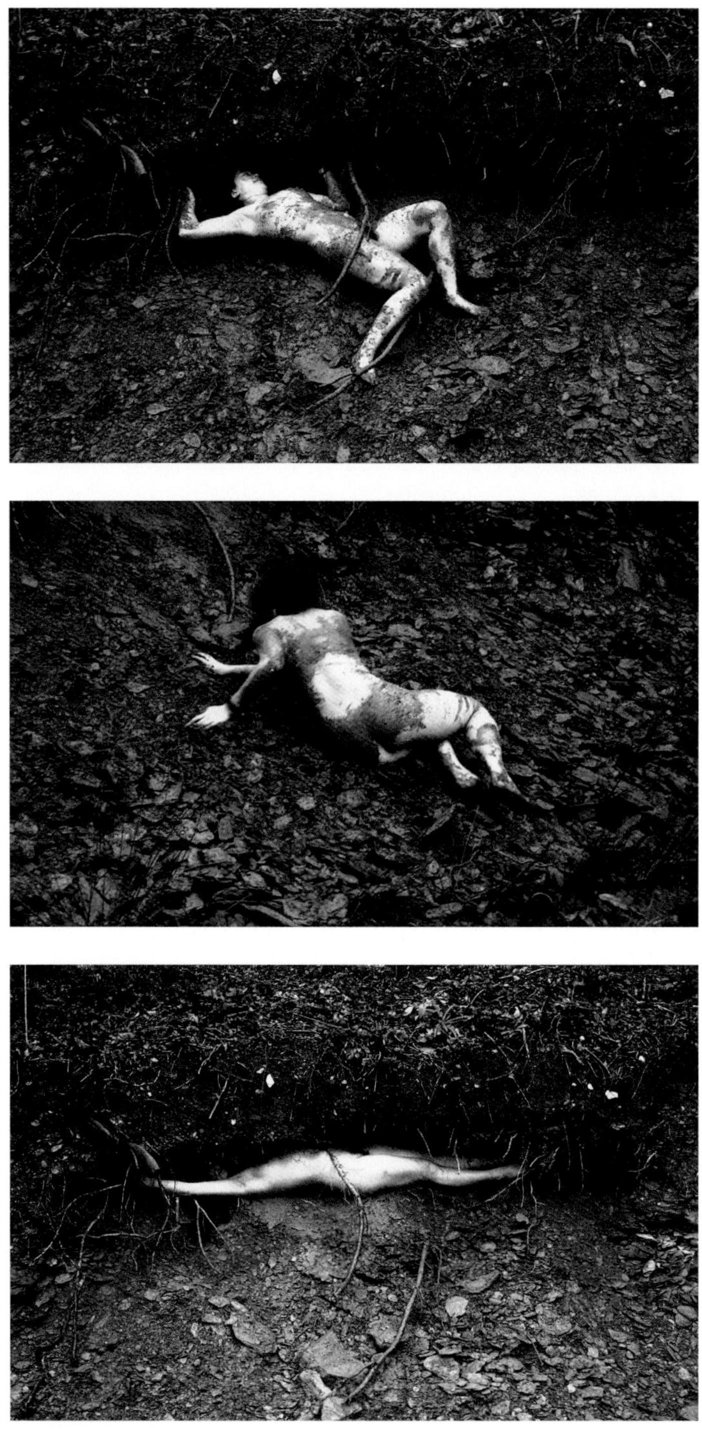

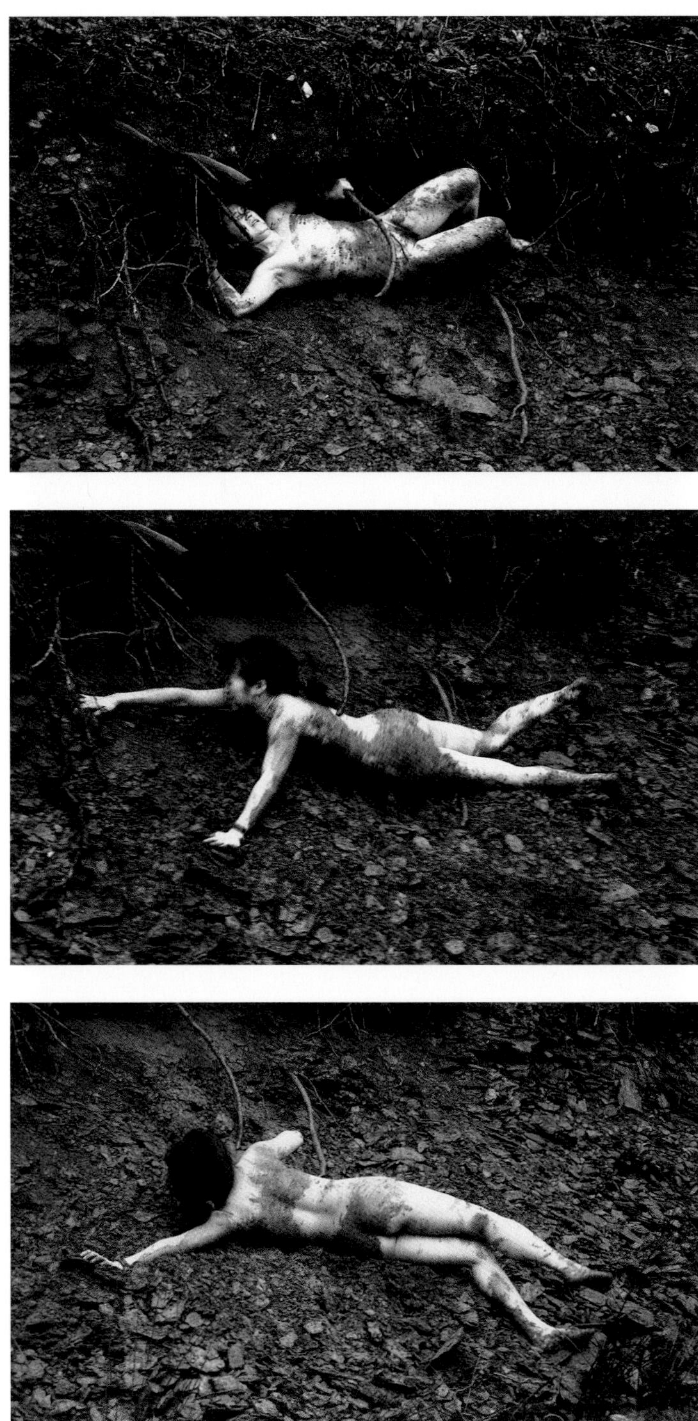

Try and Go Home,
1997

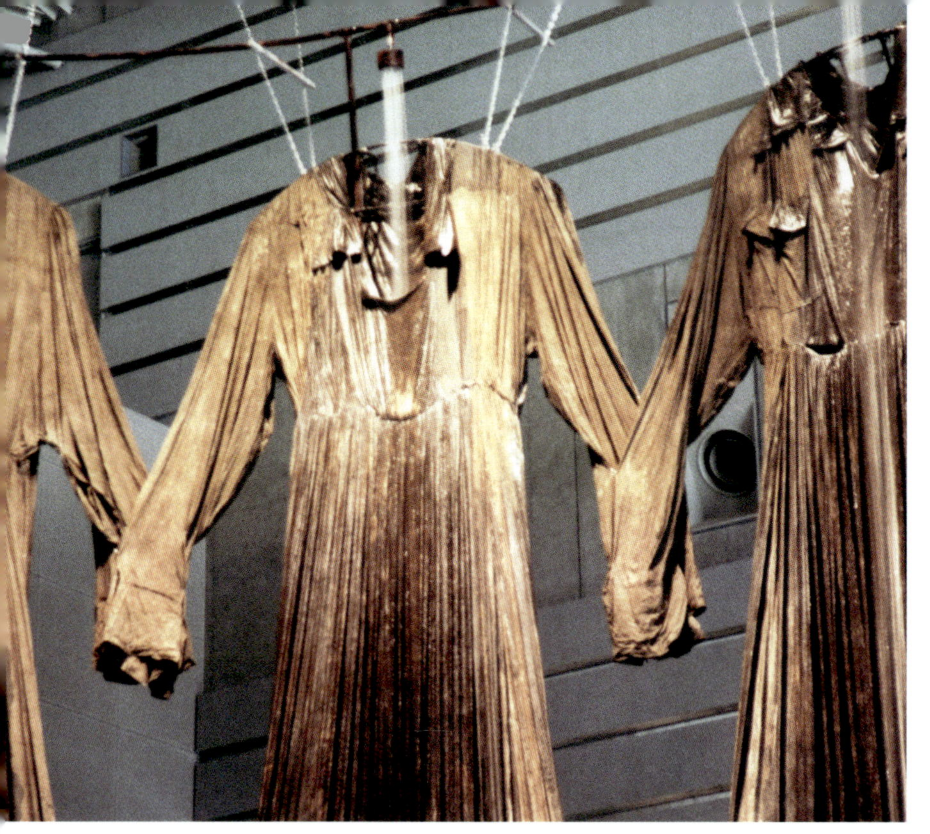

Memory of Skin,
2001

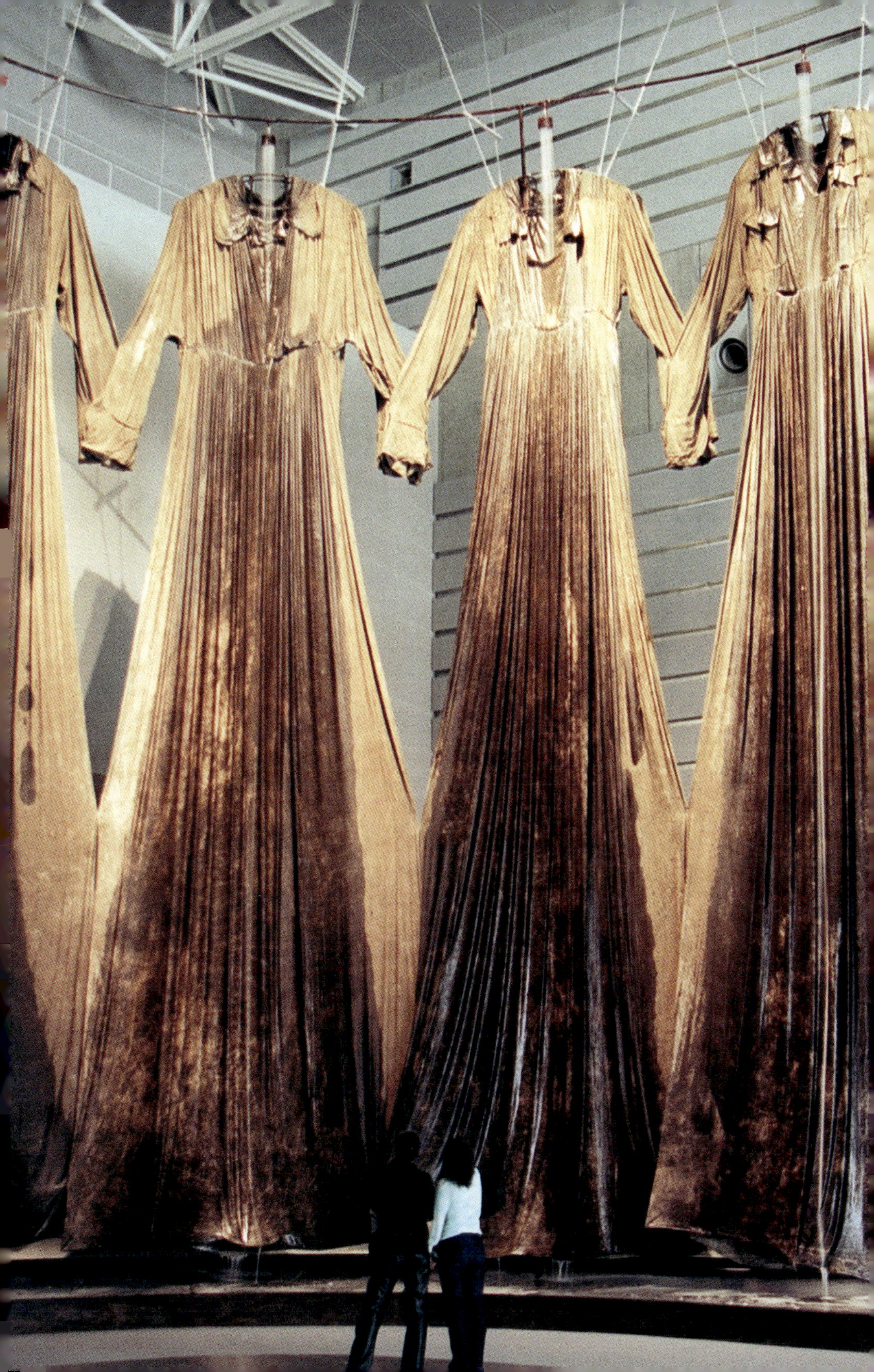

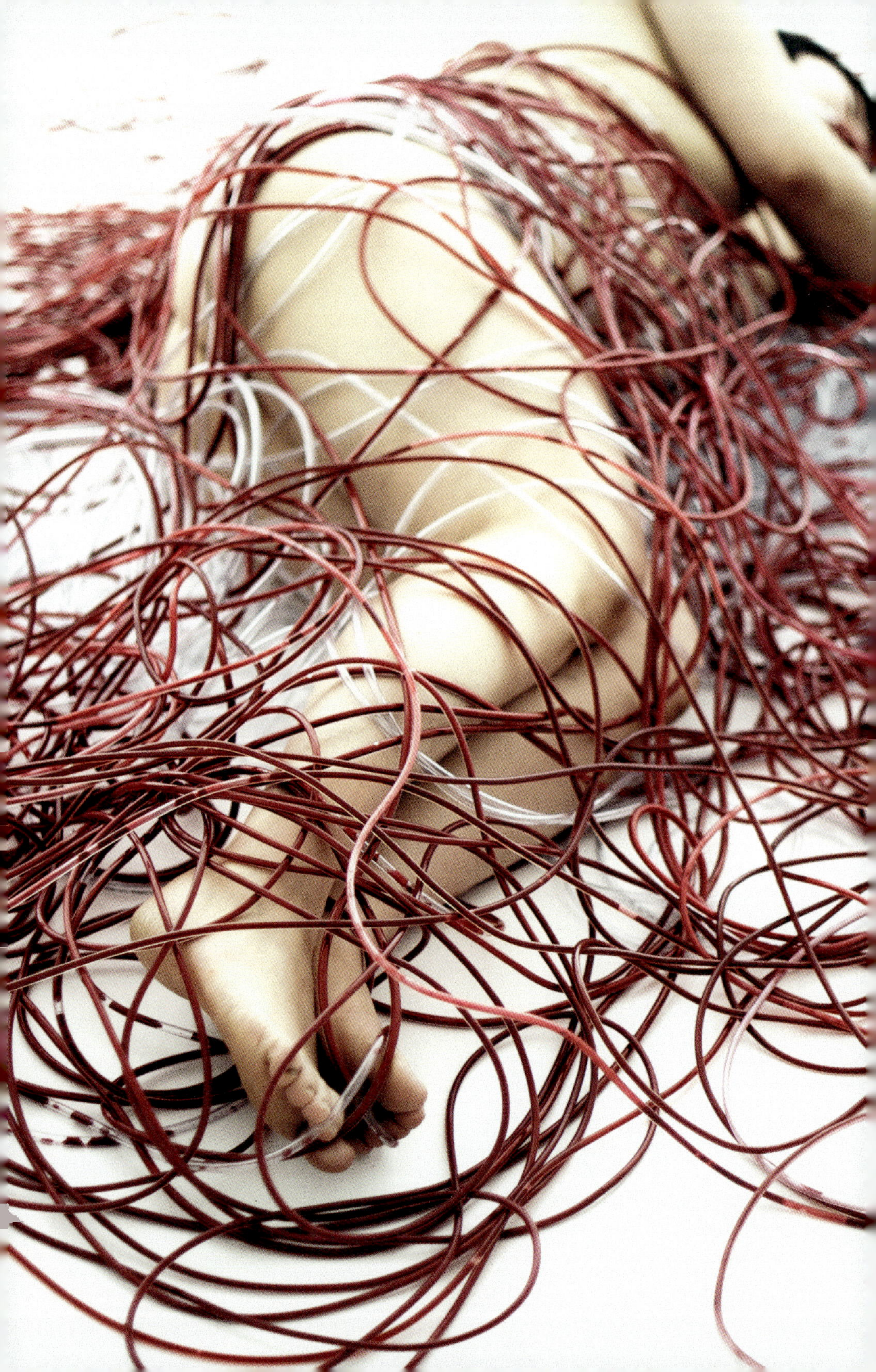

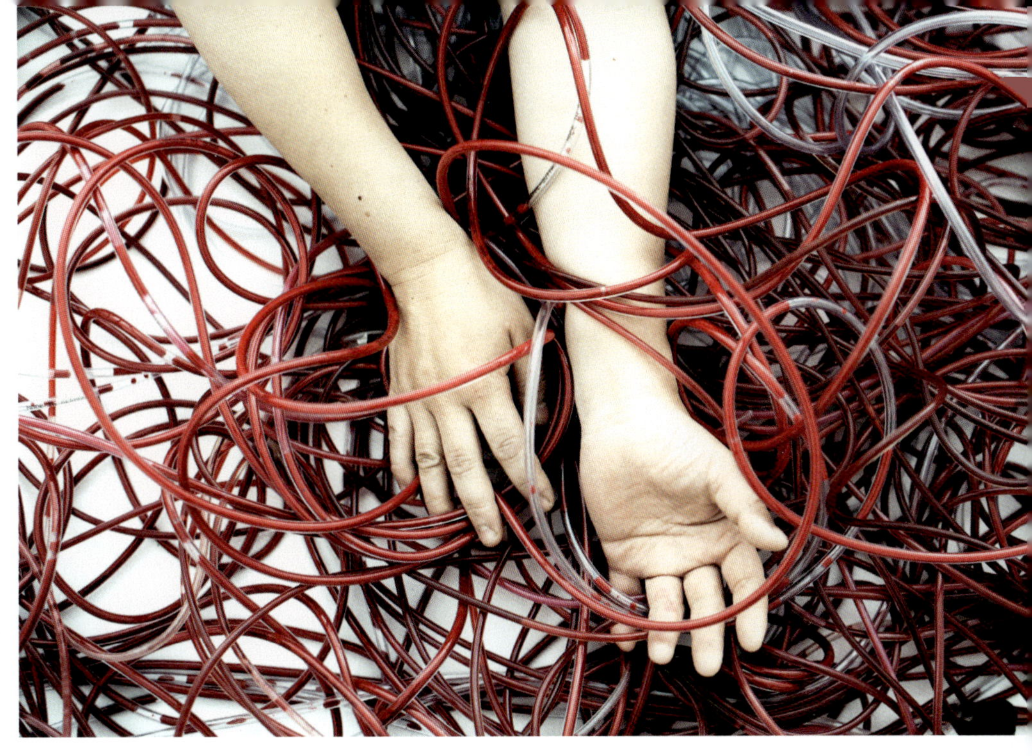

Wall,
2010

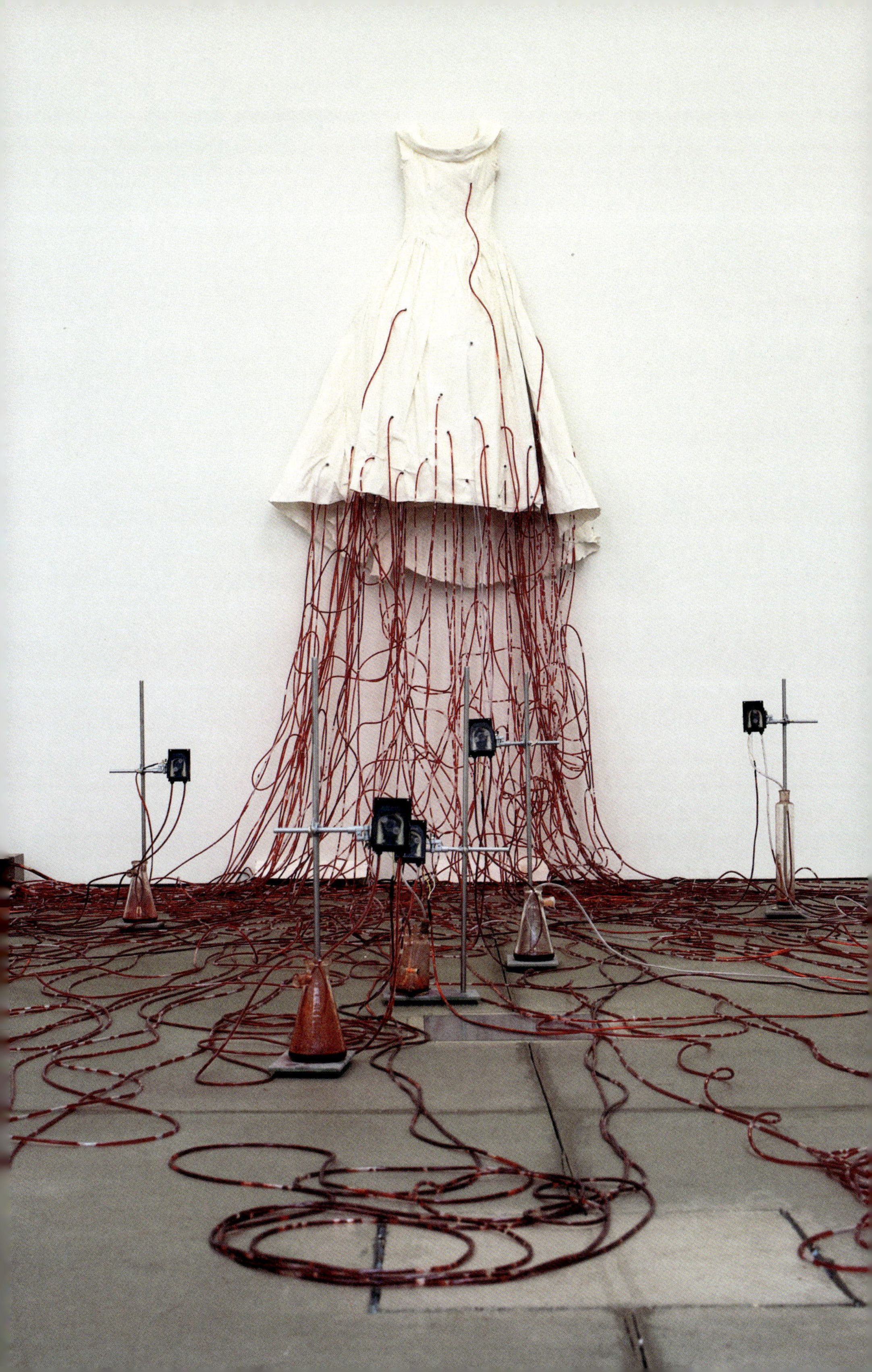

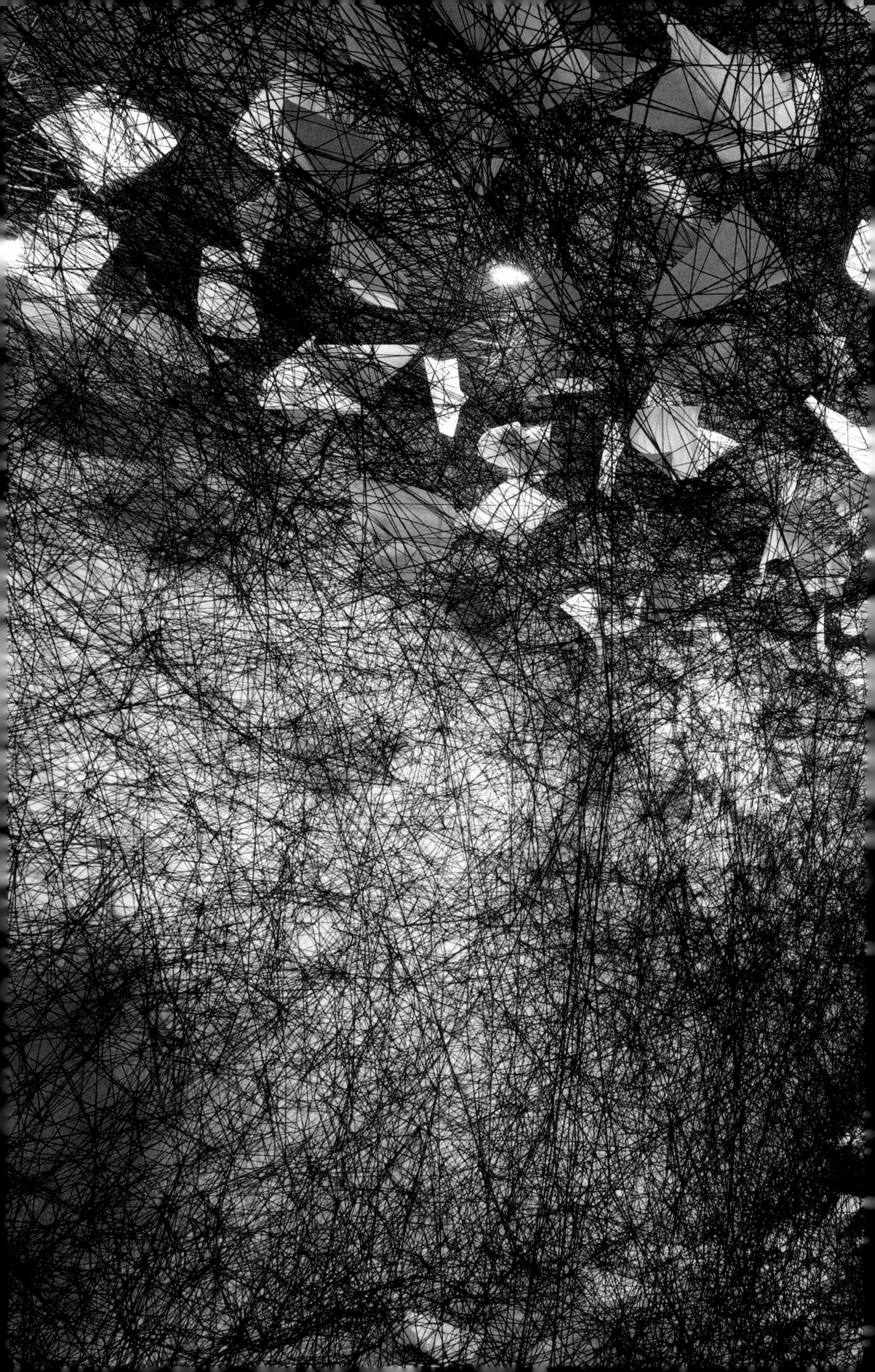

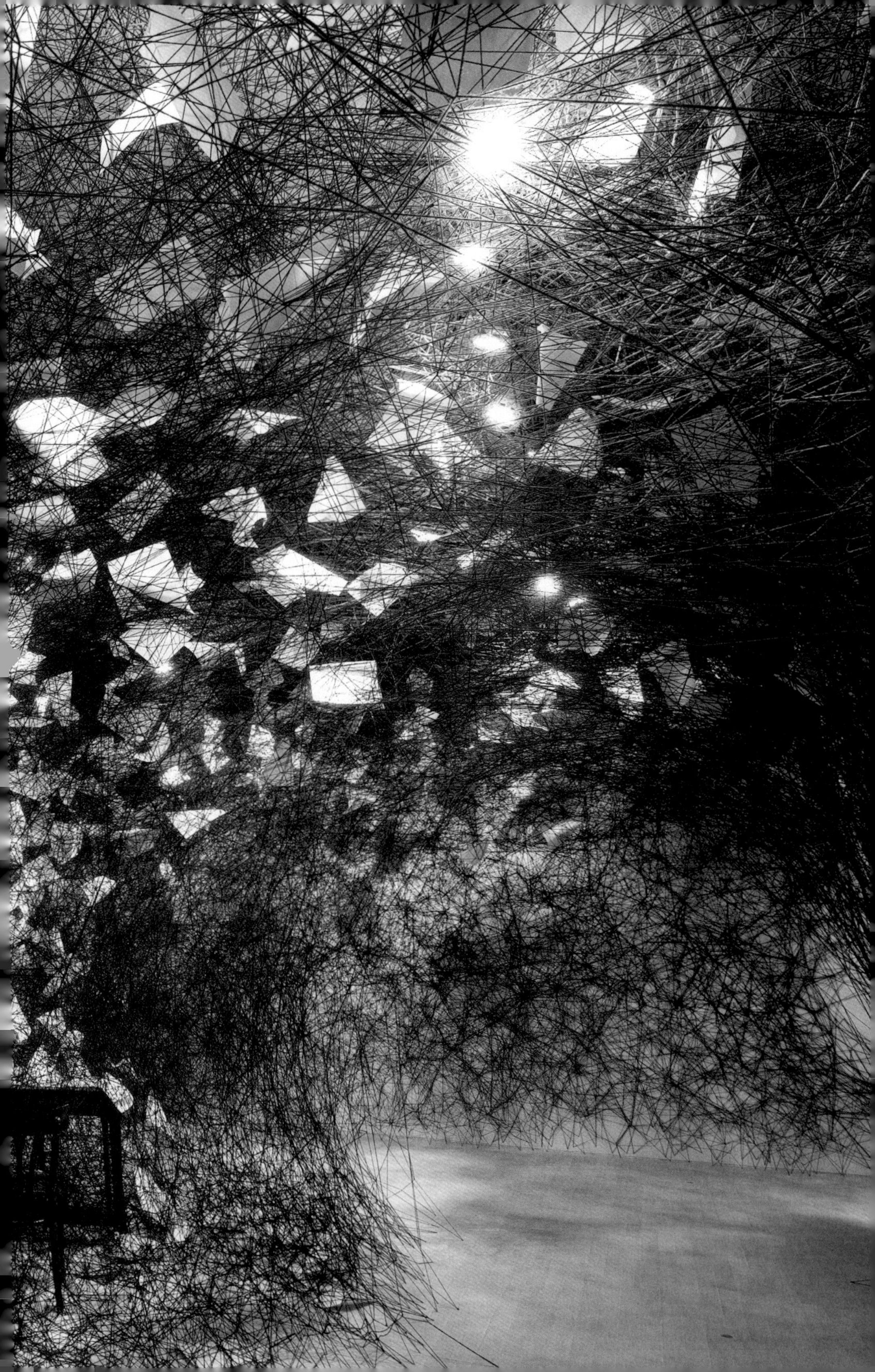

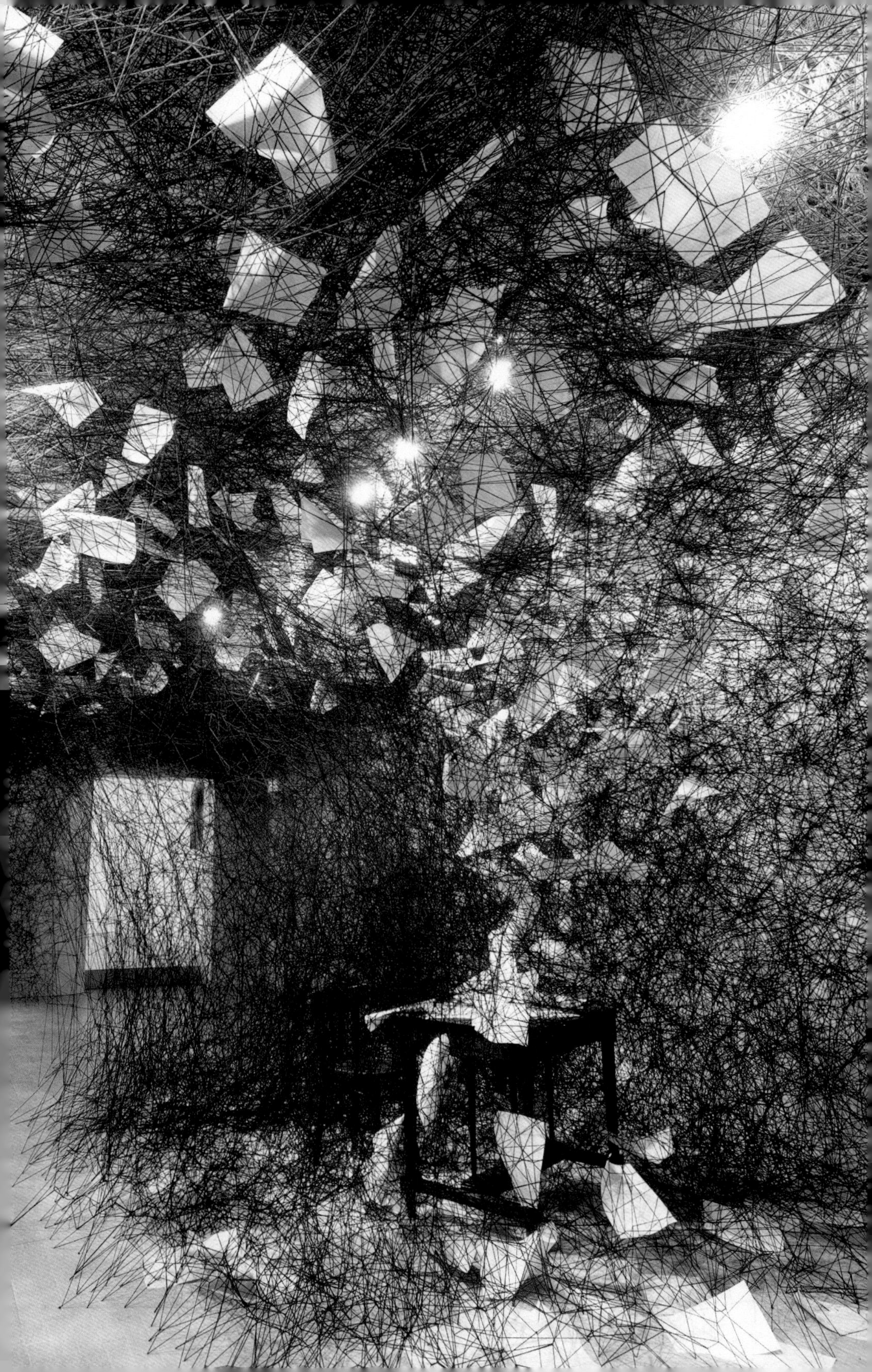

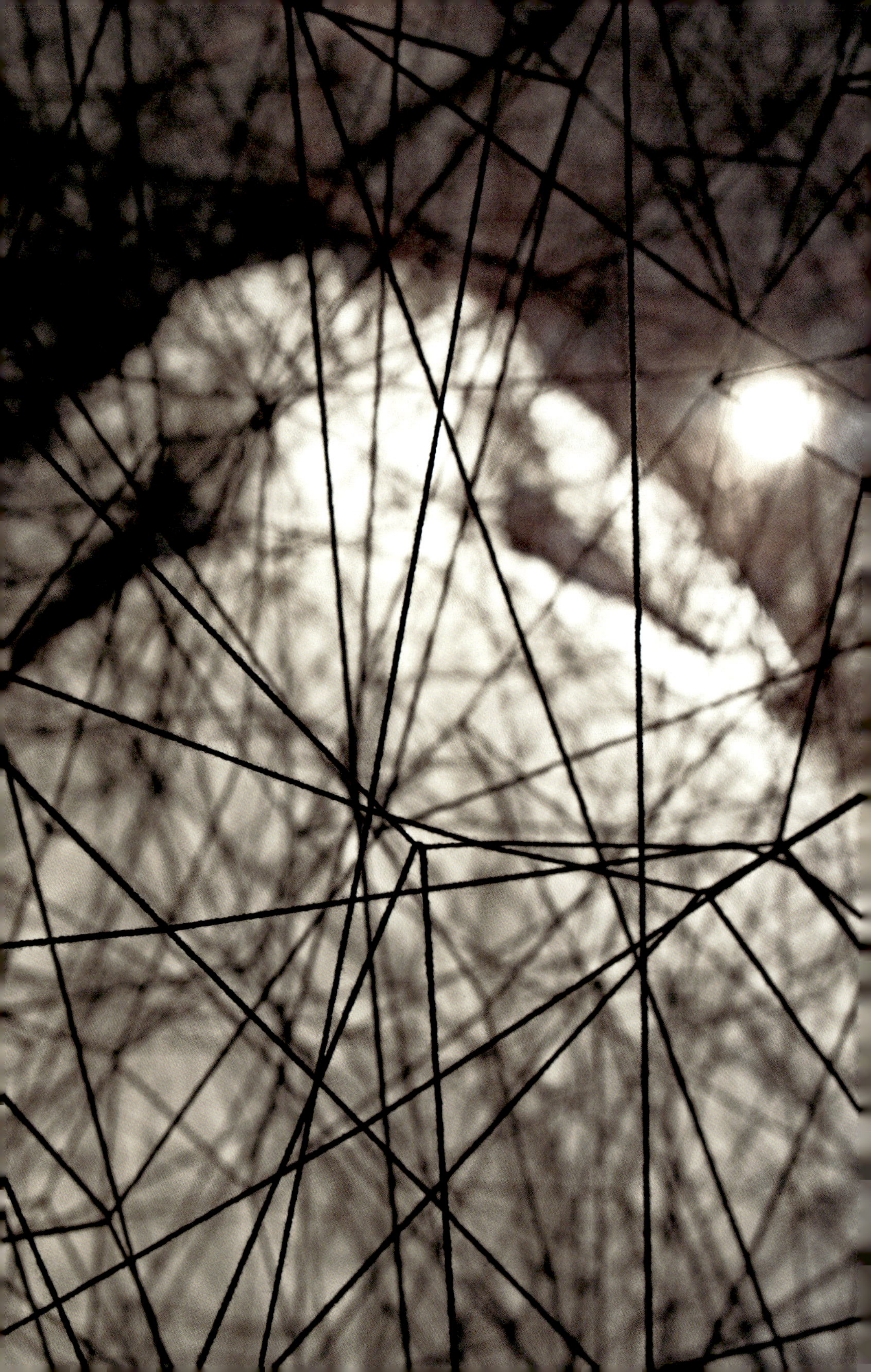

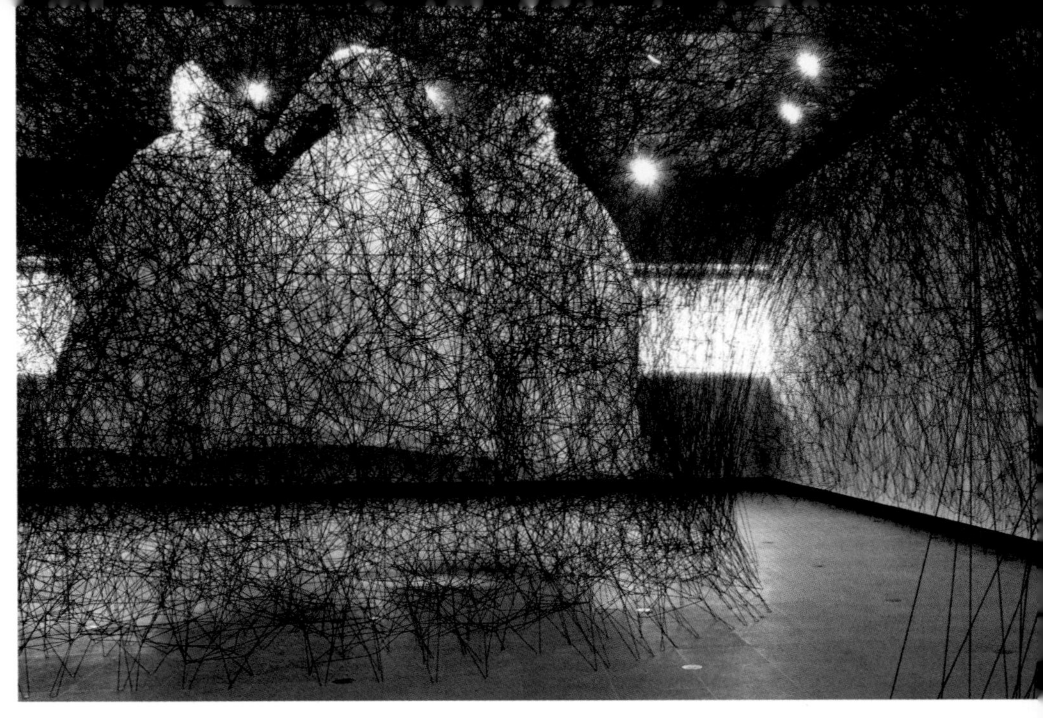

After the Dream,
2009

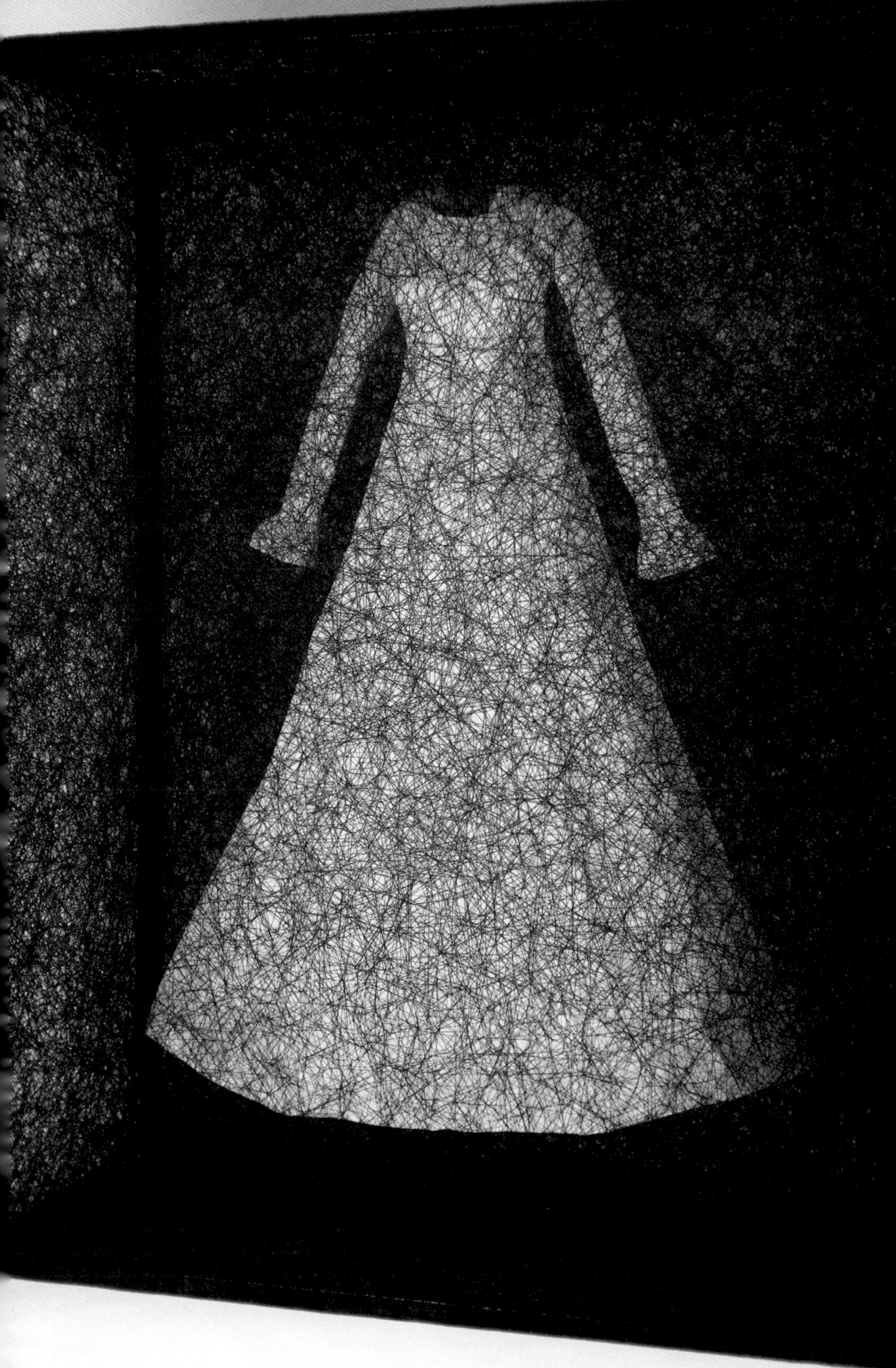

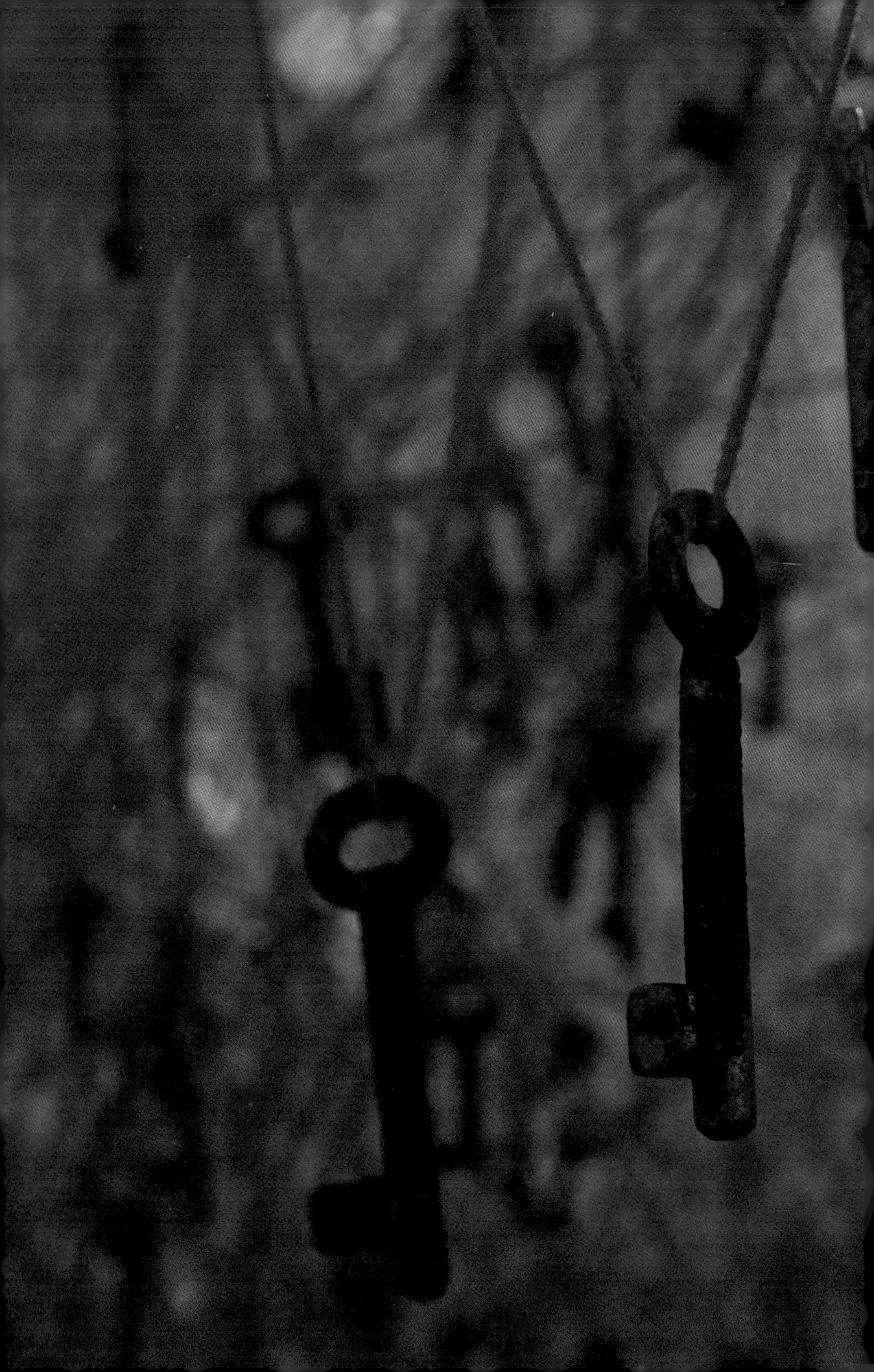

The Key in the Hand, 2015
detail, and following pages

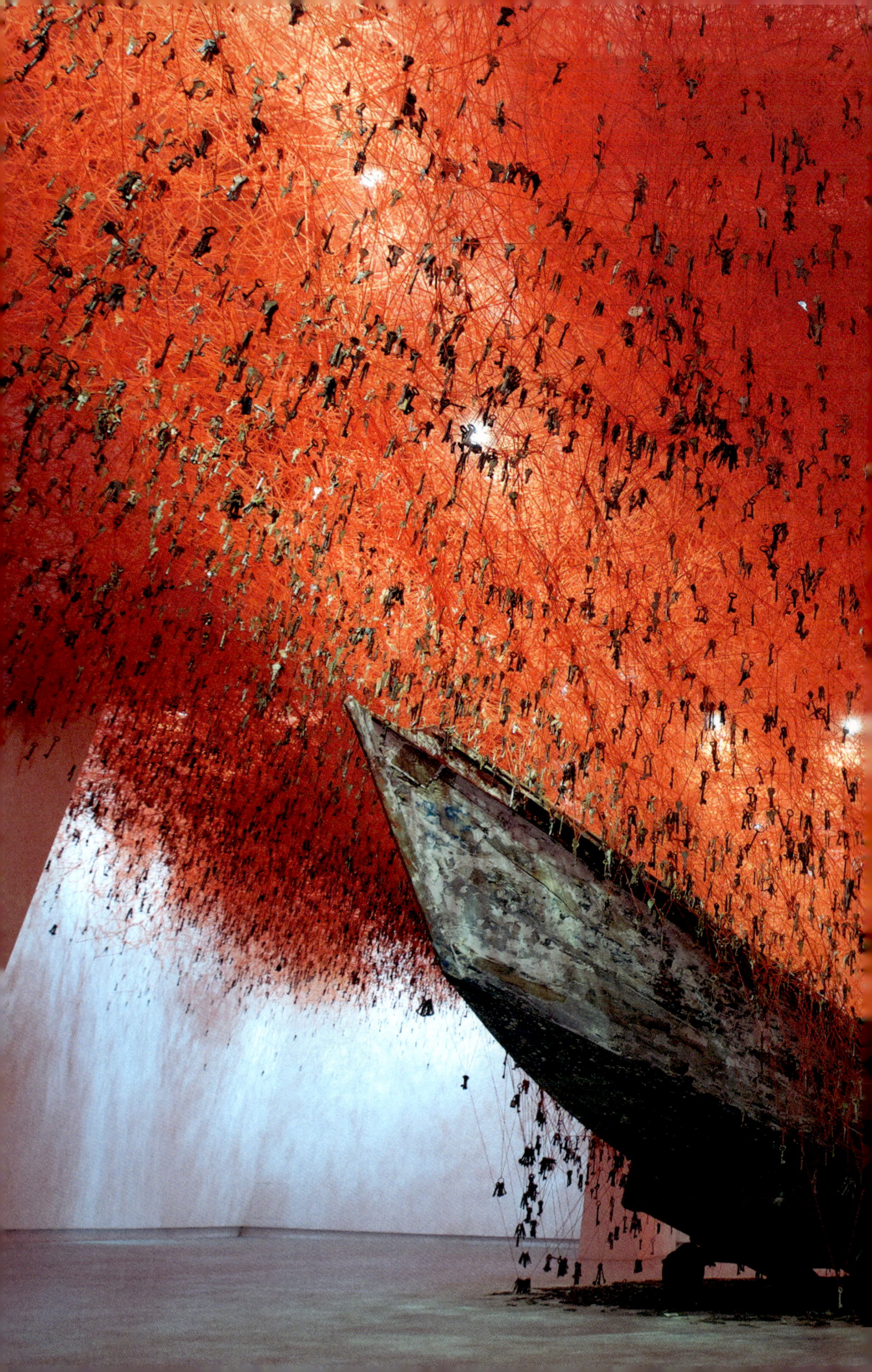

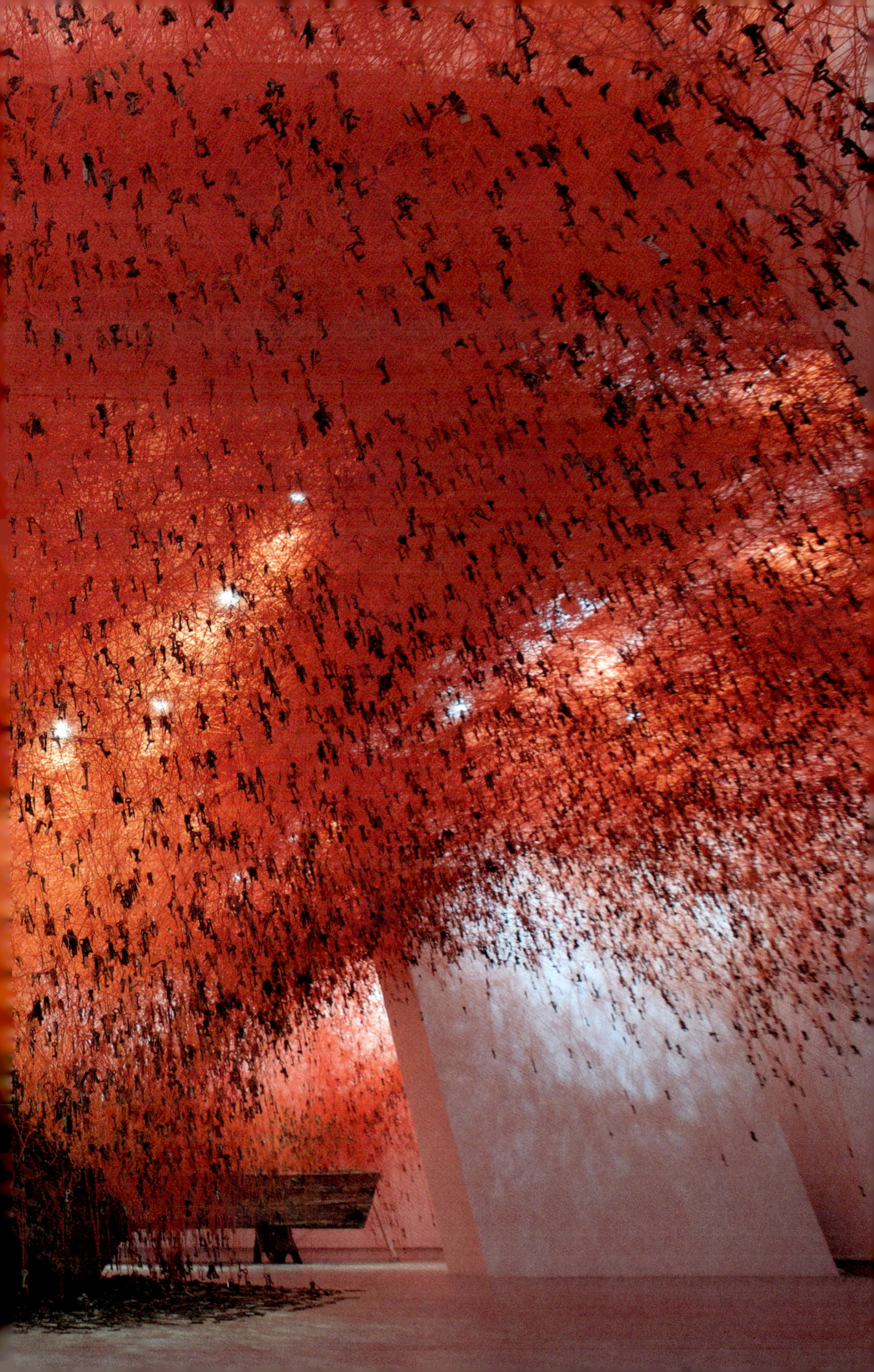

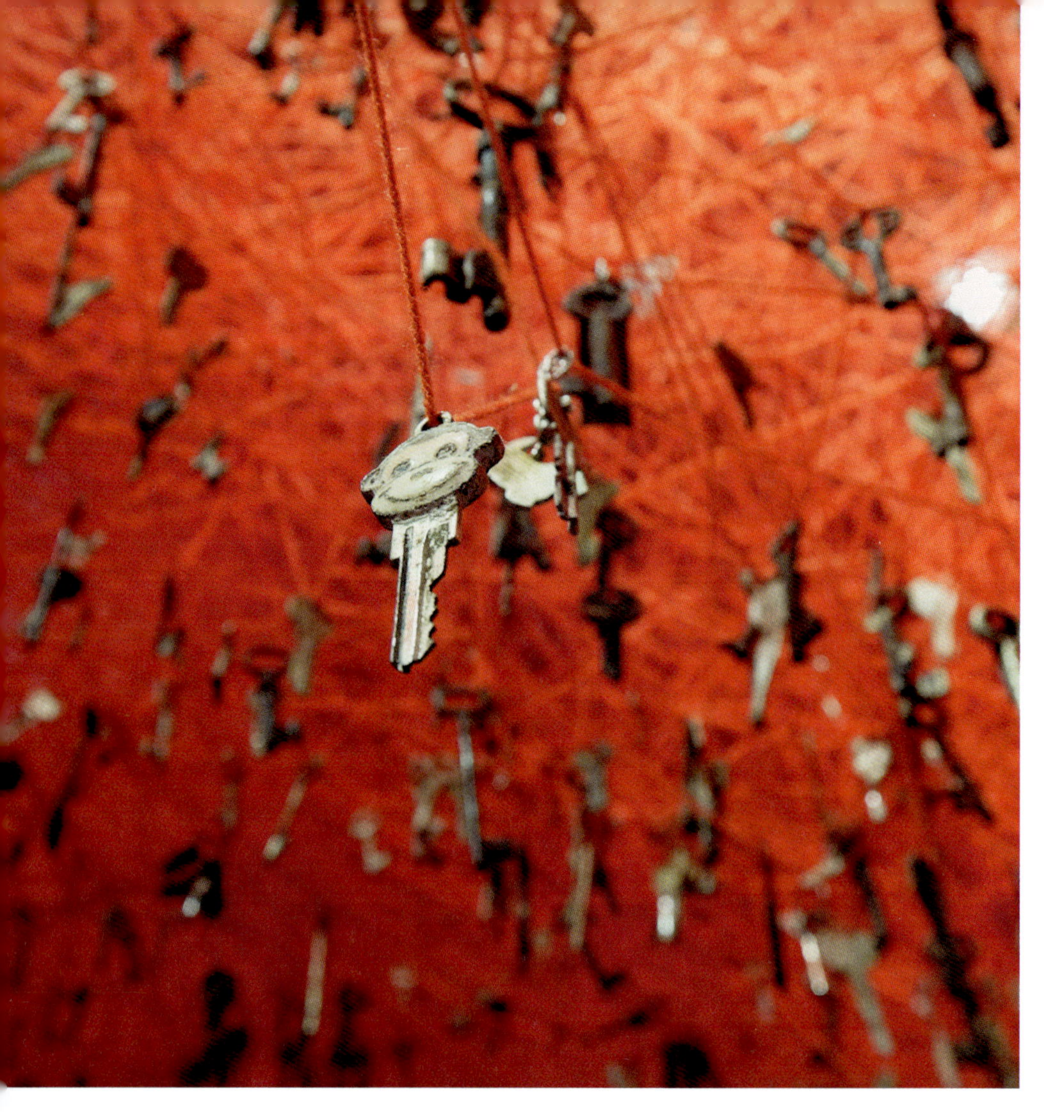

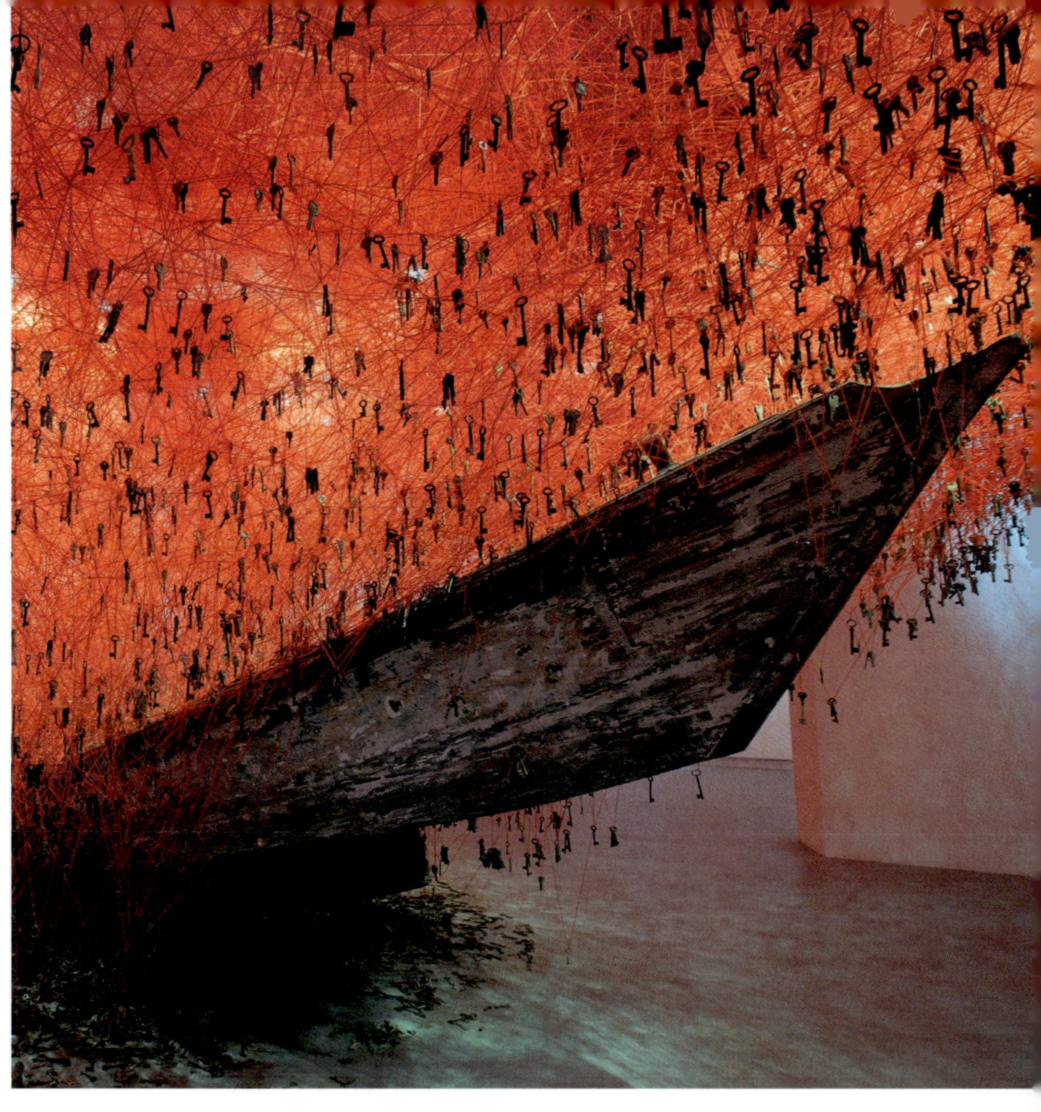

The Locked Room, 2016
and following pages

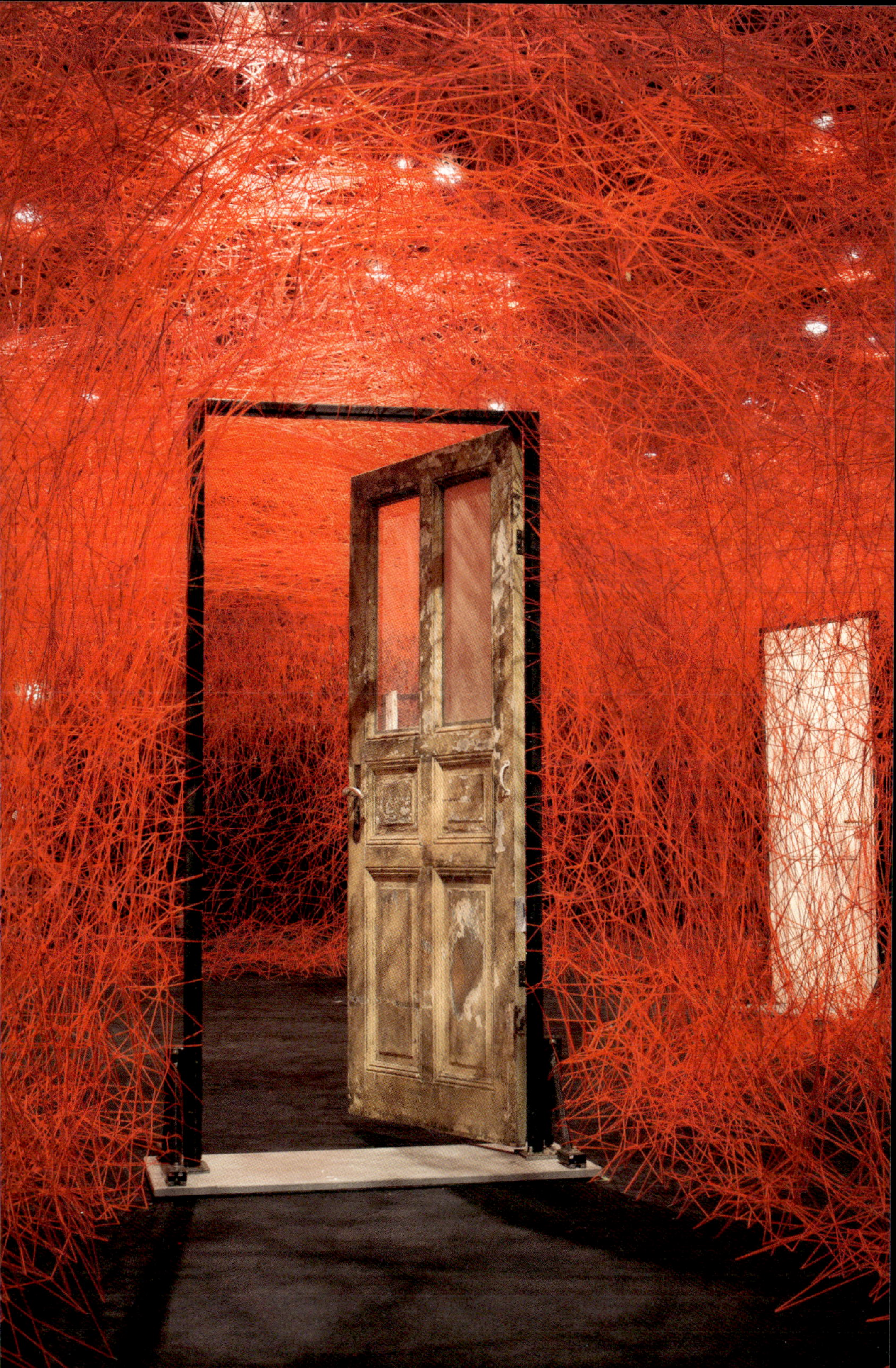

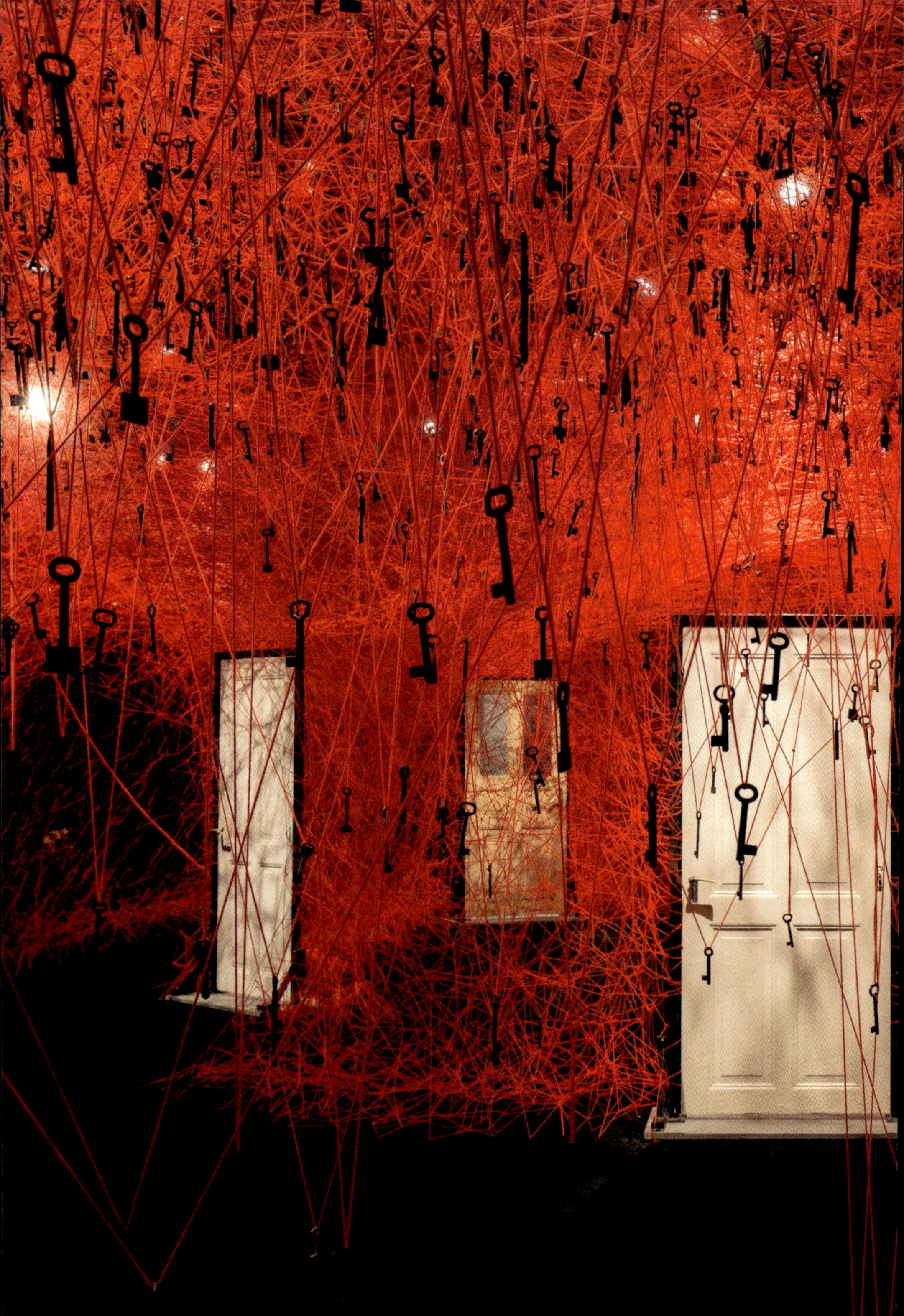

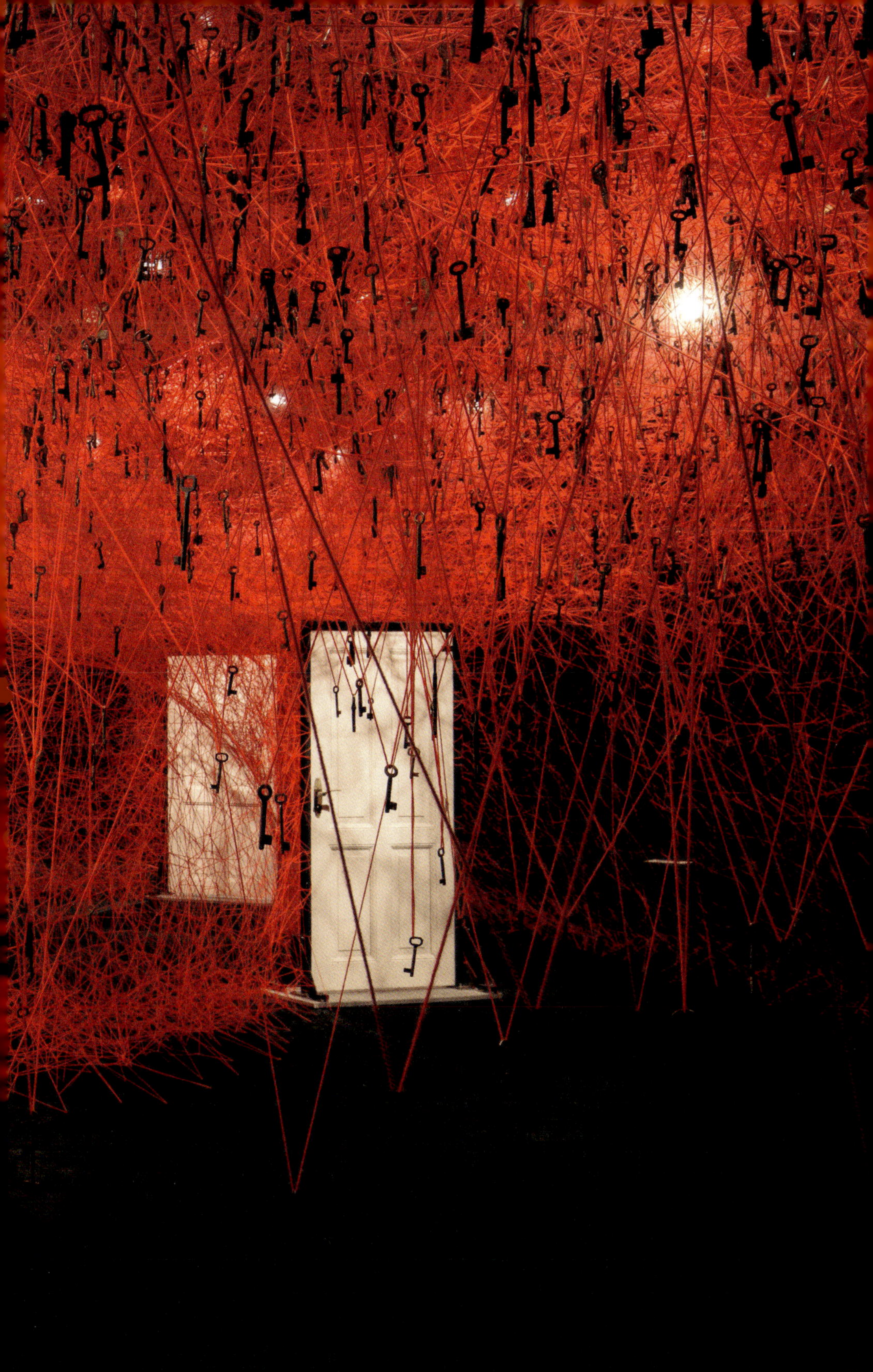

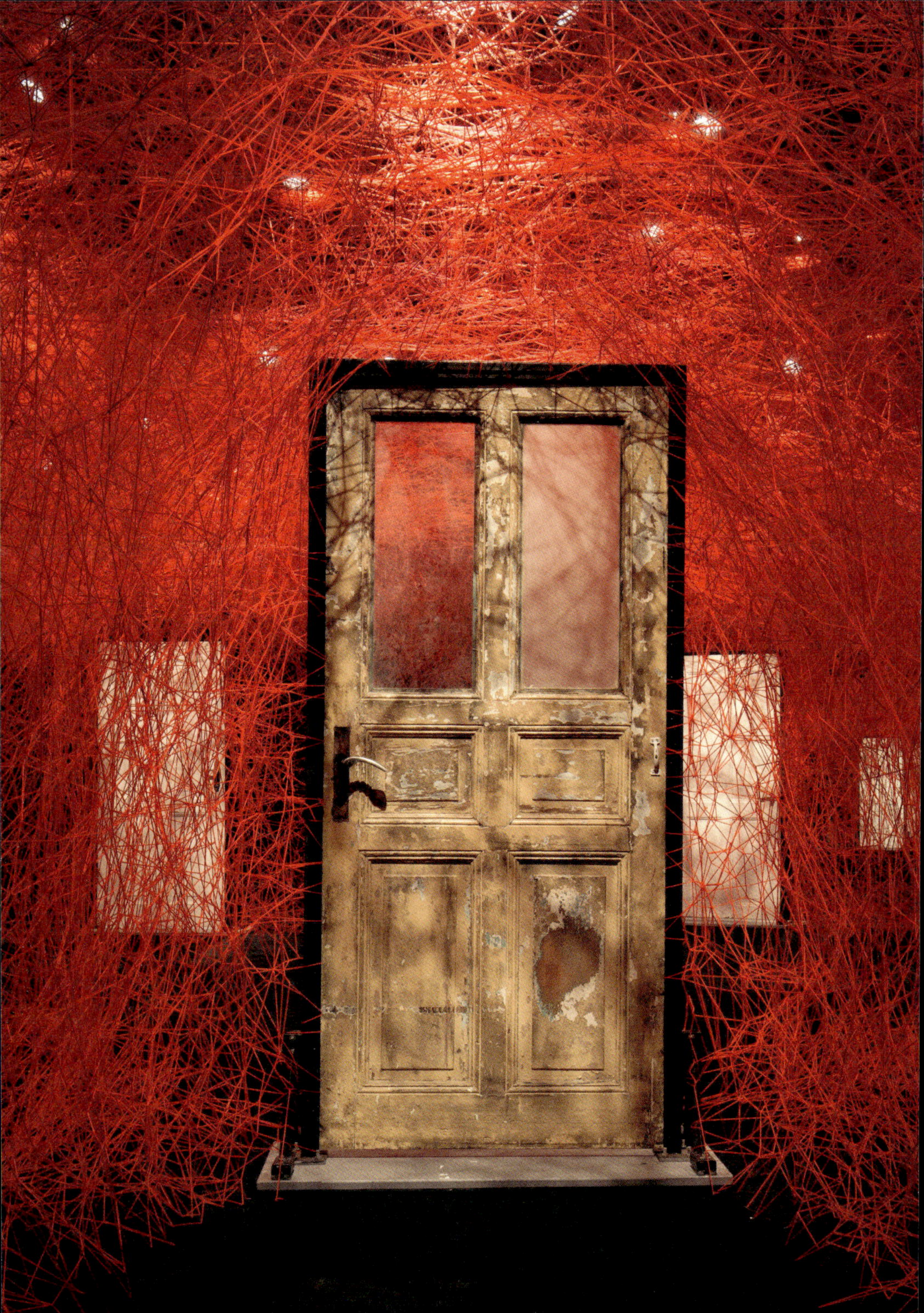

The Locked Room,
2016

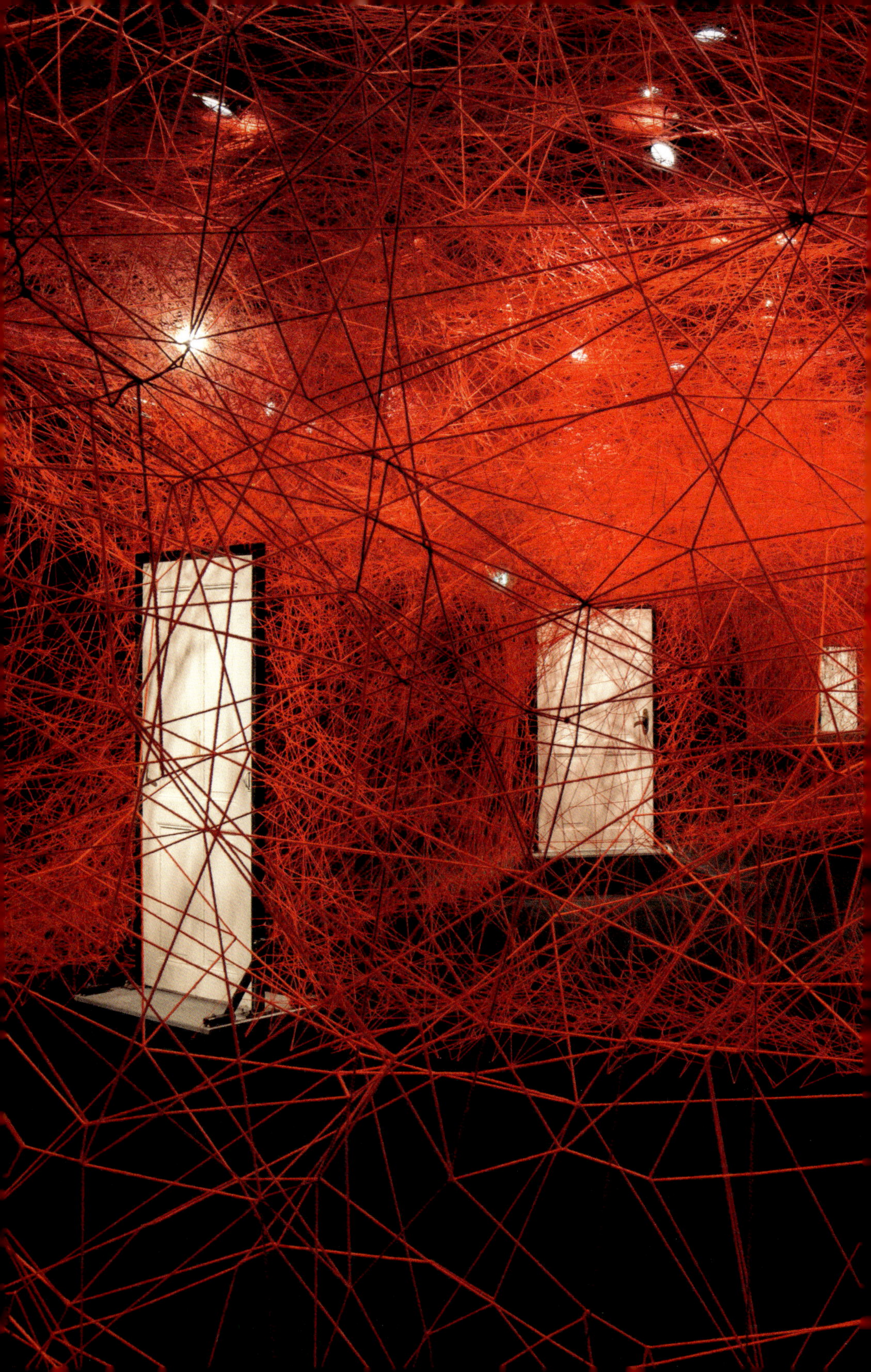

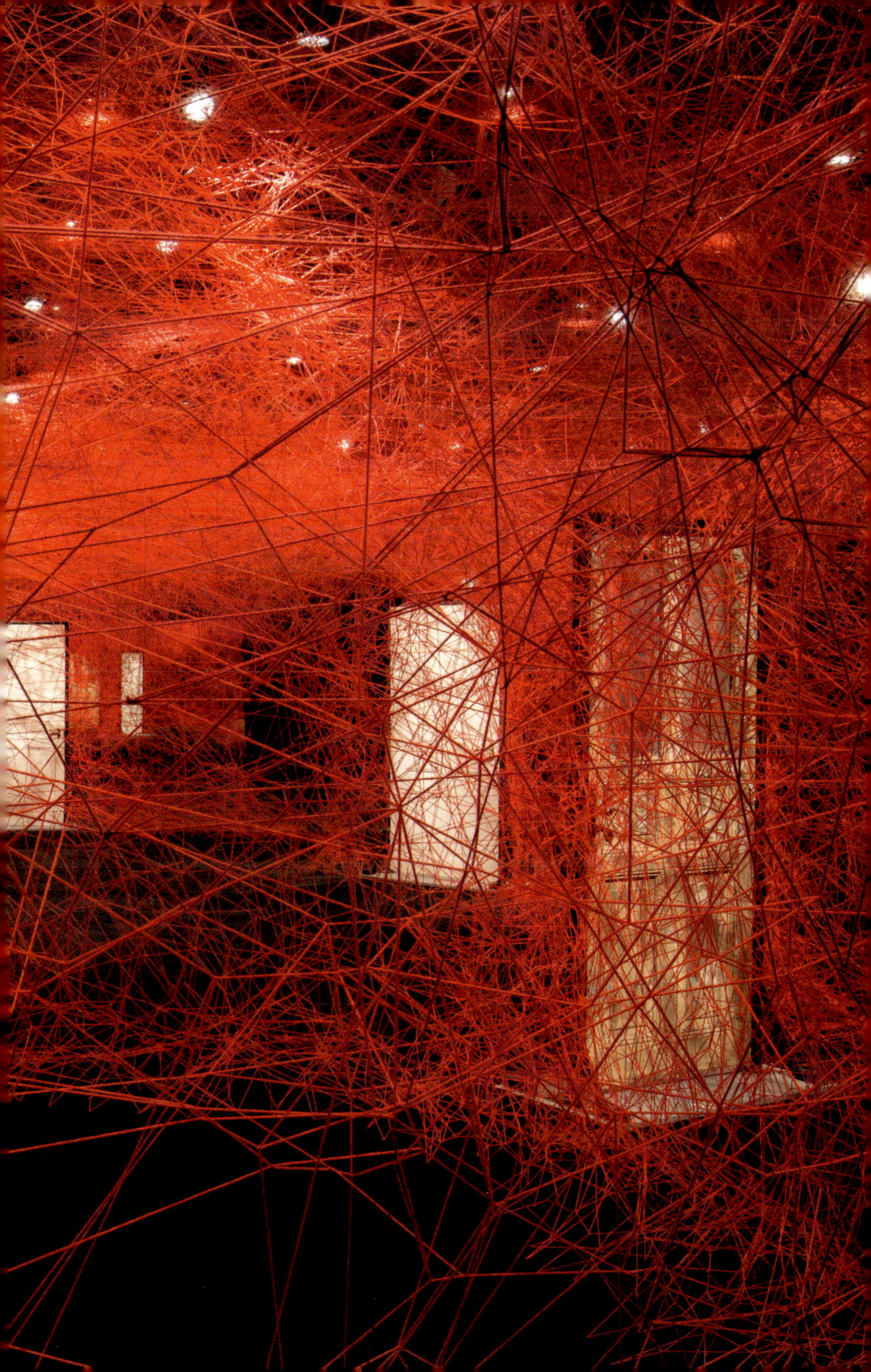

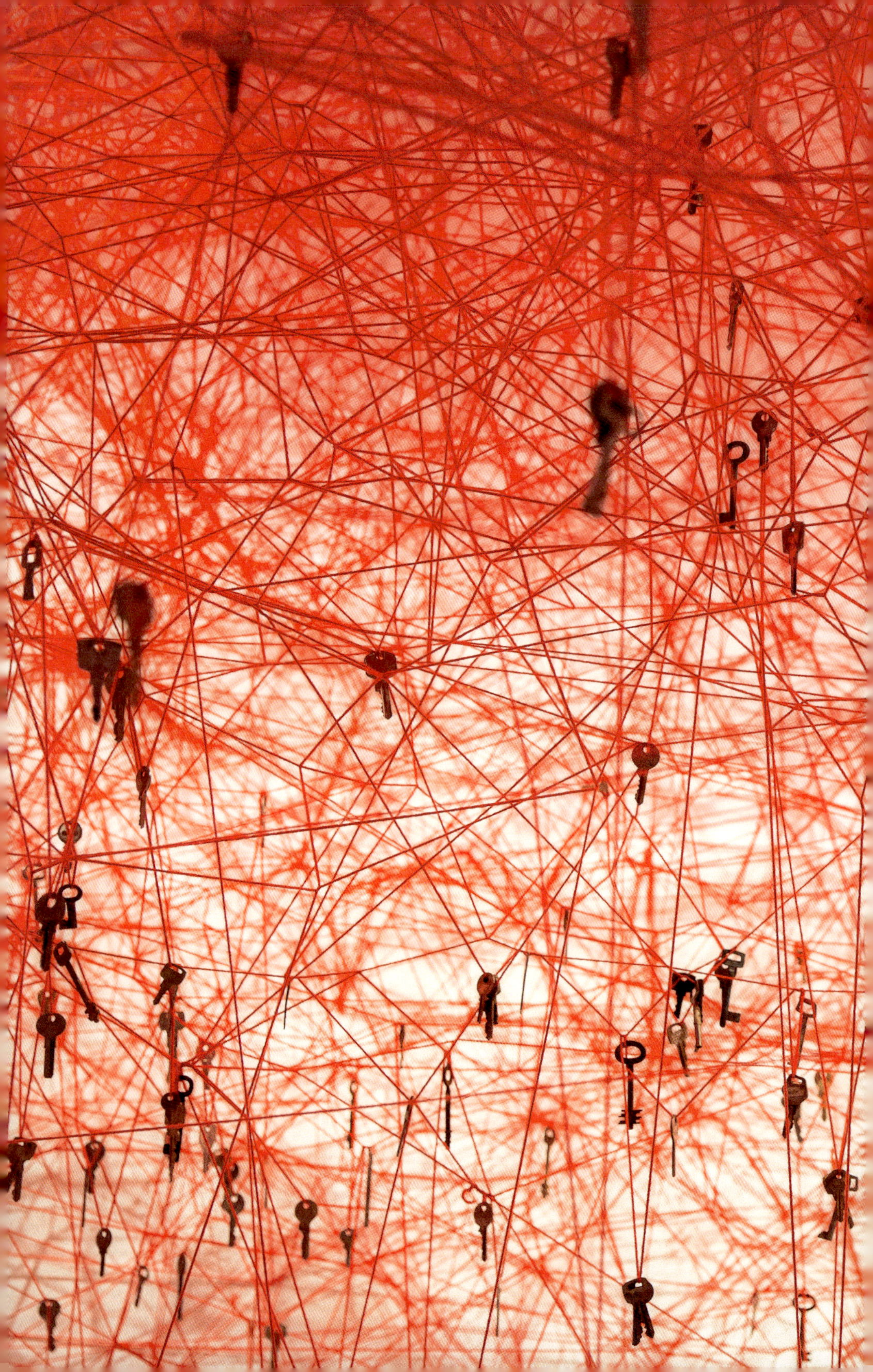

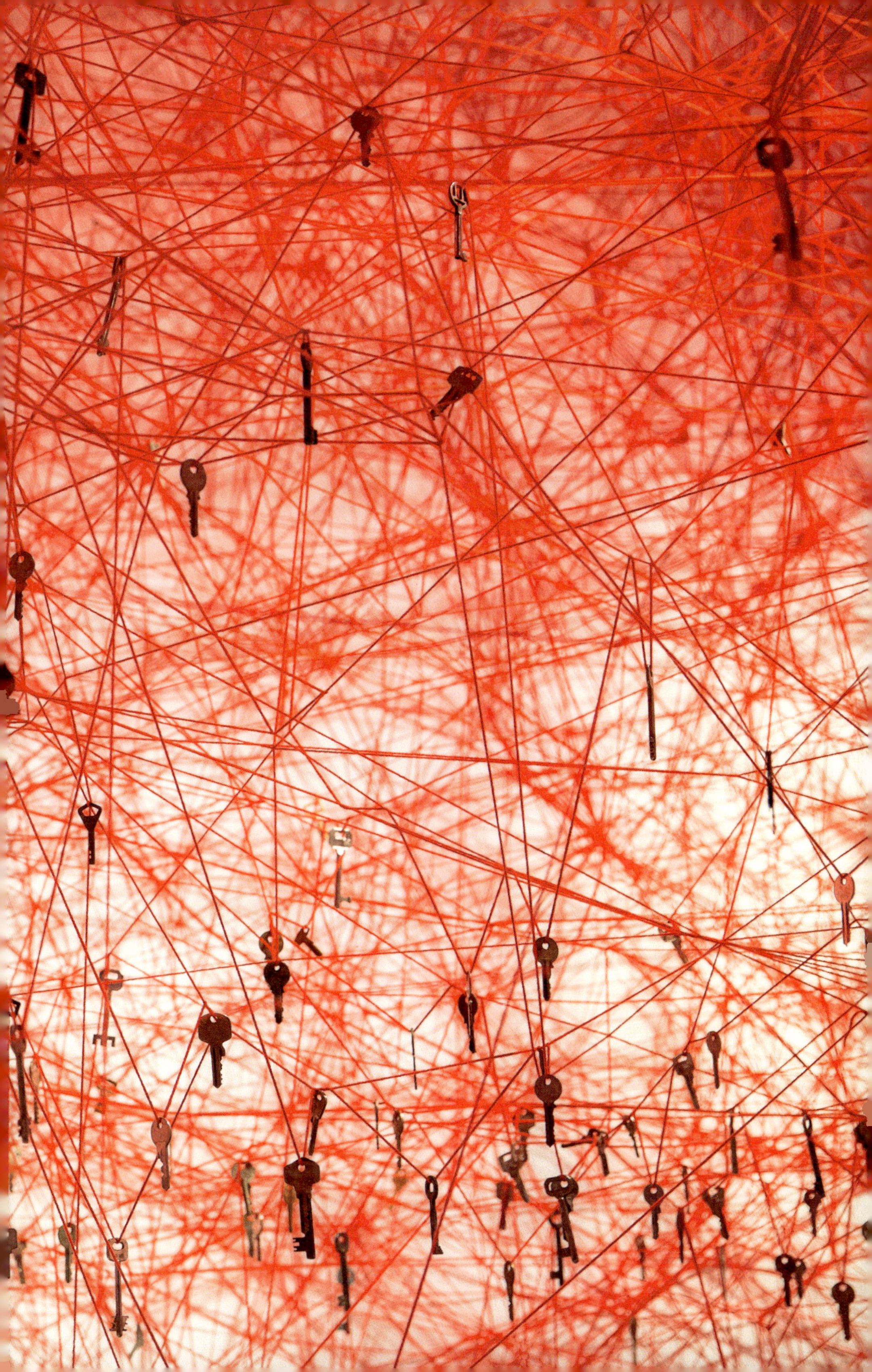

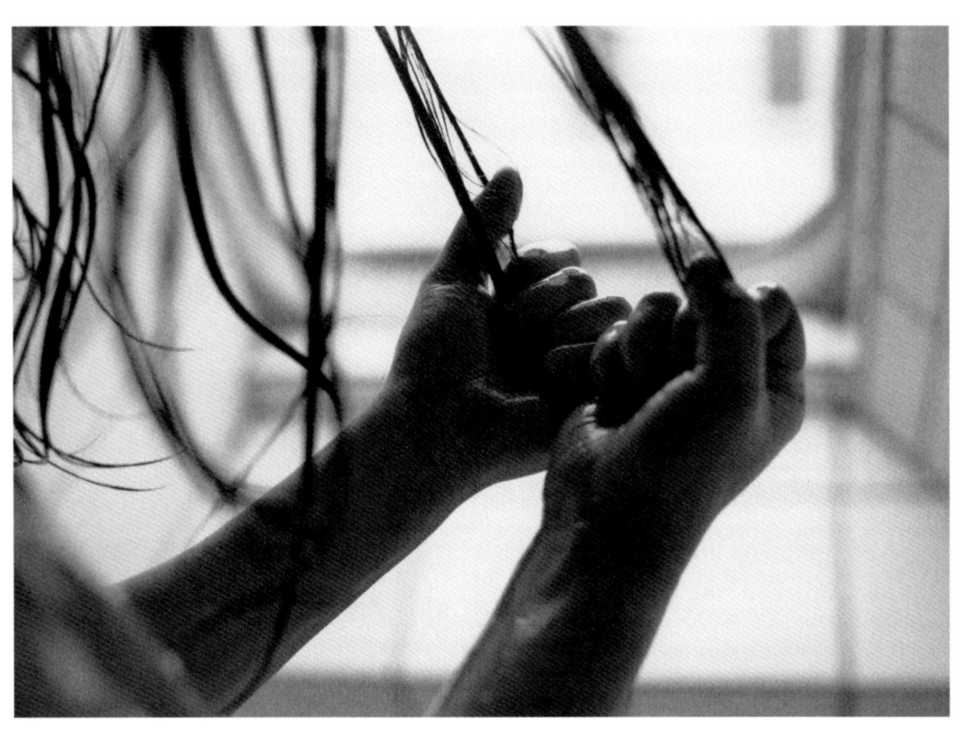

Rain of Memories, 2016
previous page

In the Bathroom,
2022

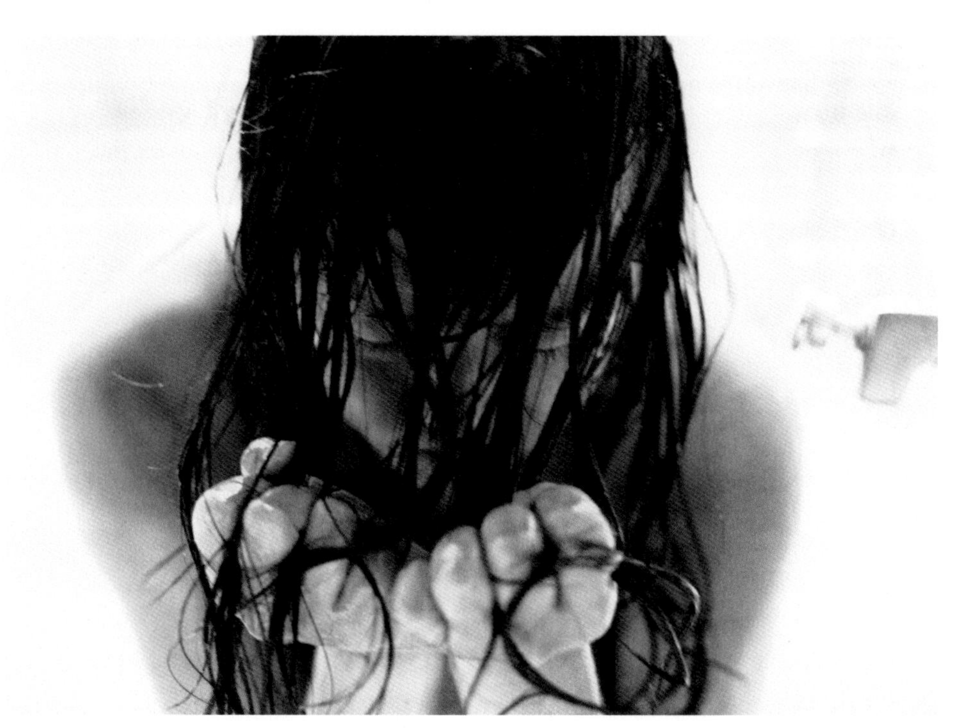

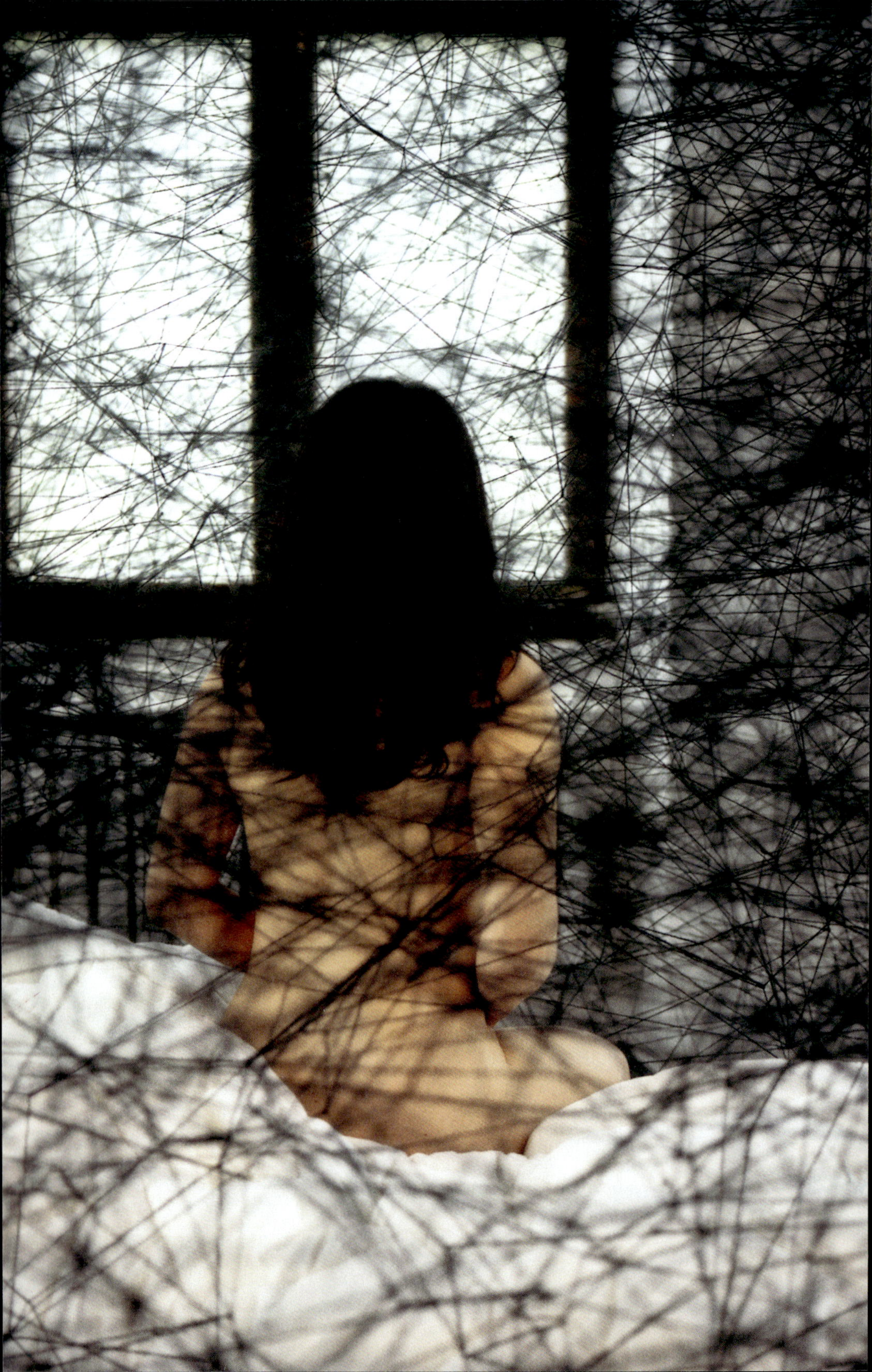

During Sleep,
2002

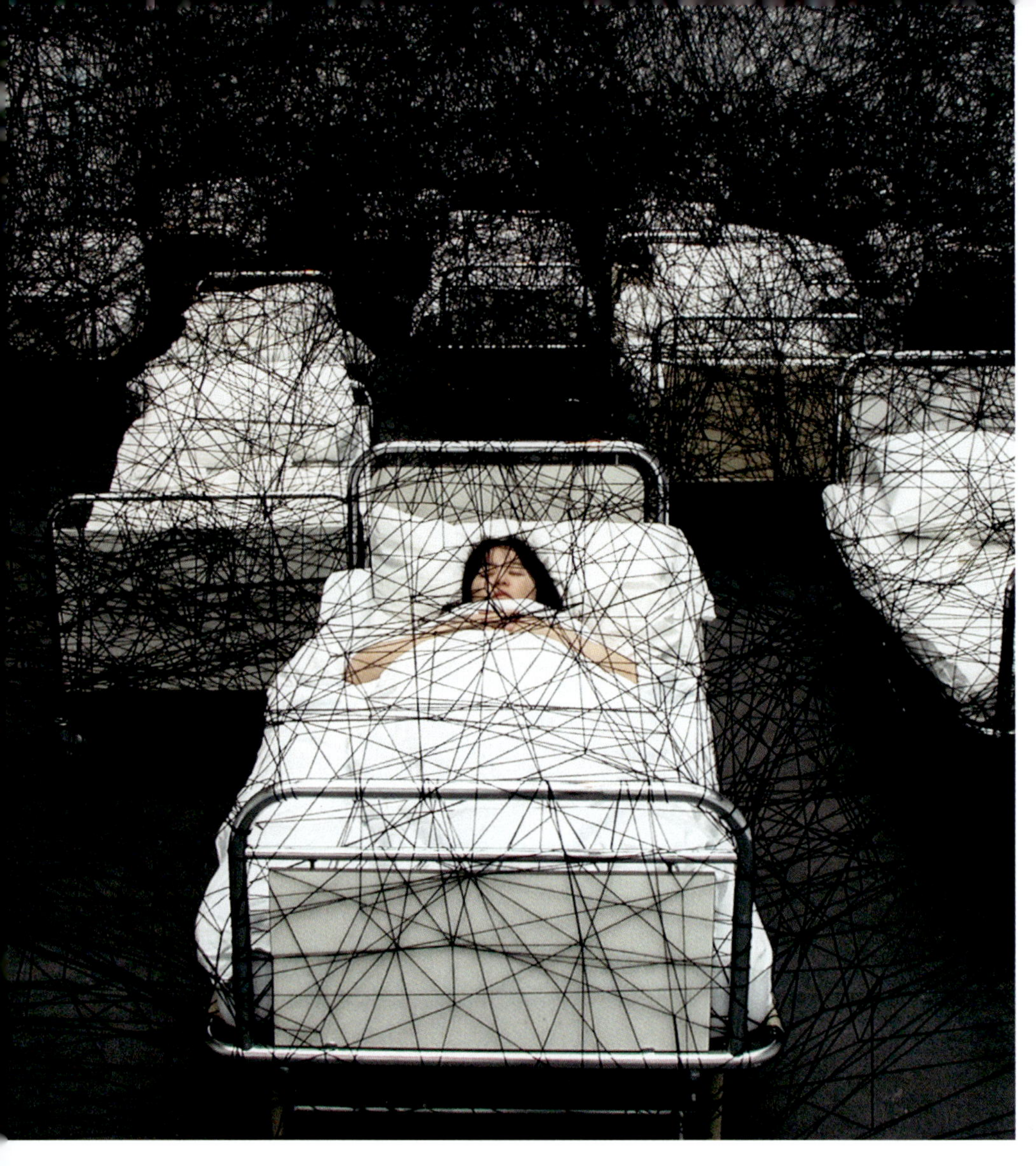

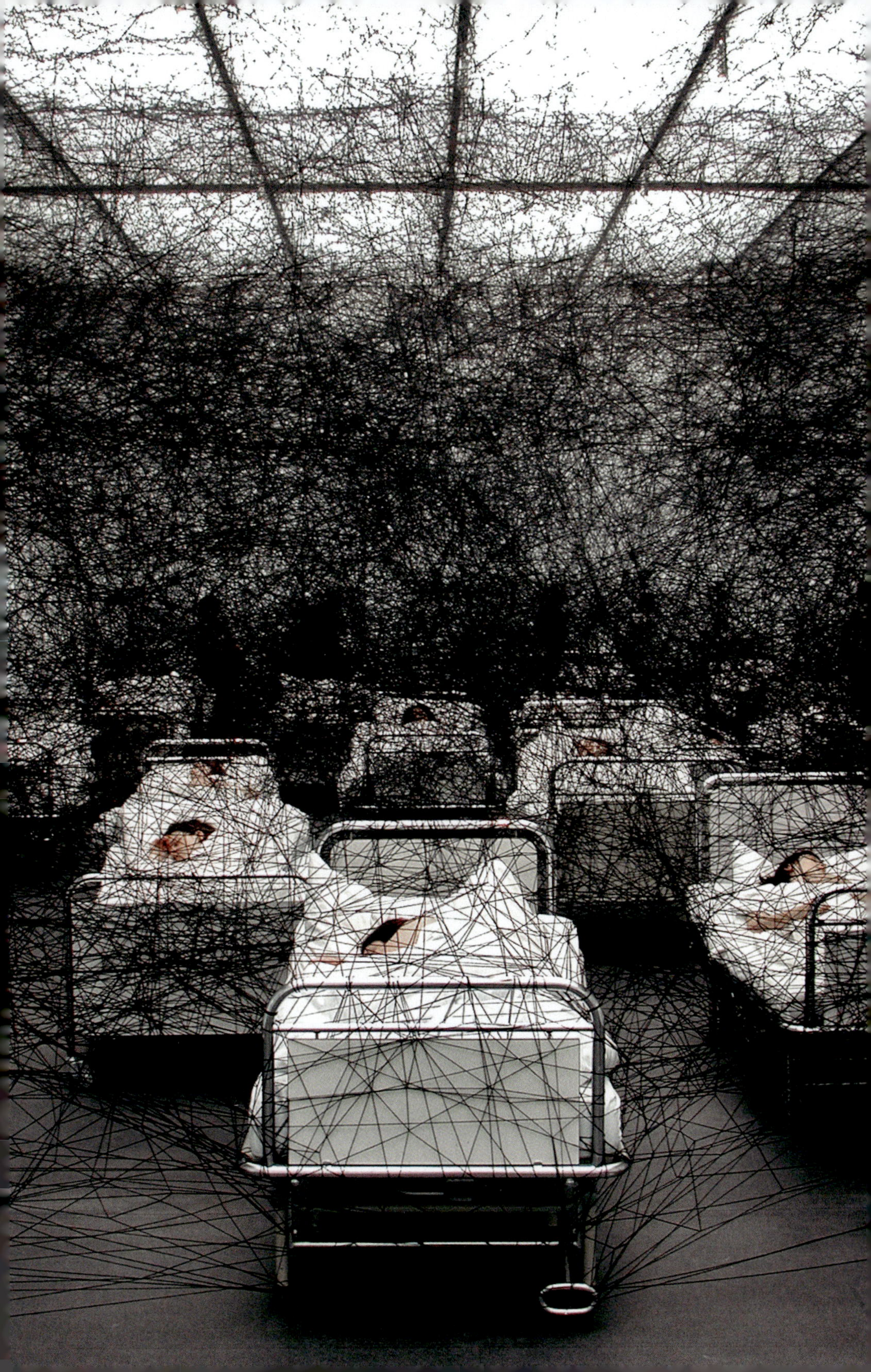

Flowing Water,
2009

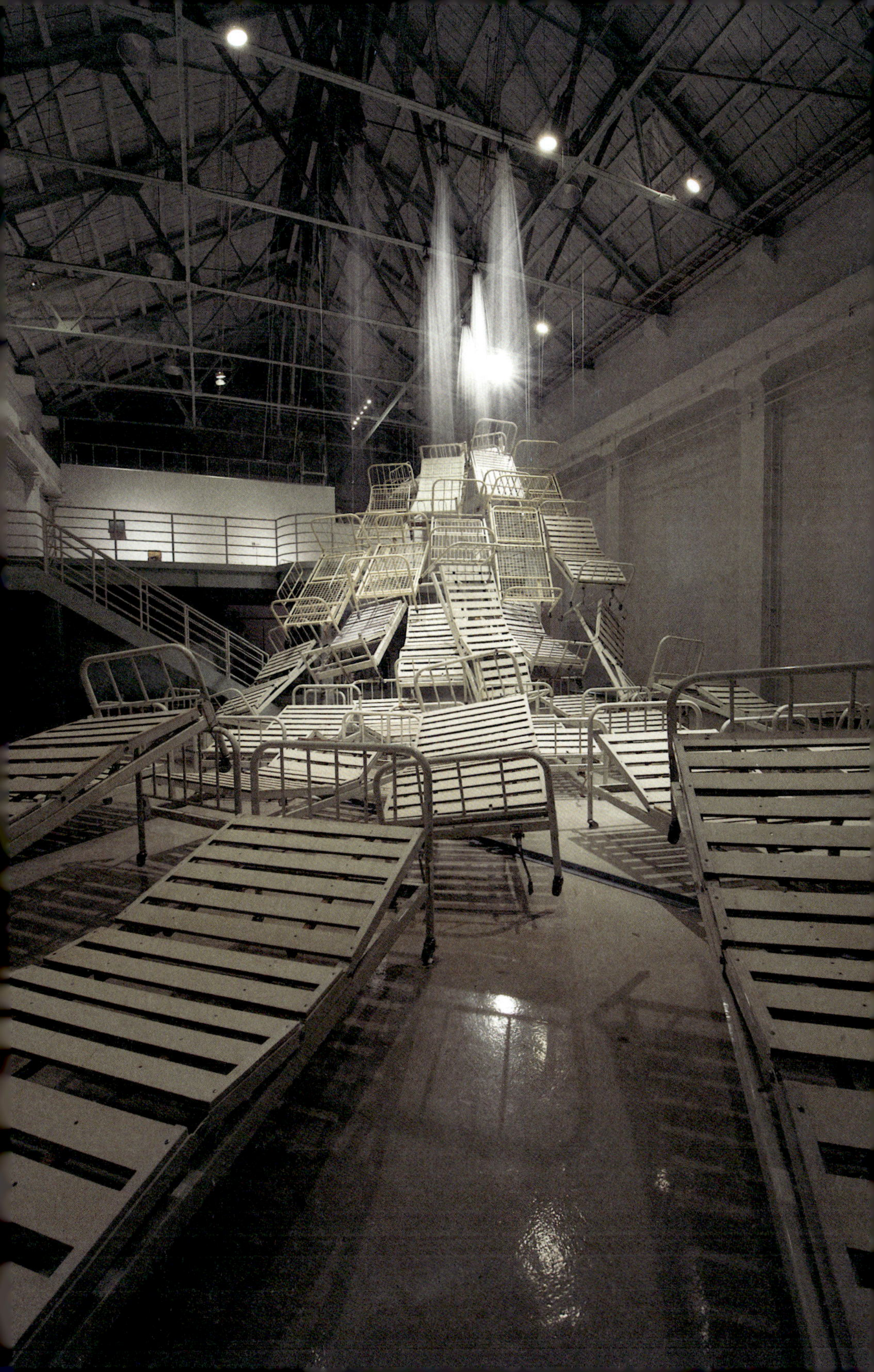

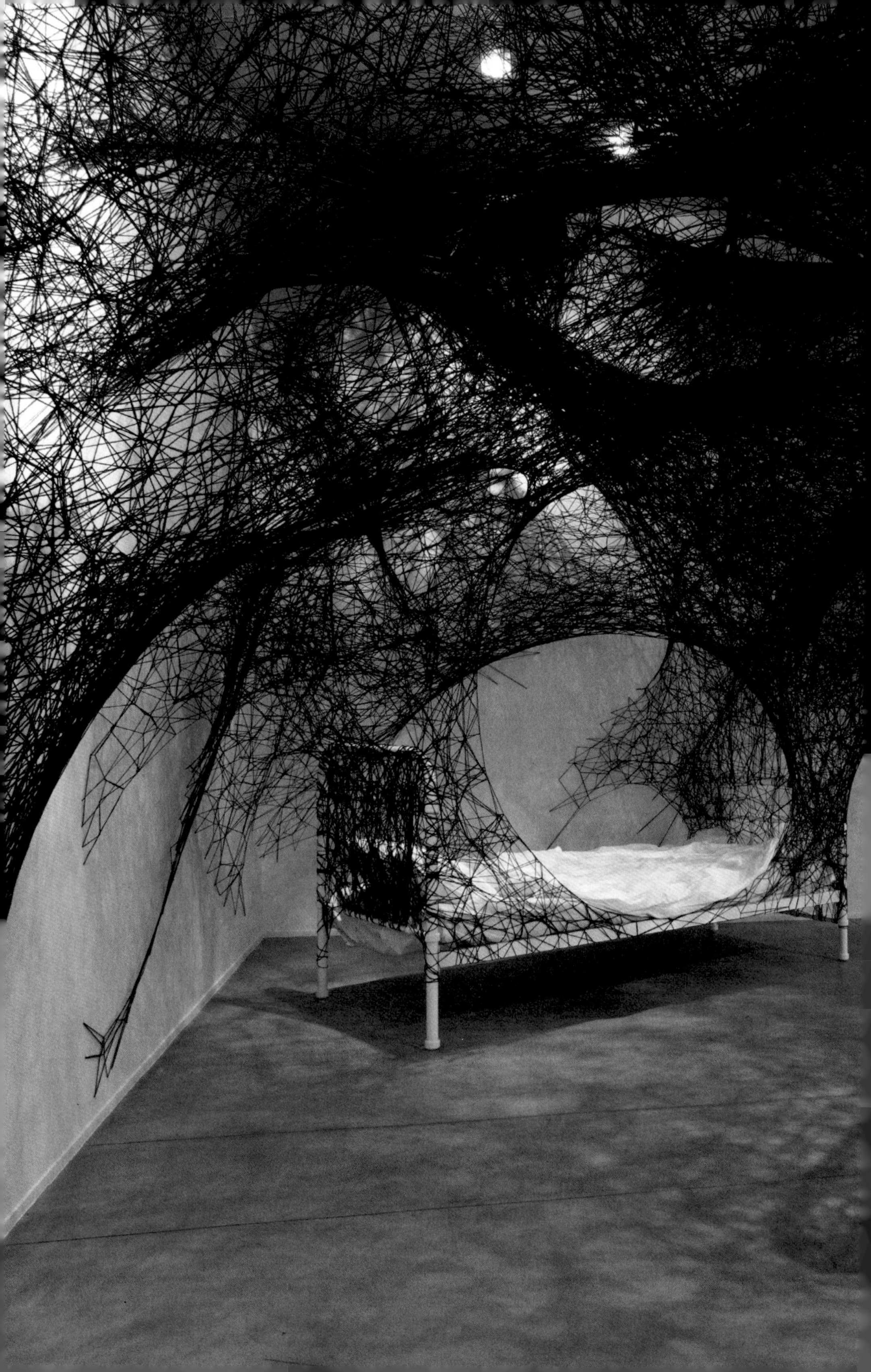

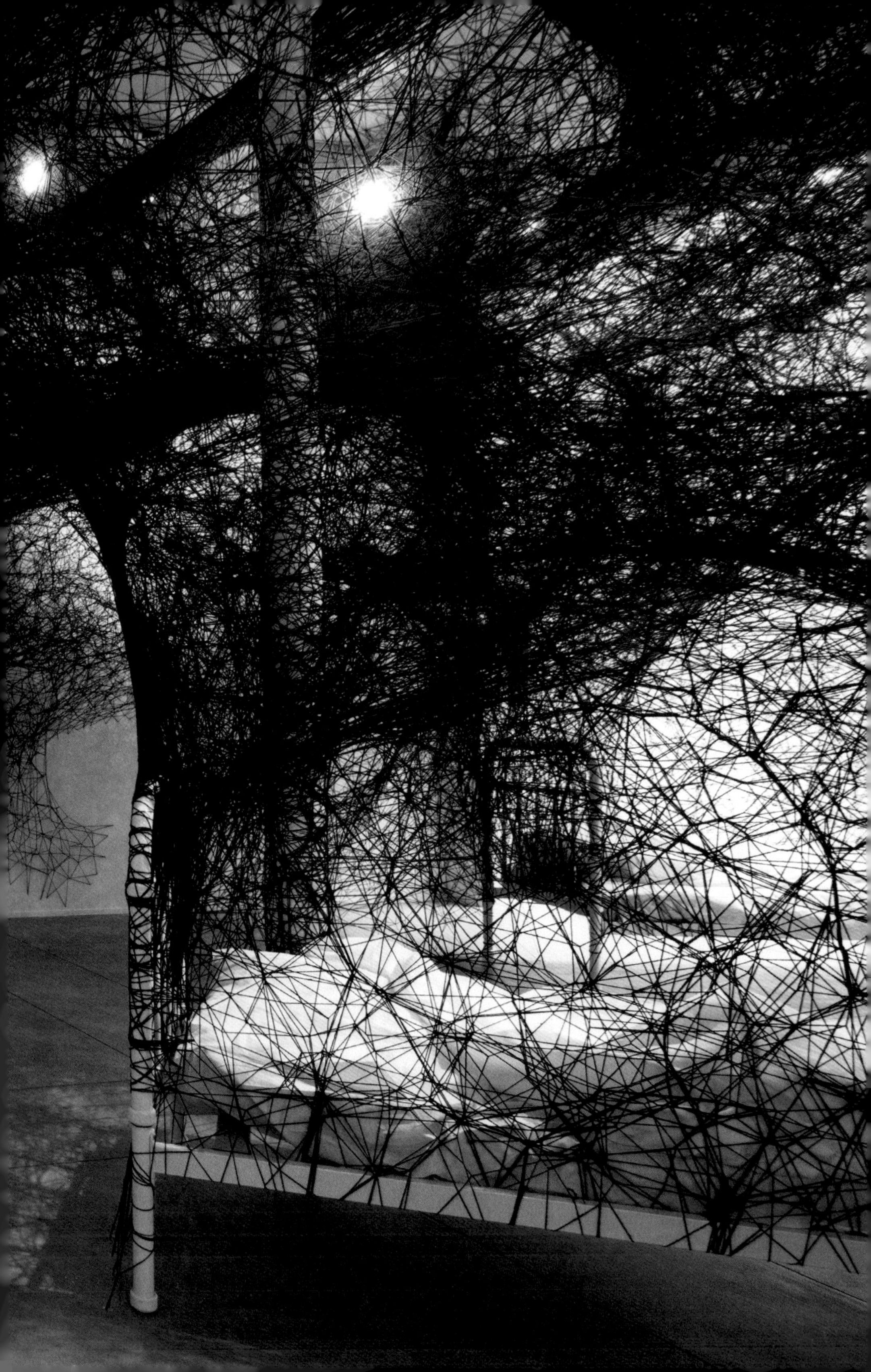

Sleeping is like Death, 2016
previous page

Conscious Sleep,
2016

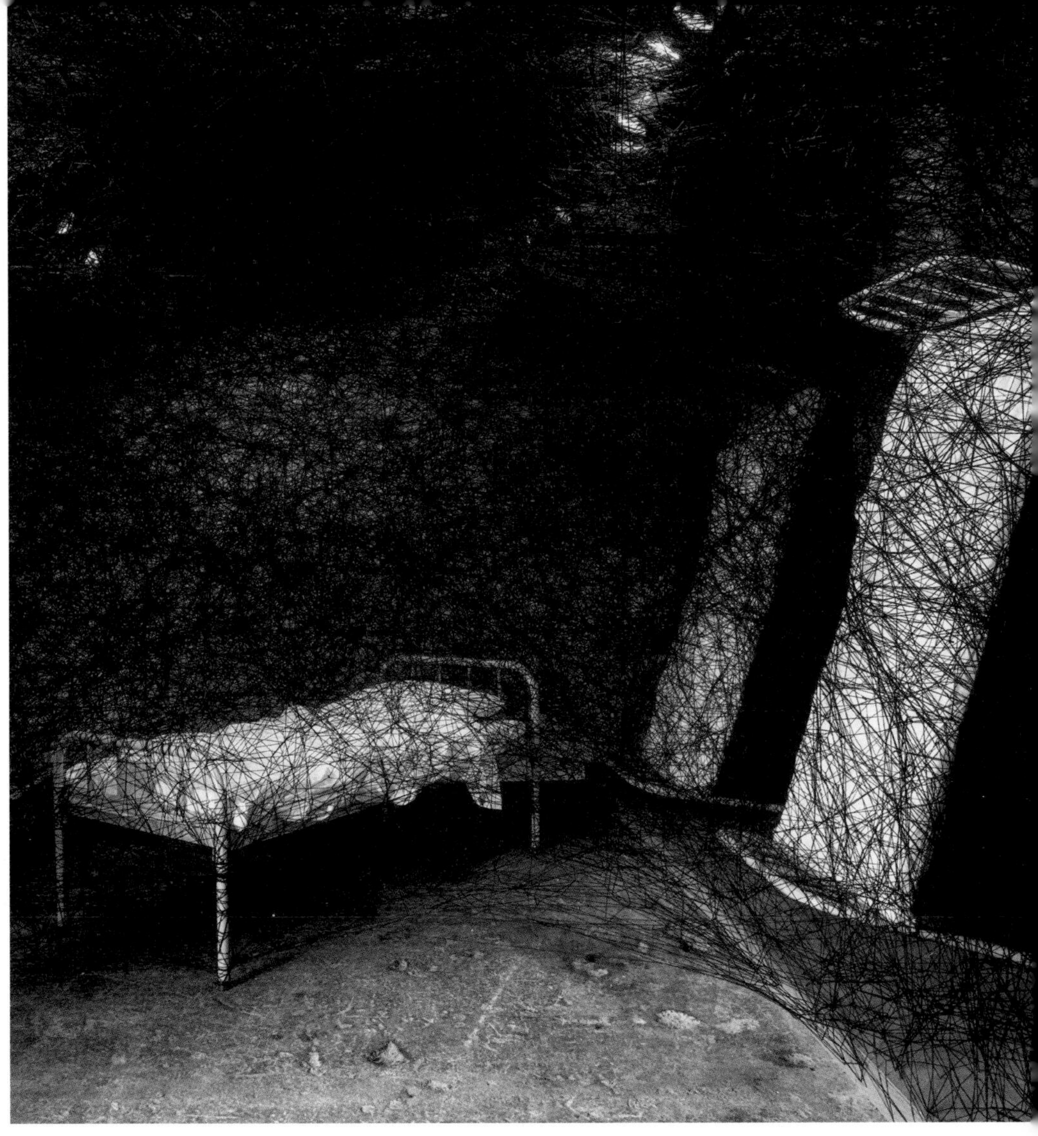

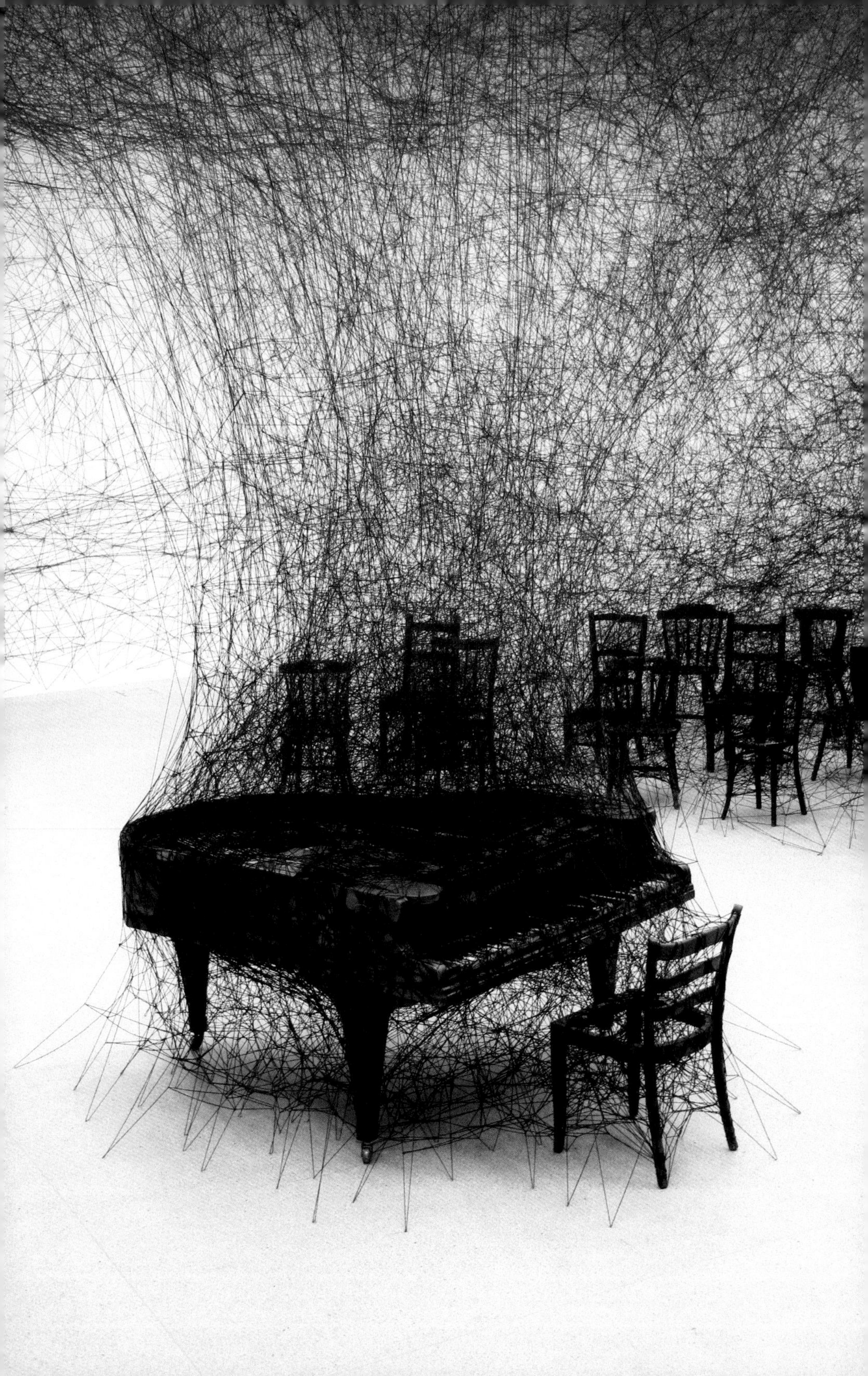

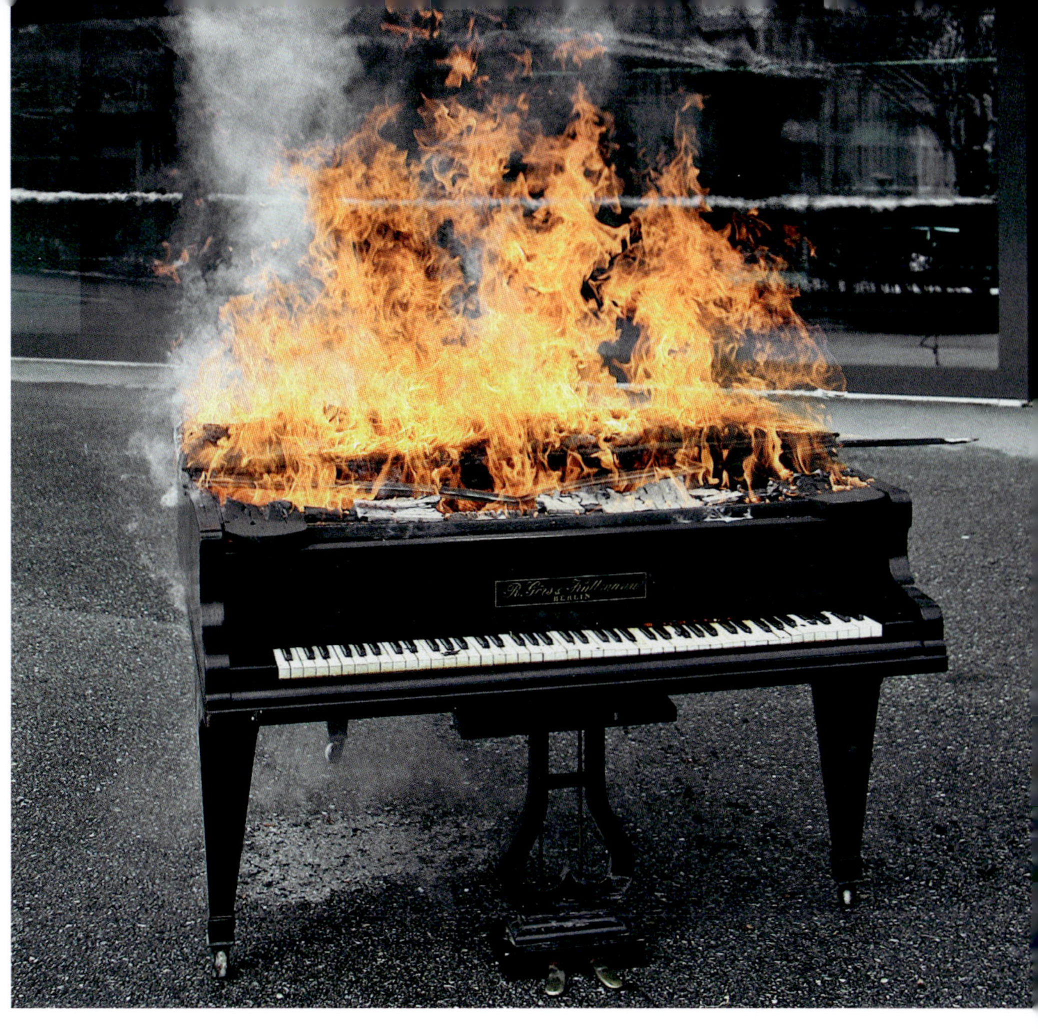

In Silence,
2008

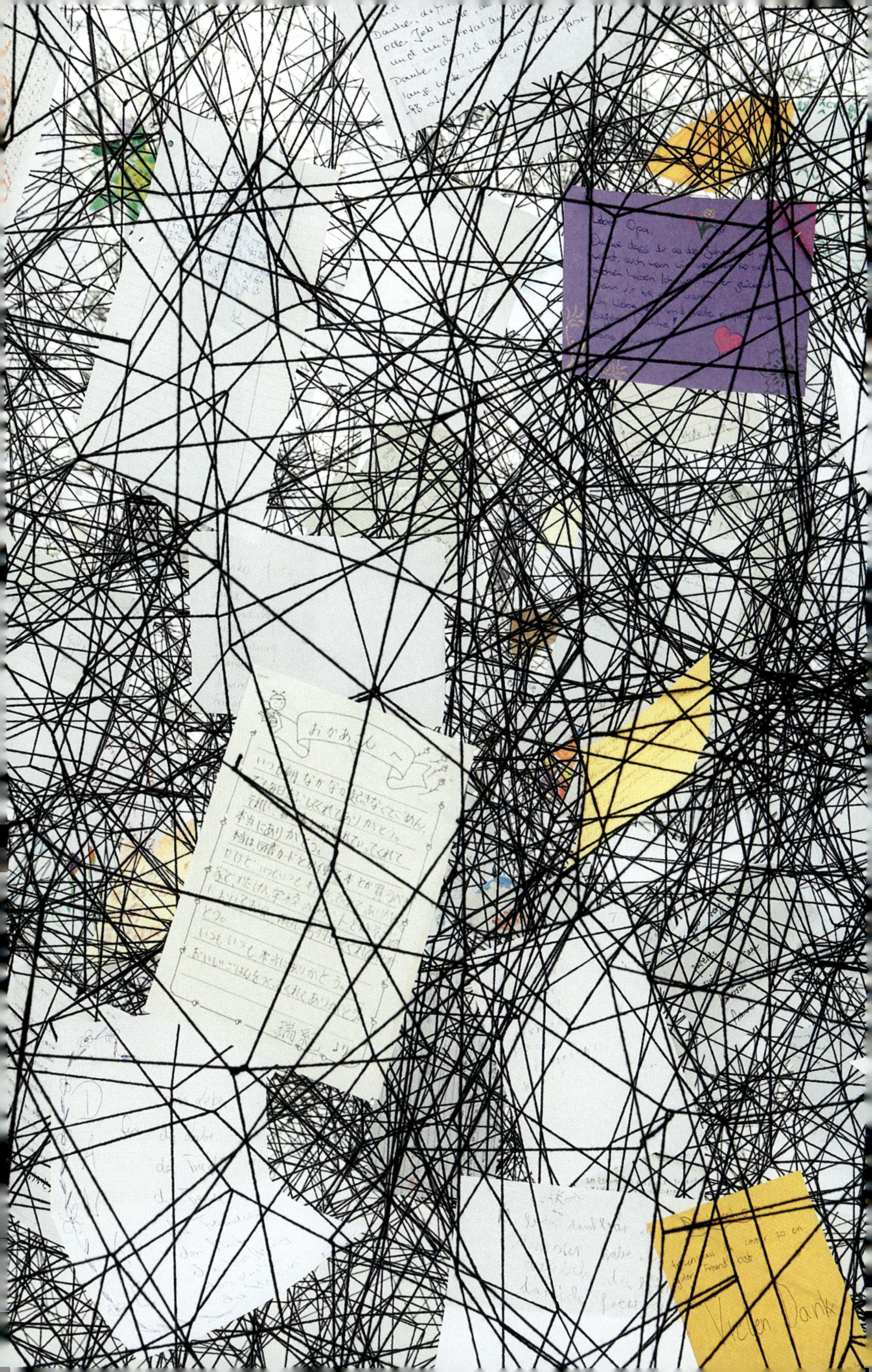

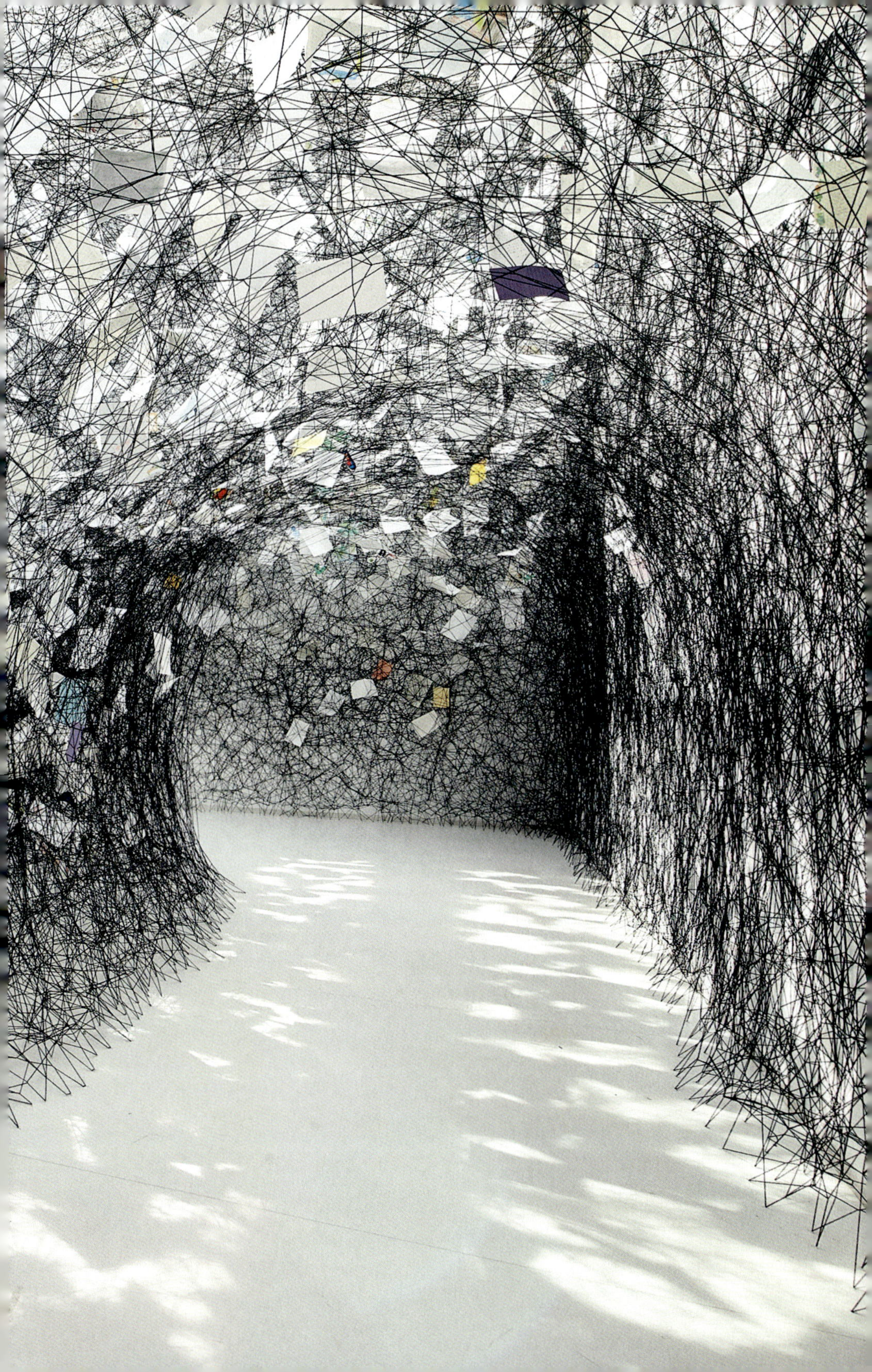

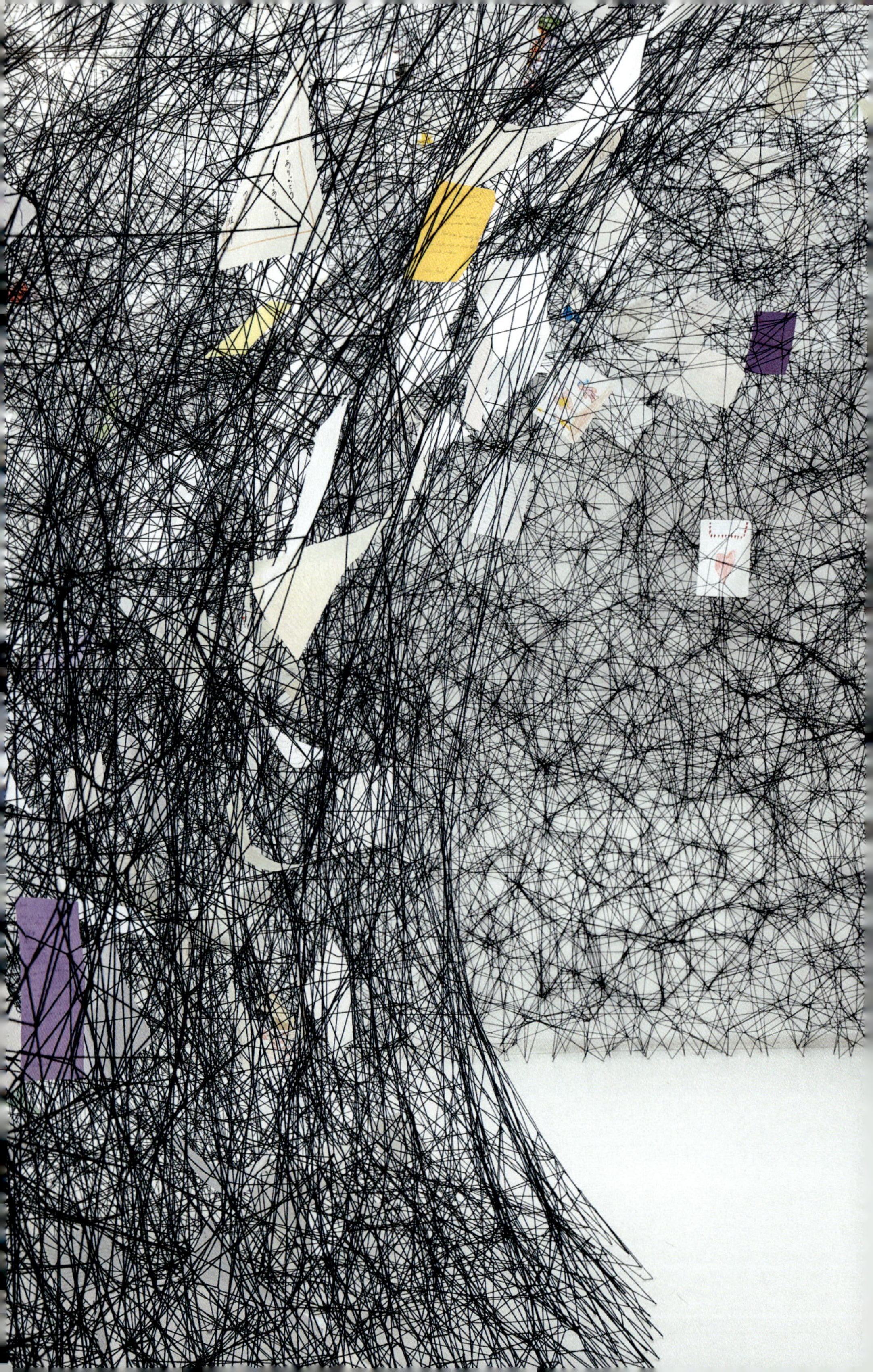

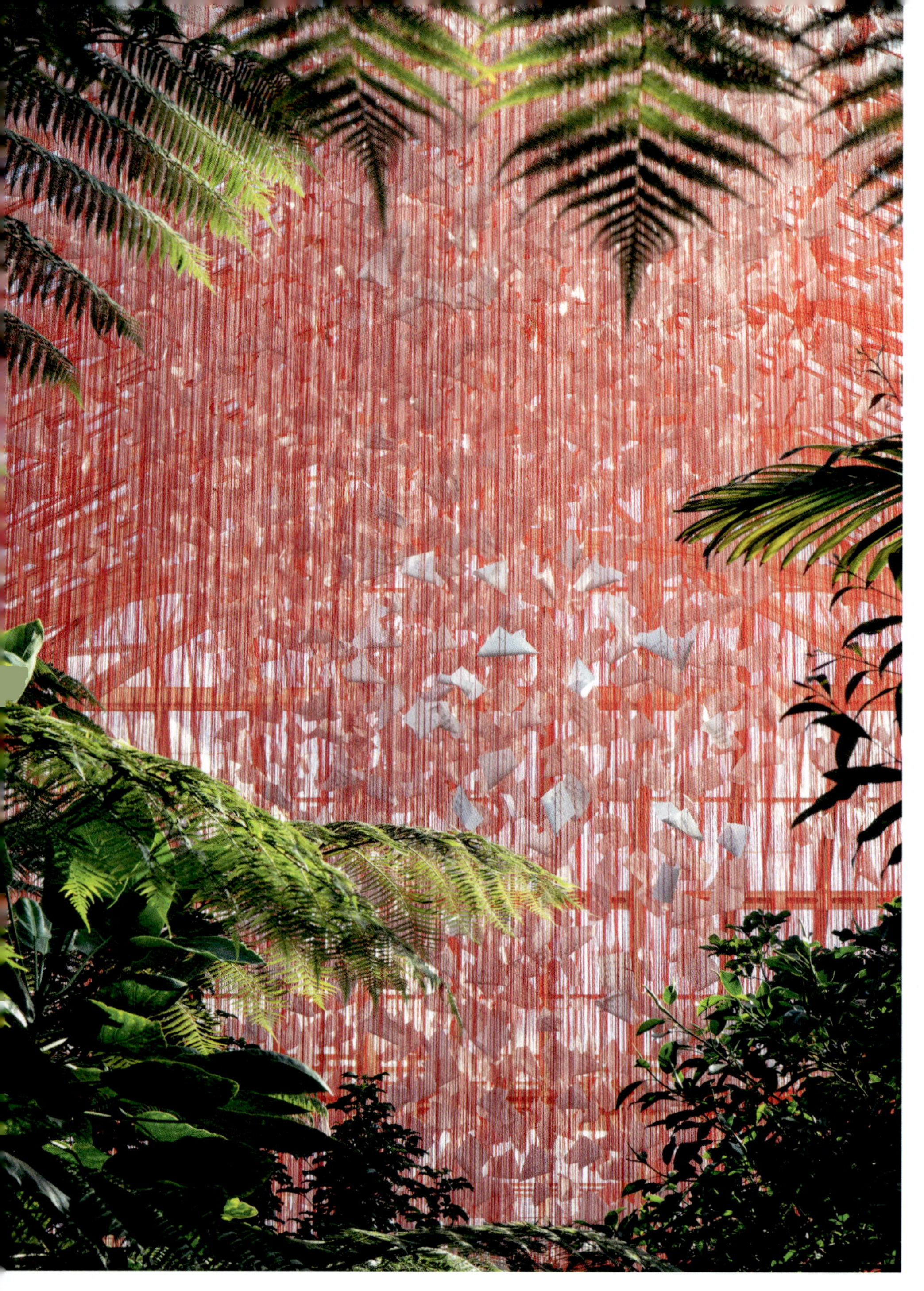

One Thousand Springs,
2021

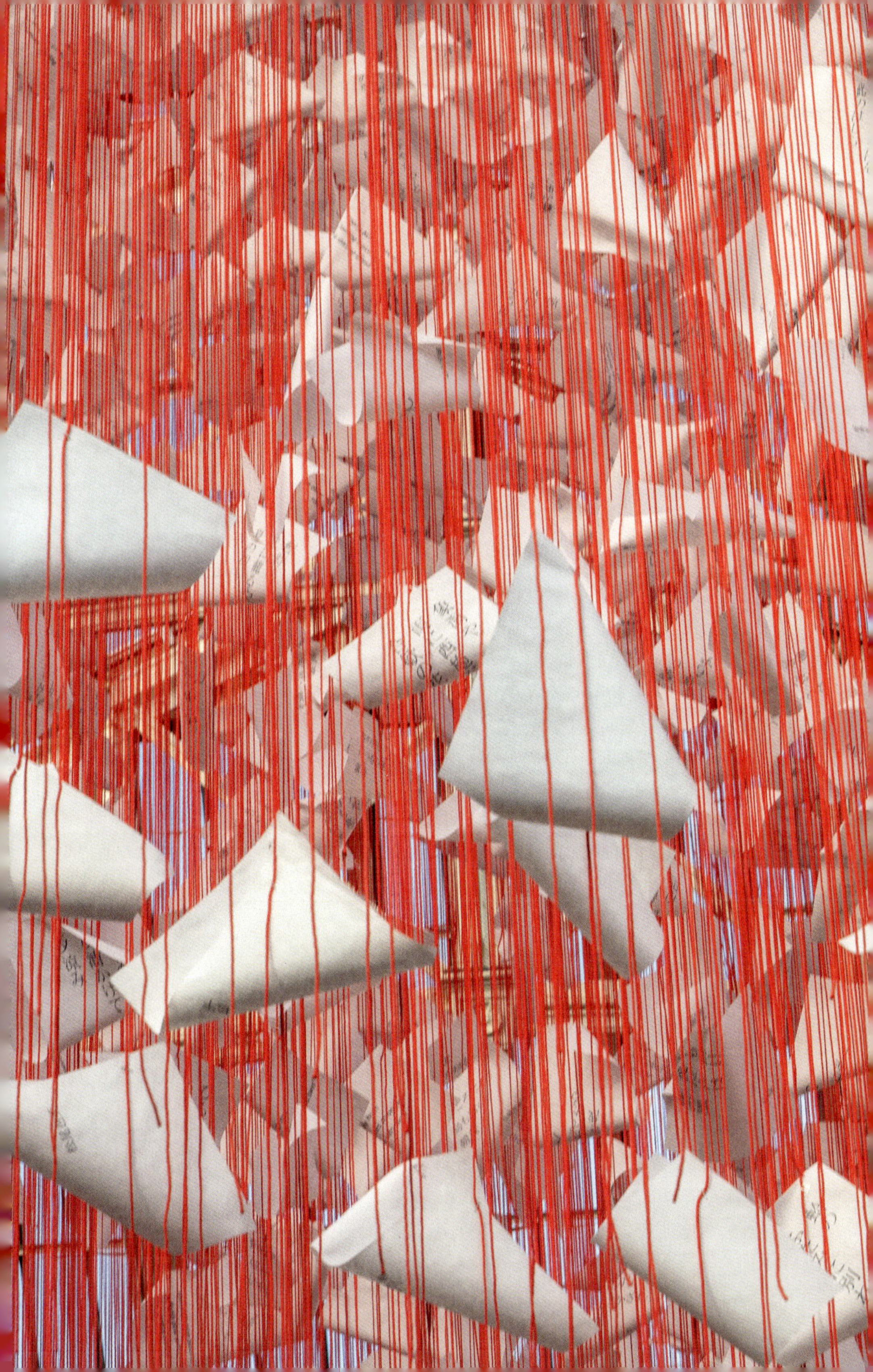

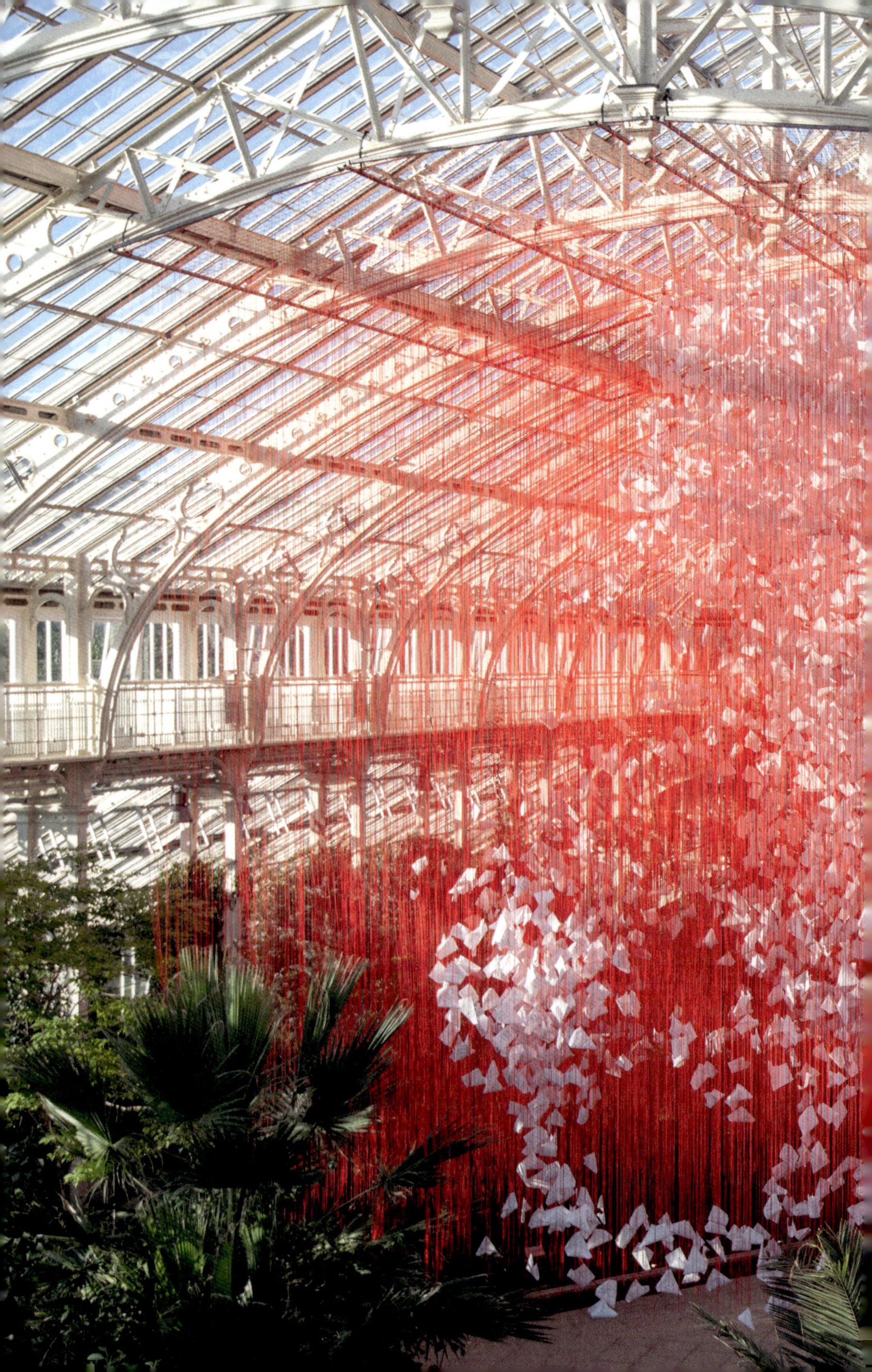

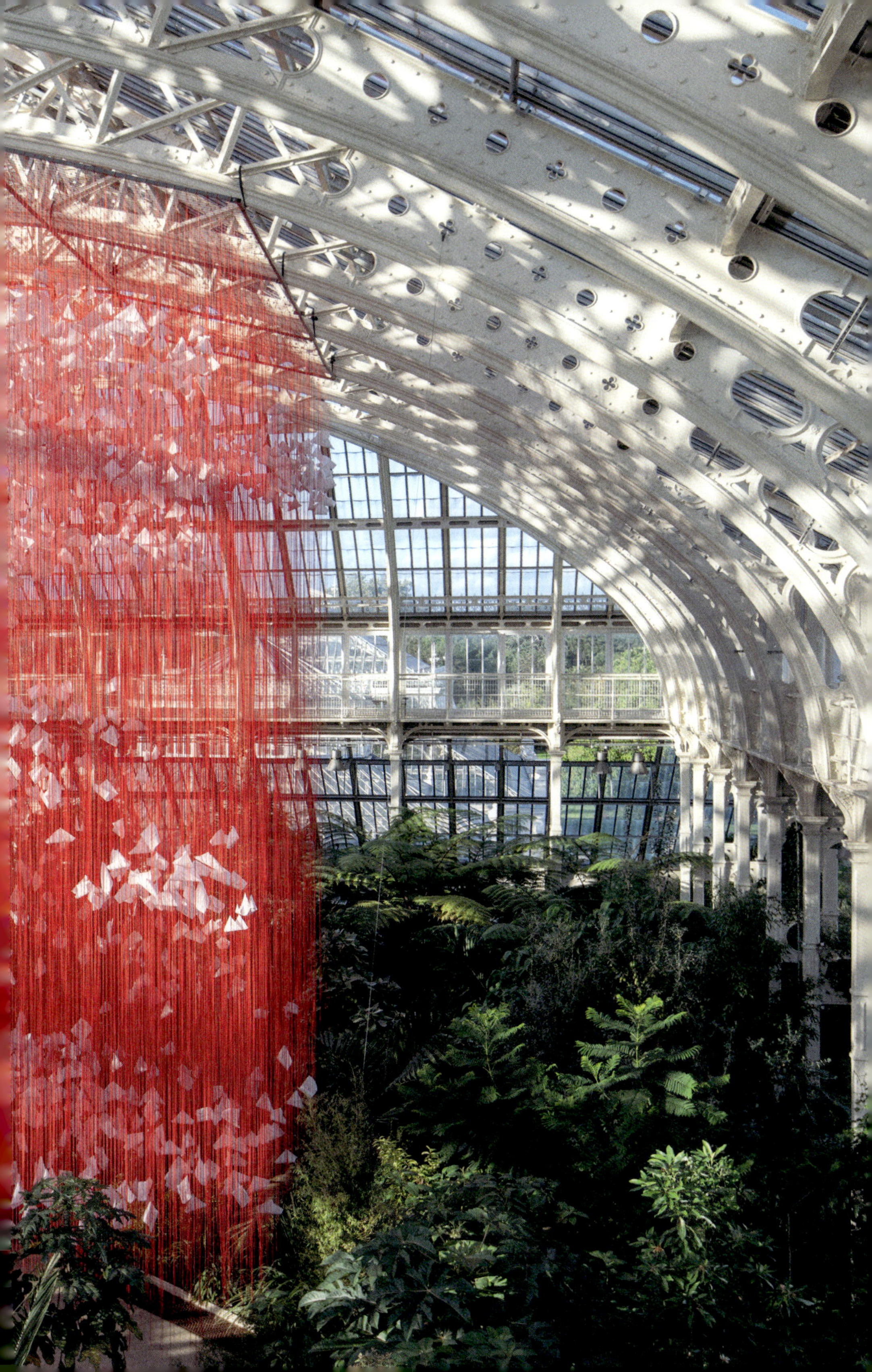

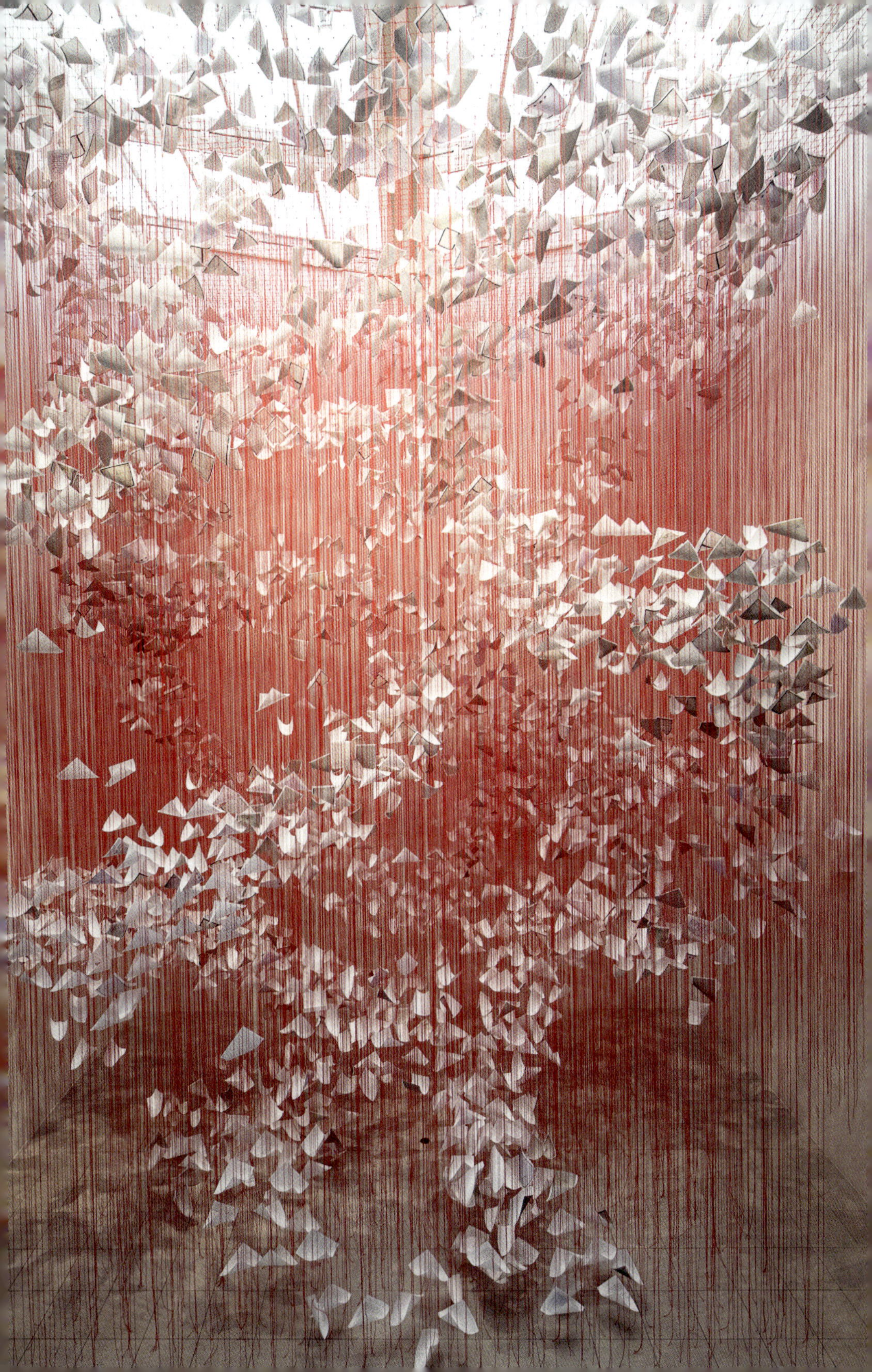

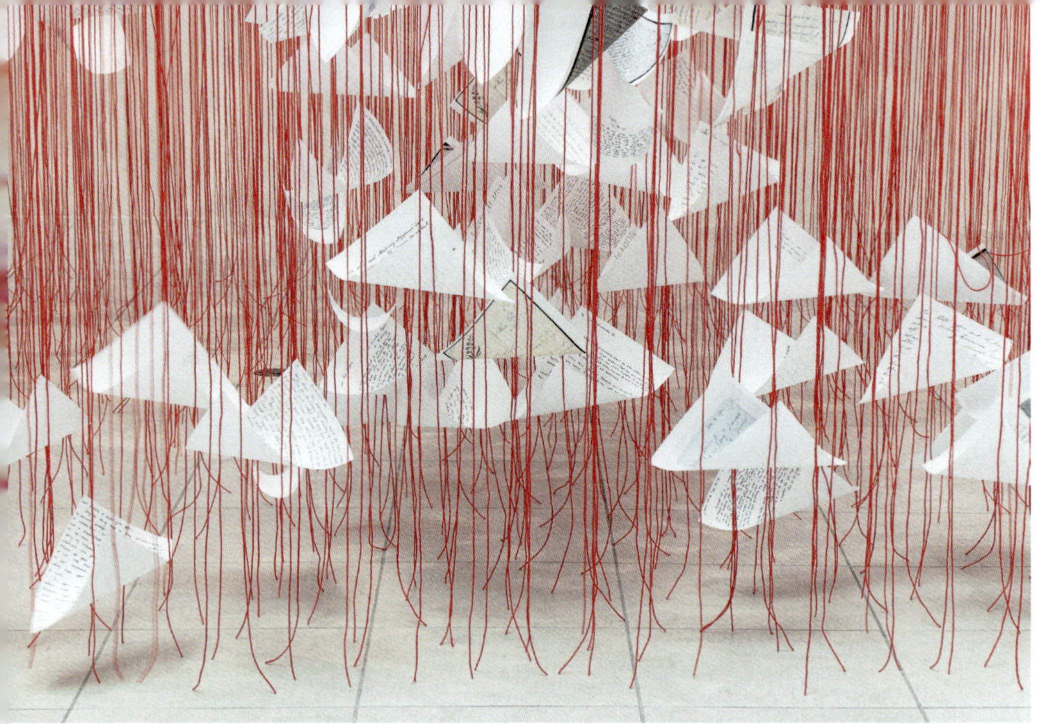

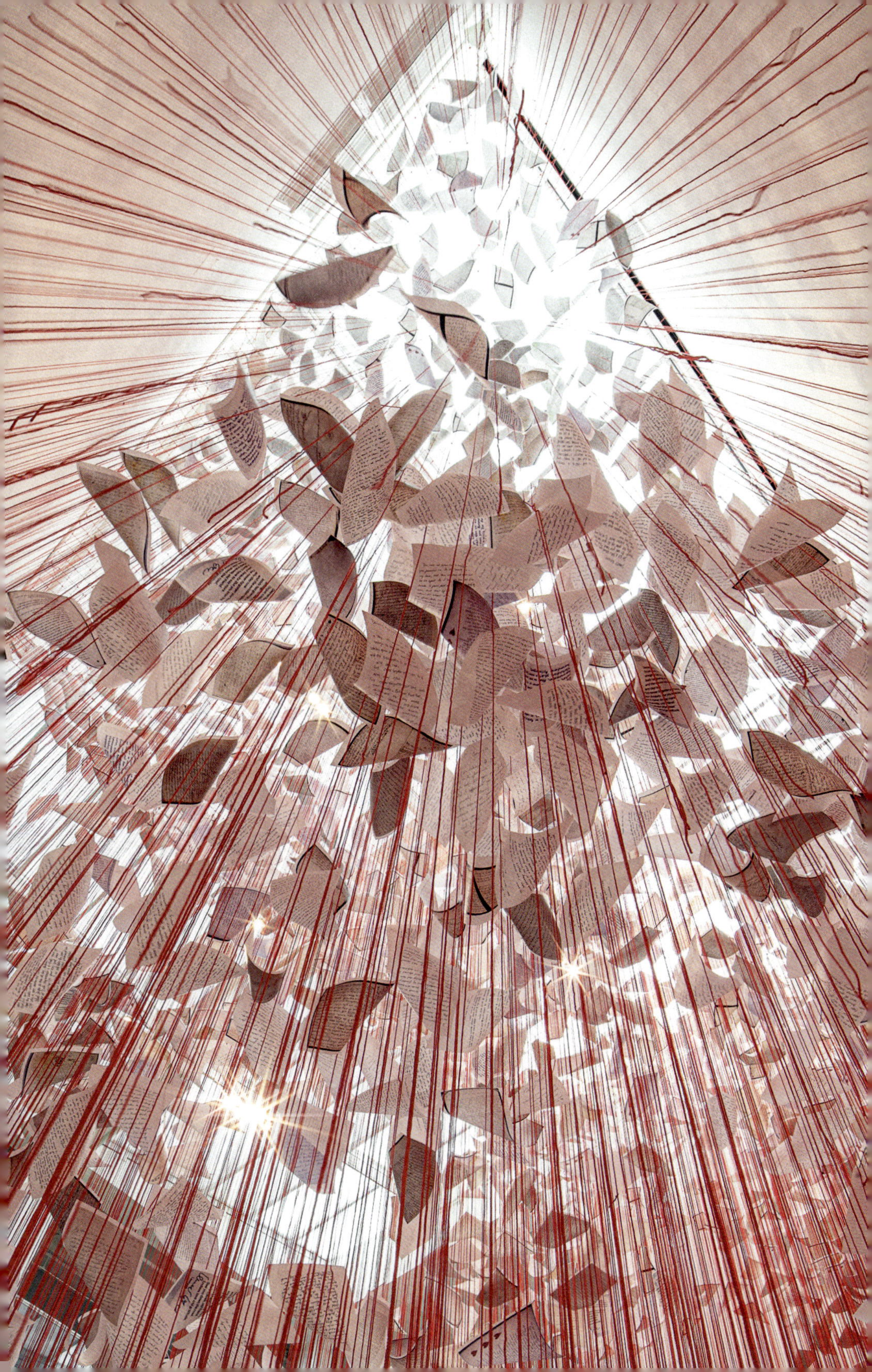

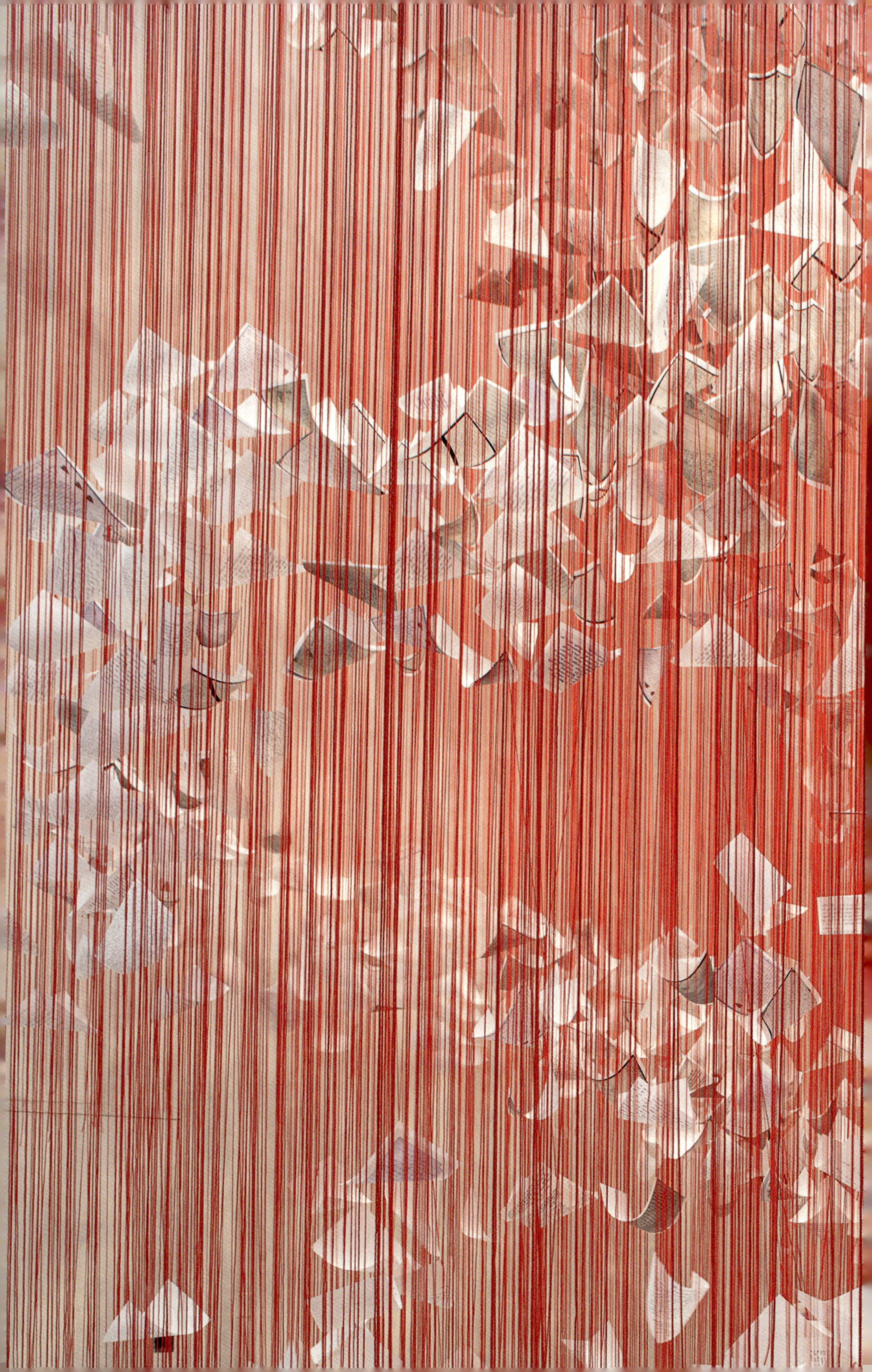

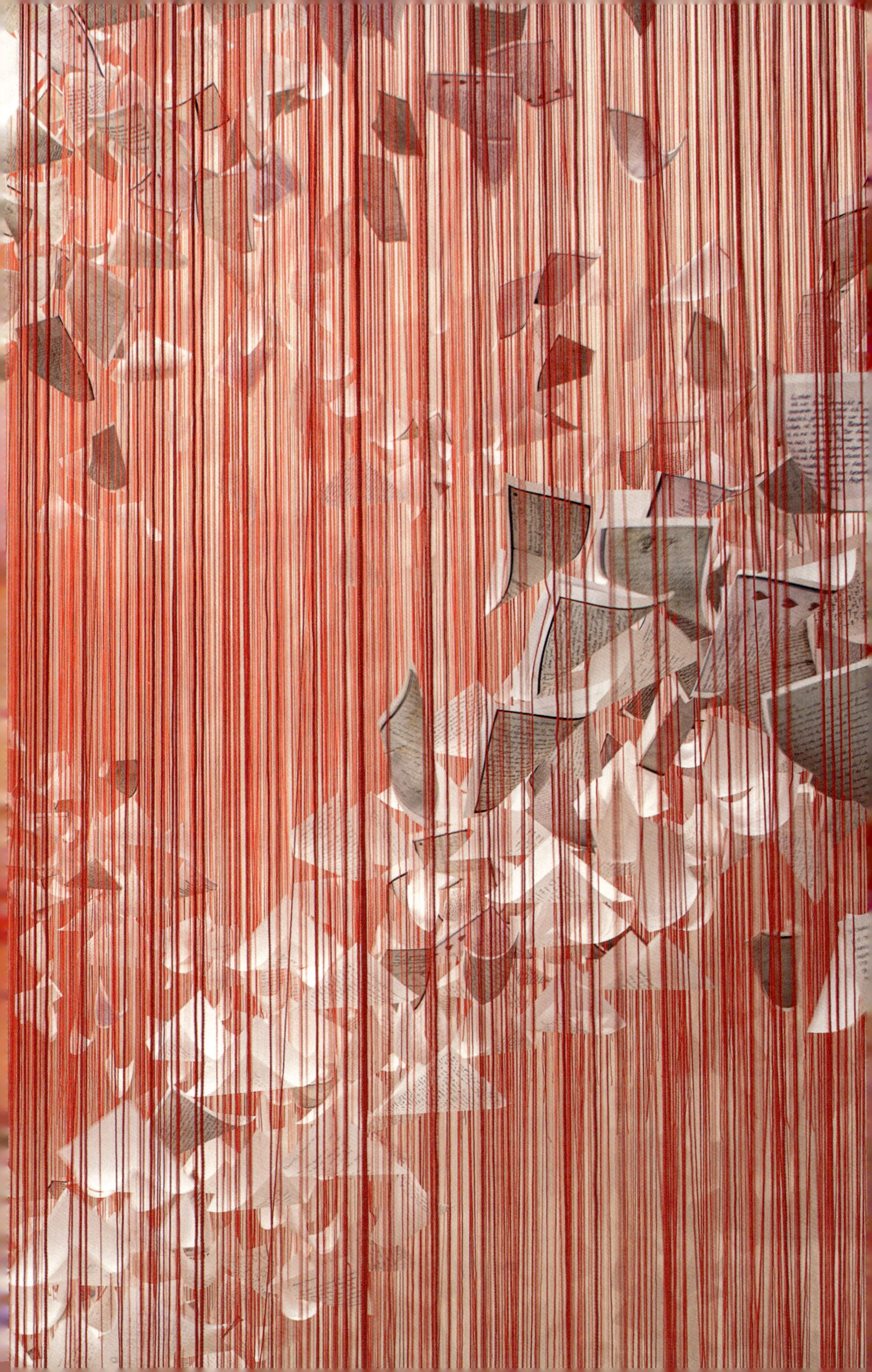

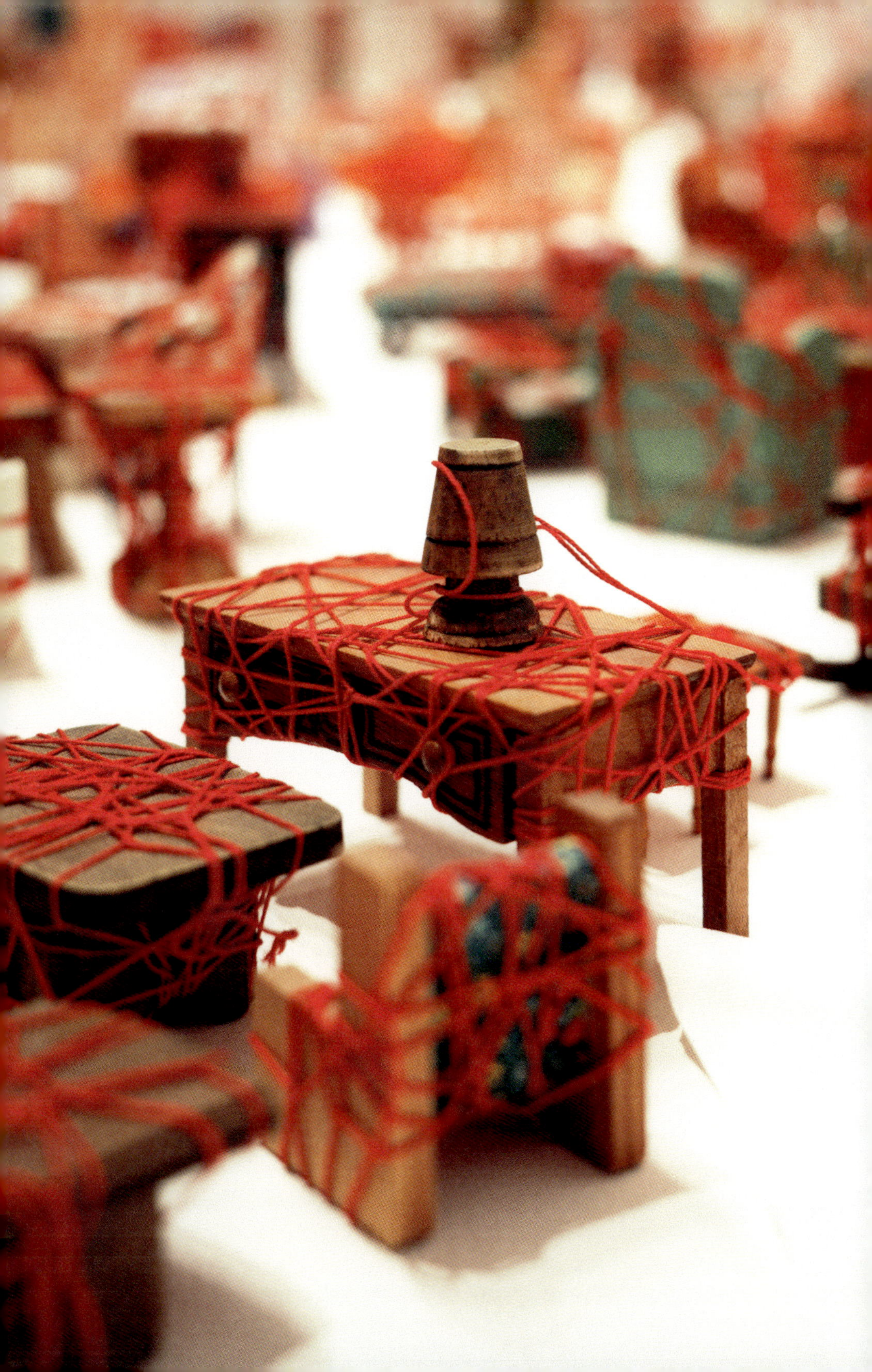

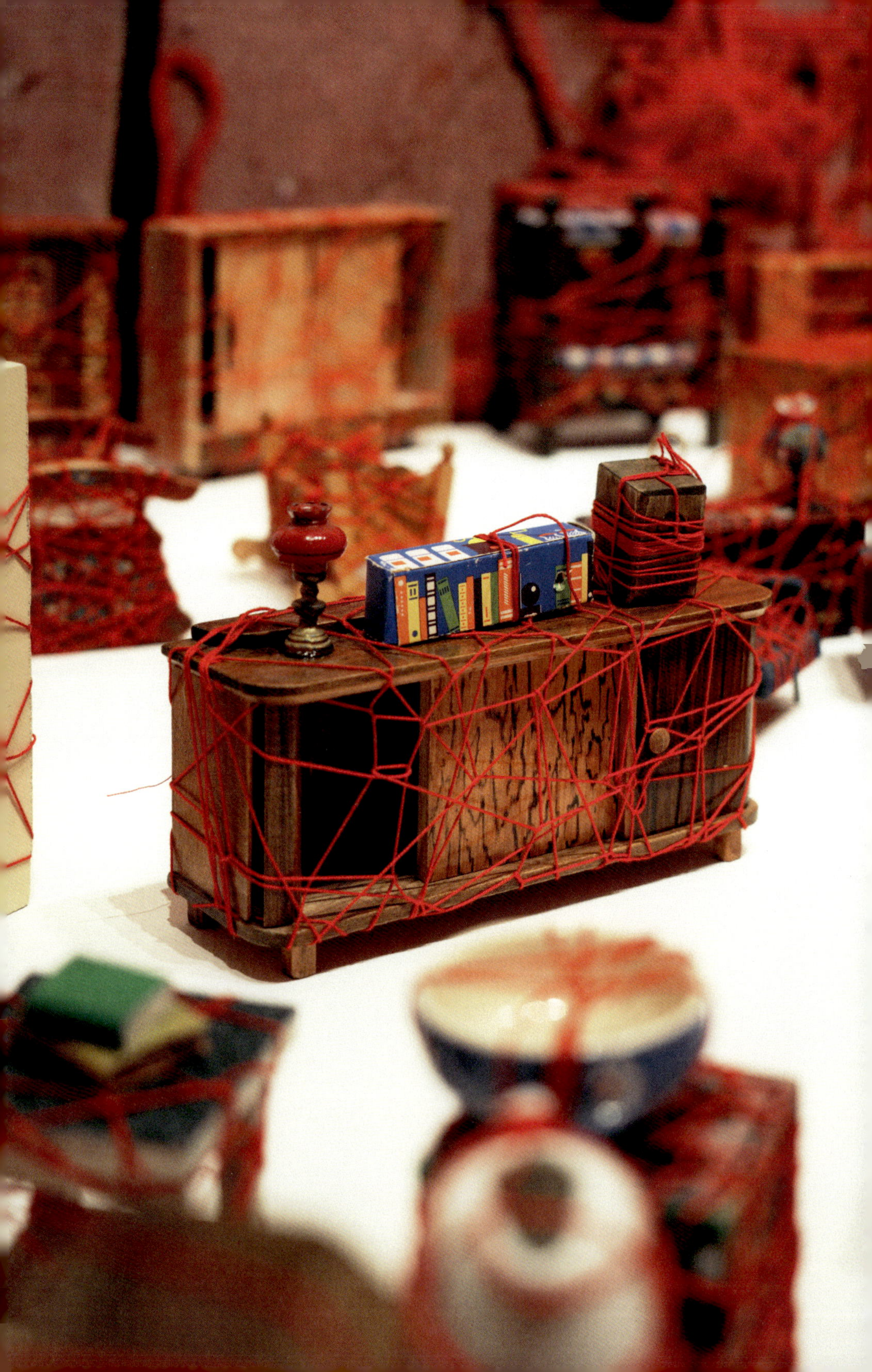

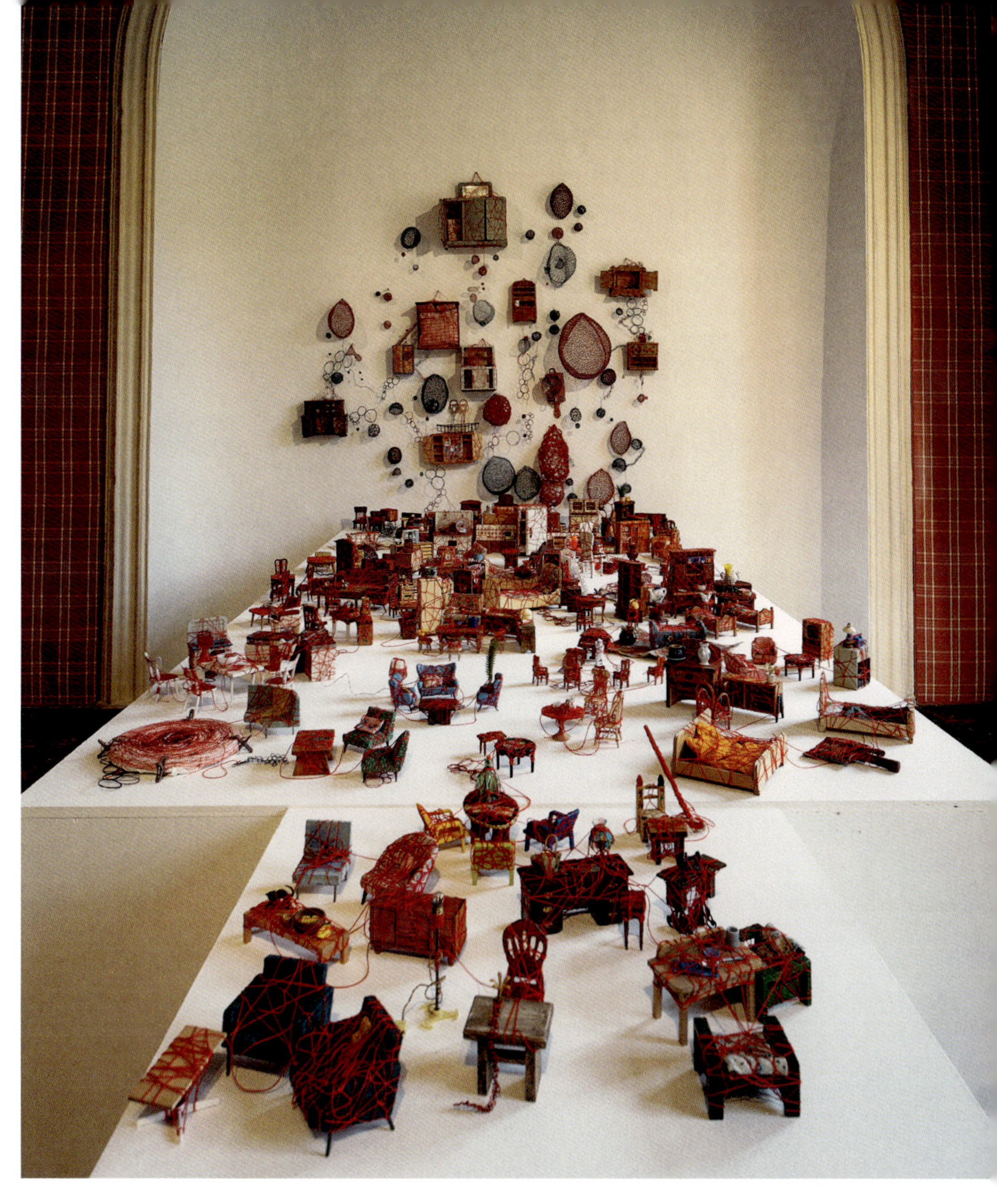

Living Inside,
2025

Internal Line,
2019

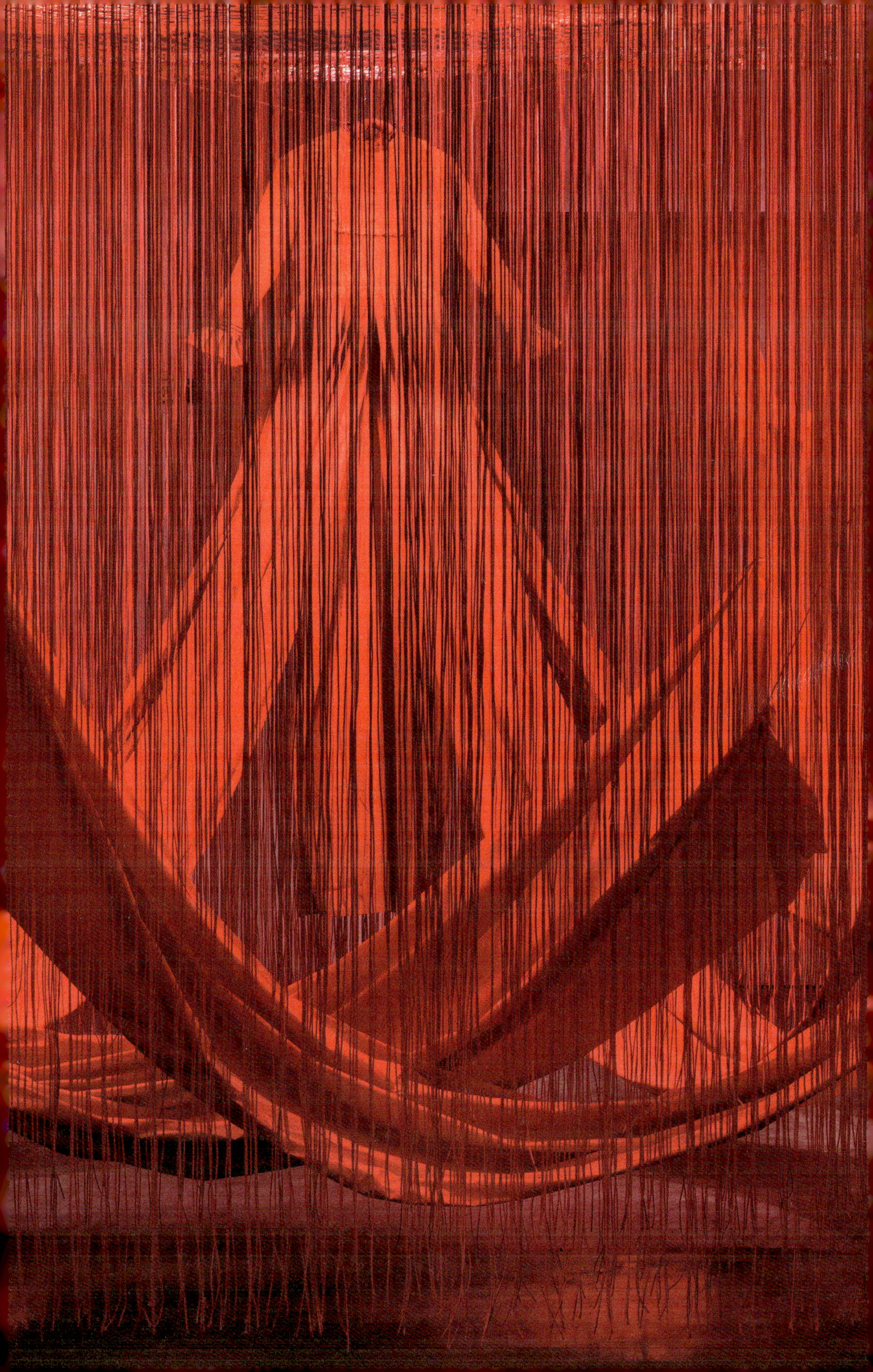

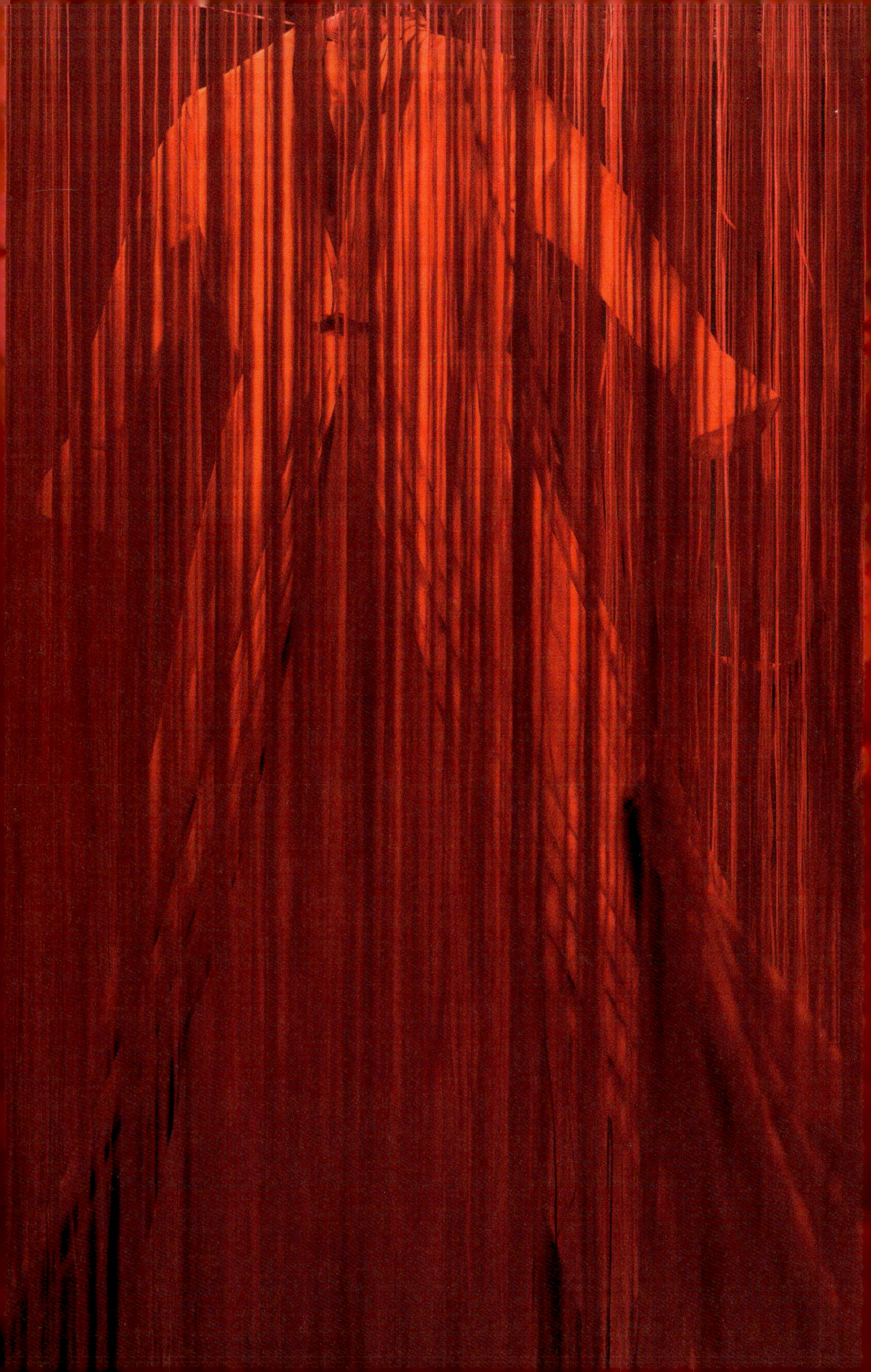

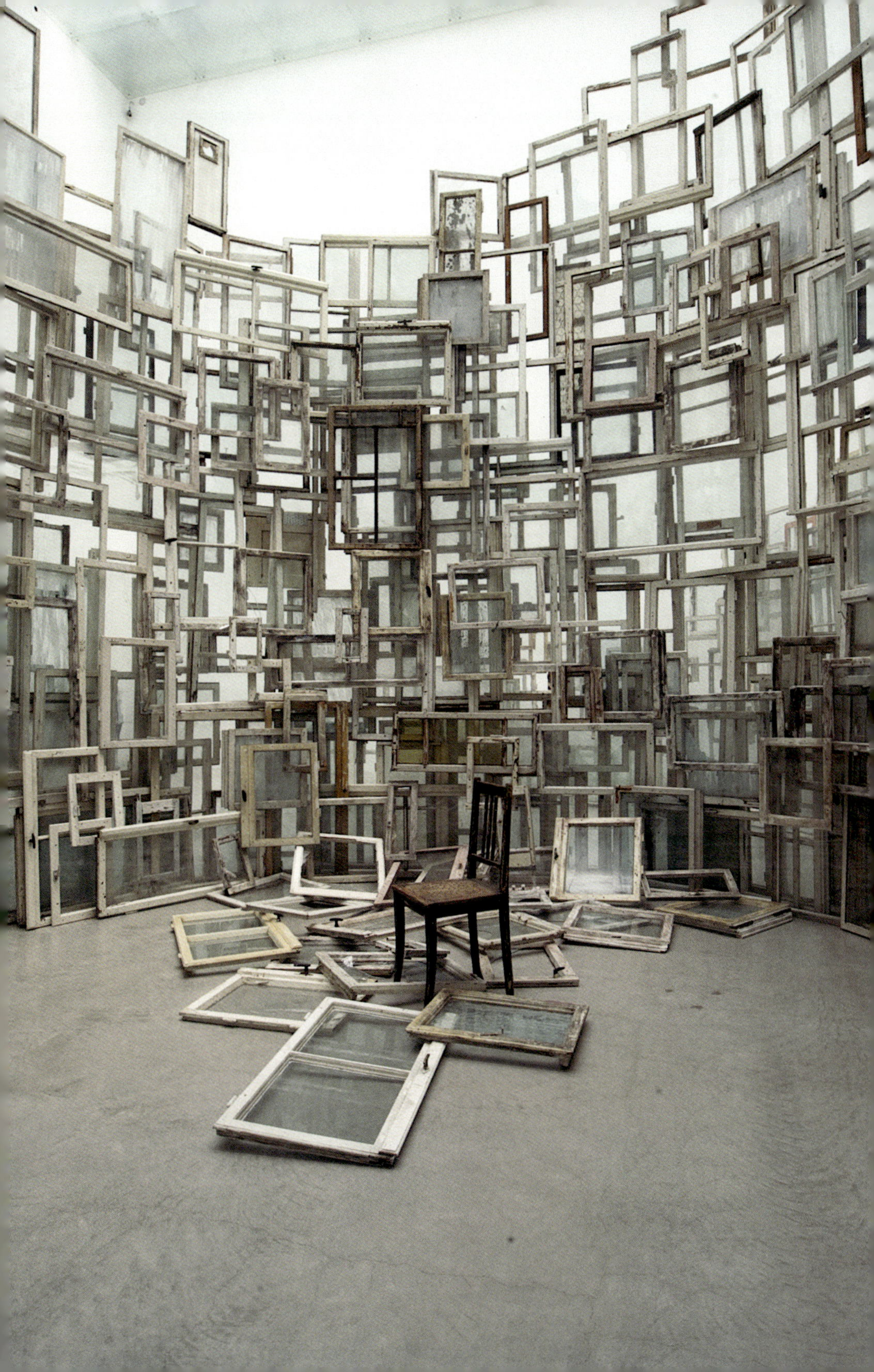

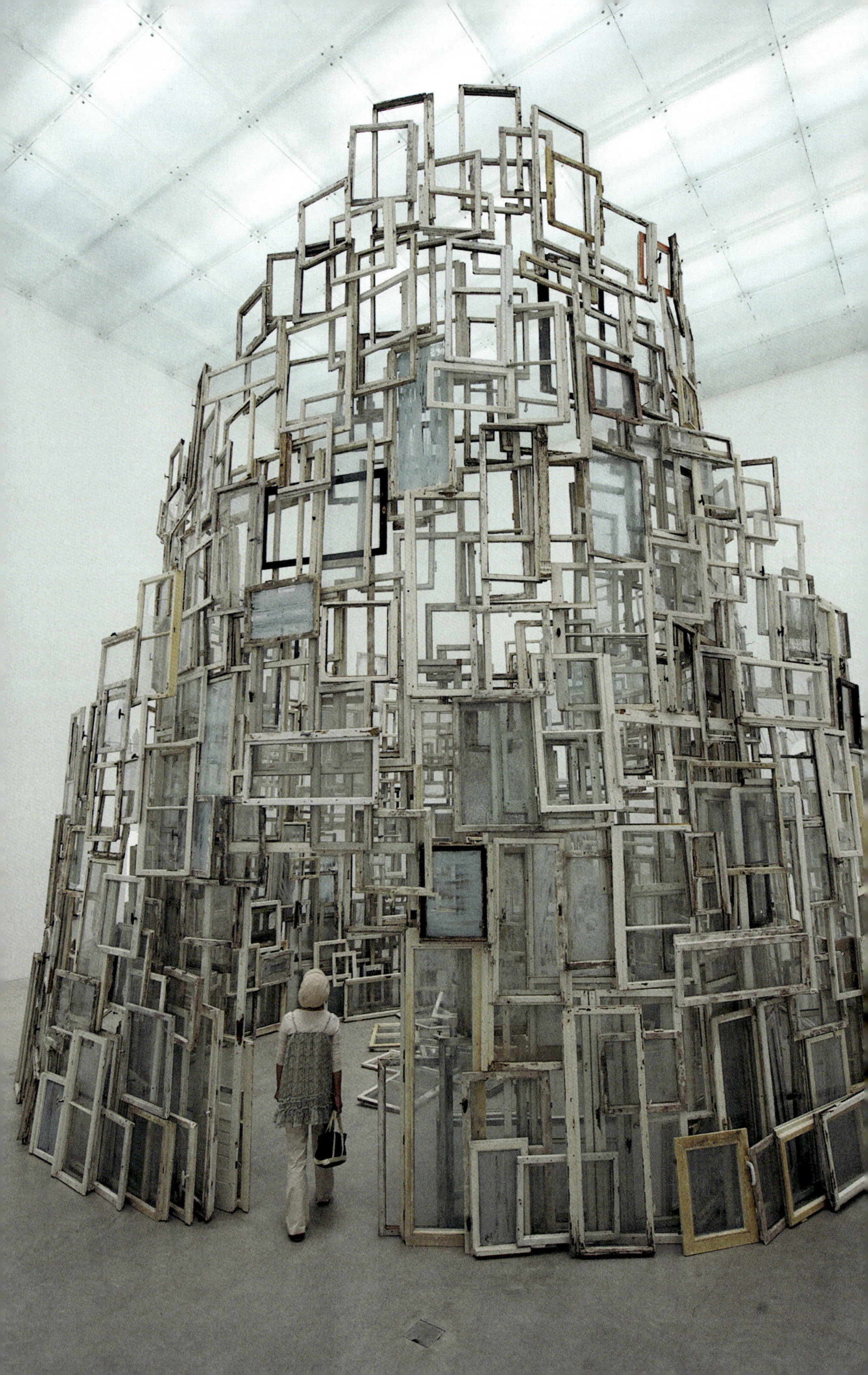

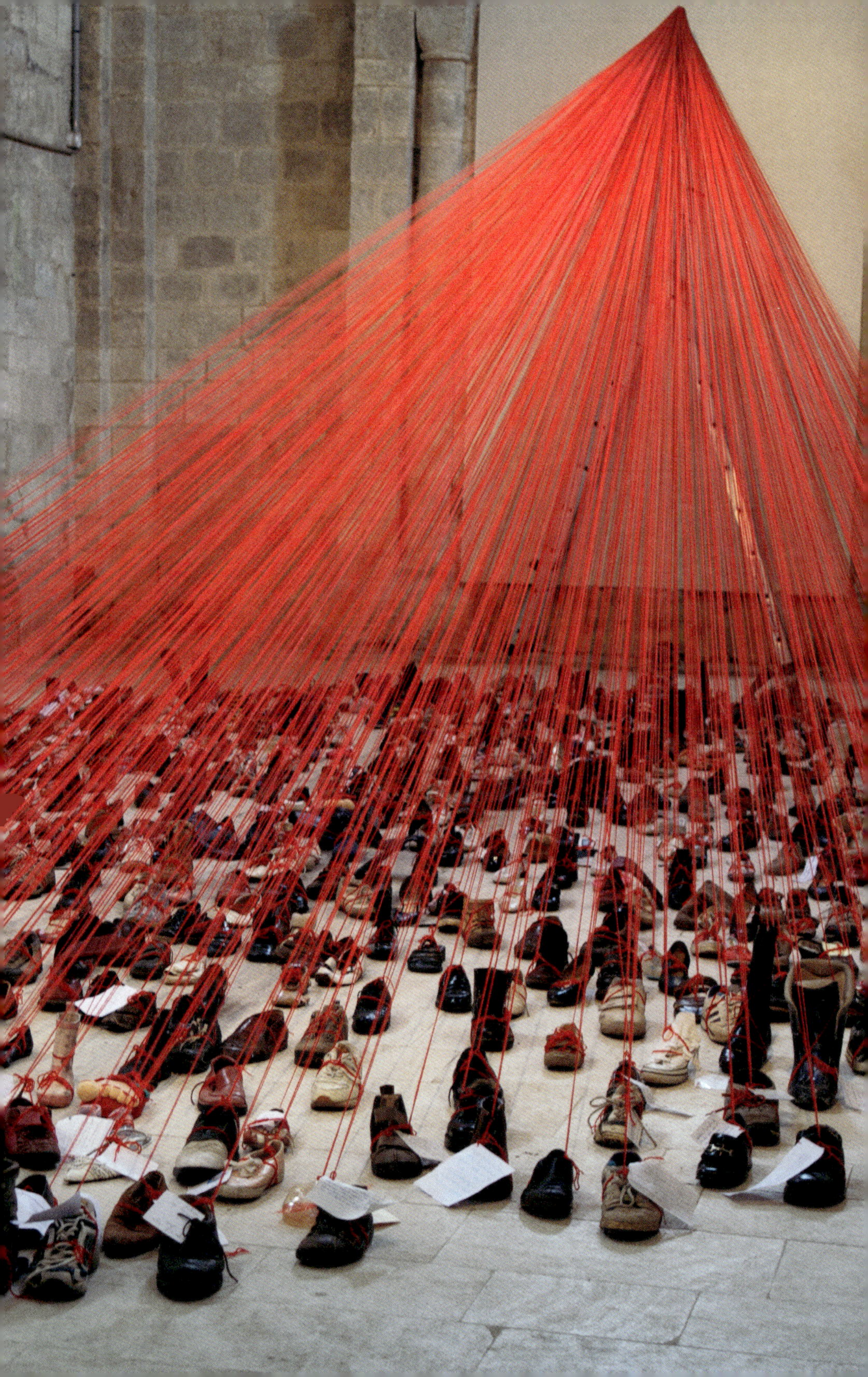

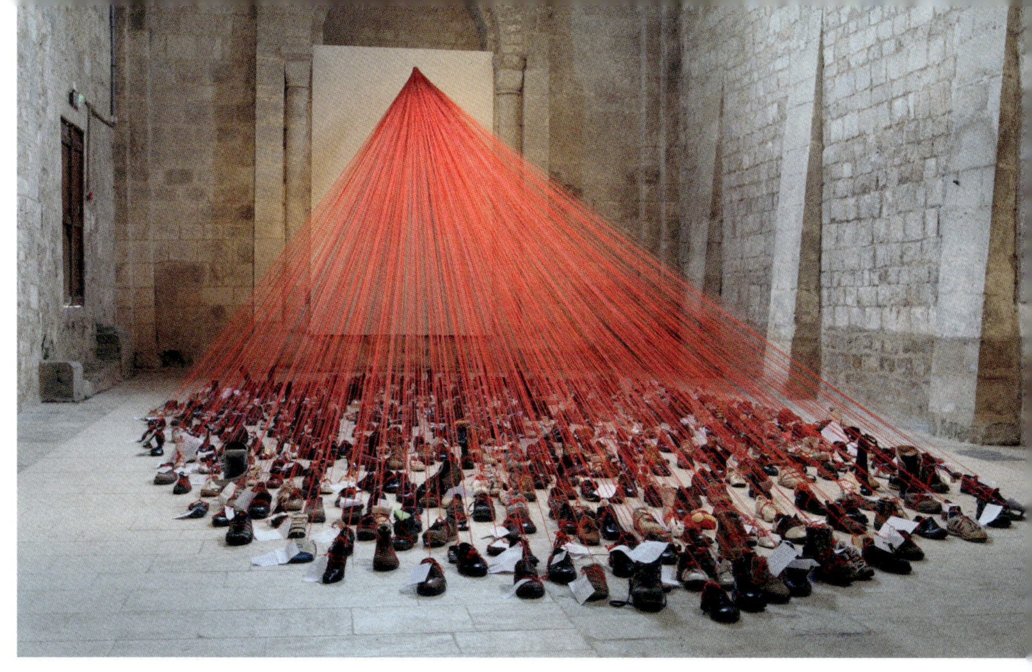

Over the Continents,
2011

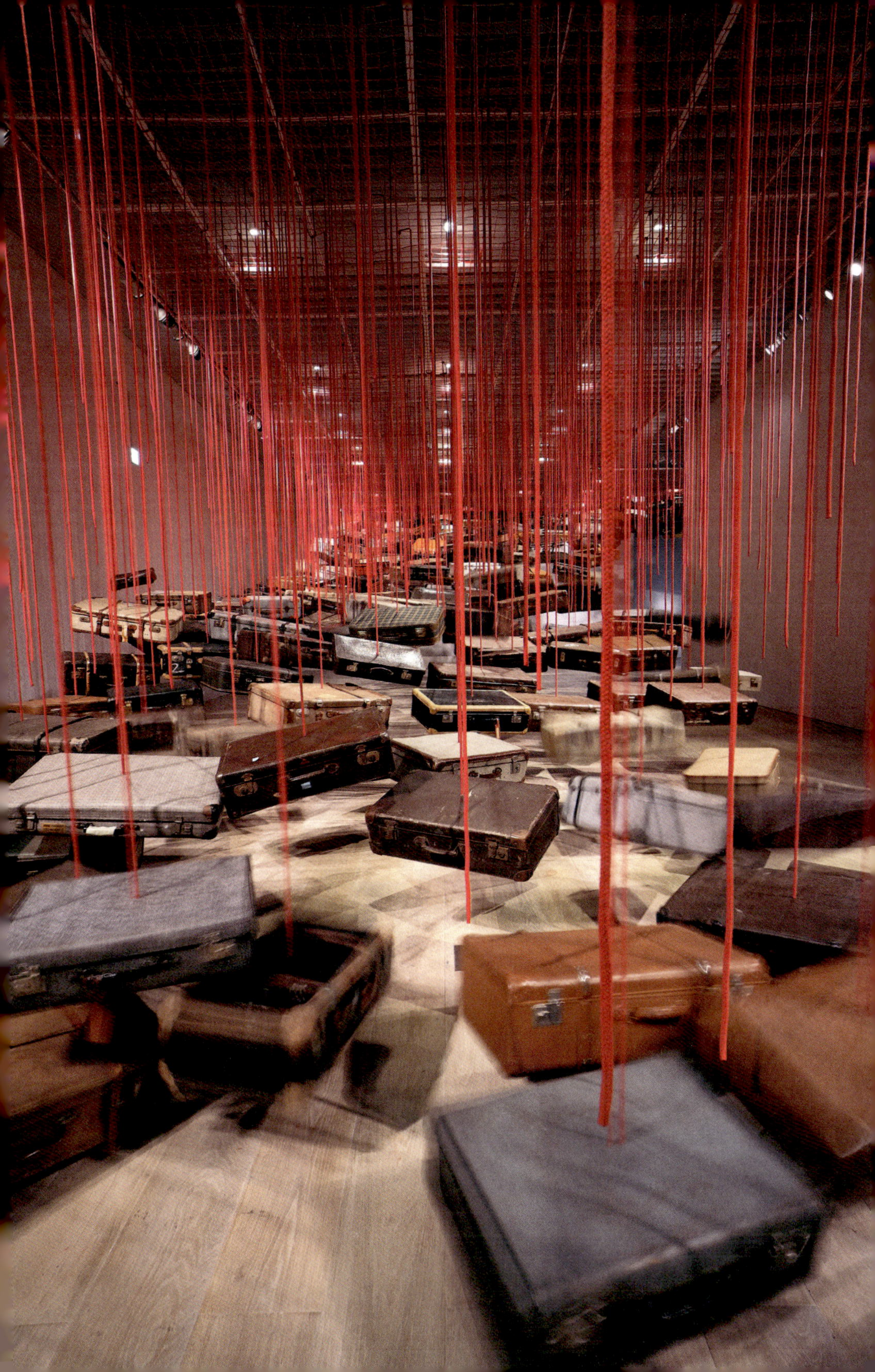

*Drawings for Yoko Tawada's Praktikantin
(The Trainee),*
2023–24

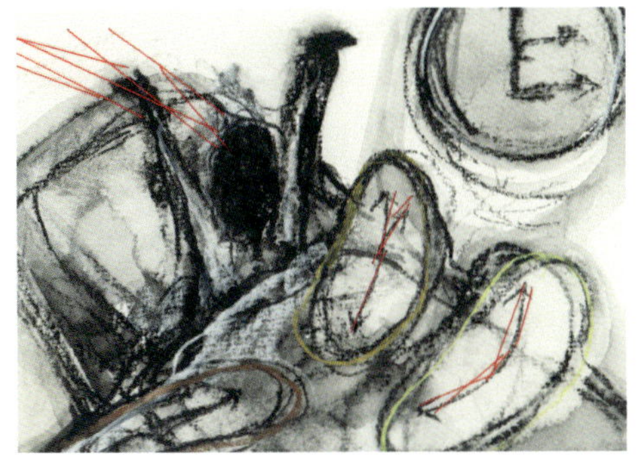
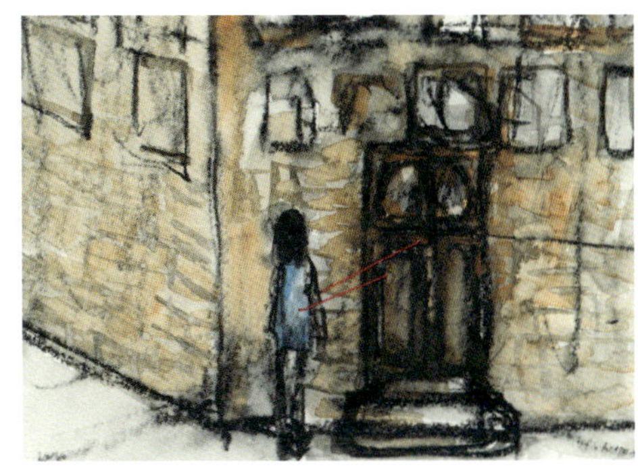
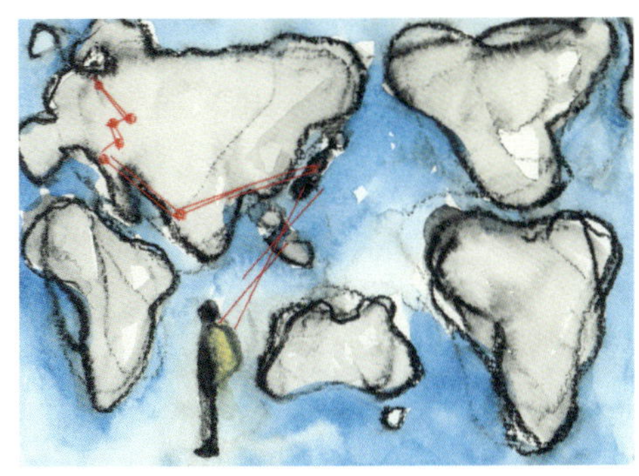
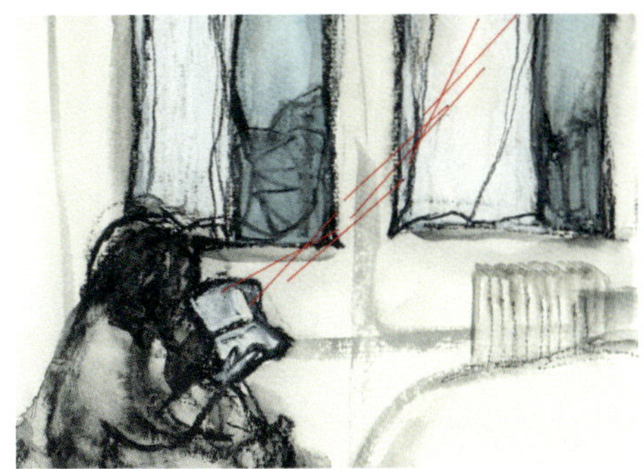
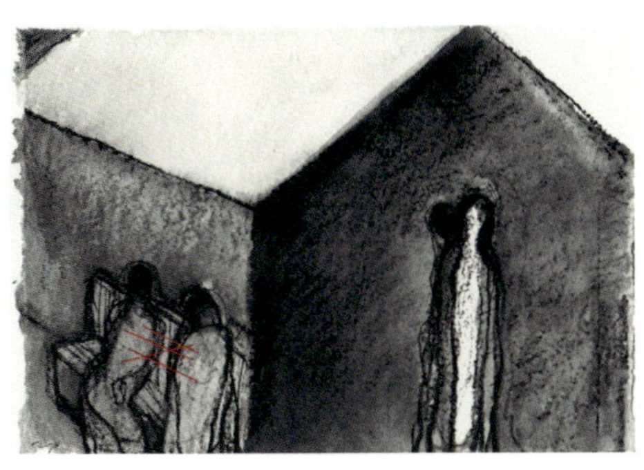
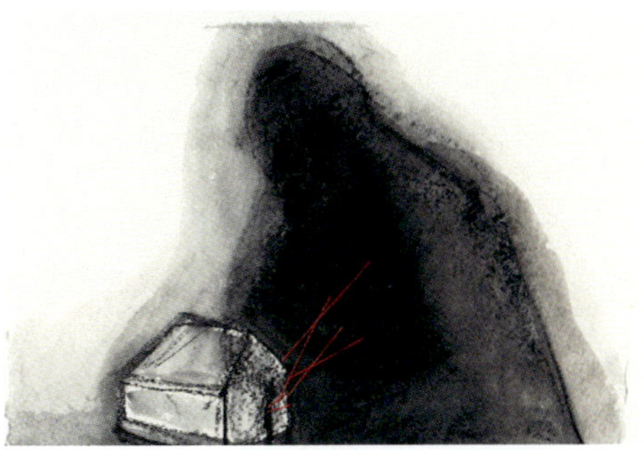
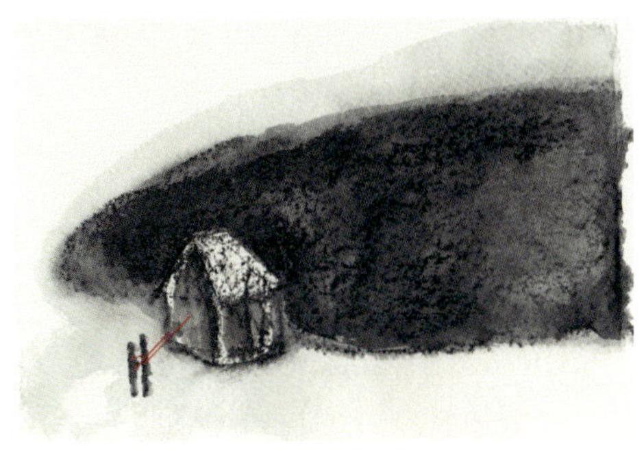
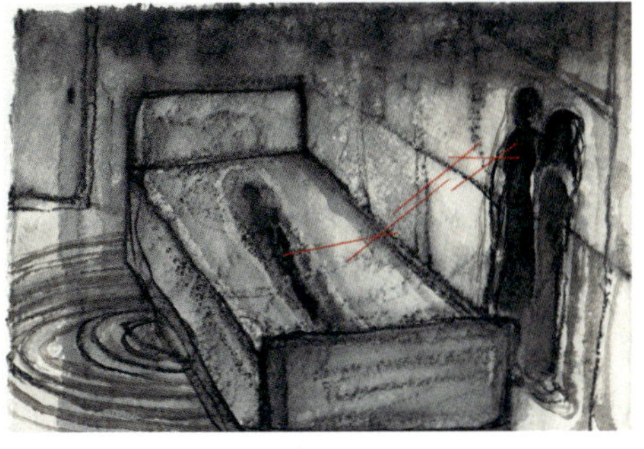

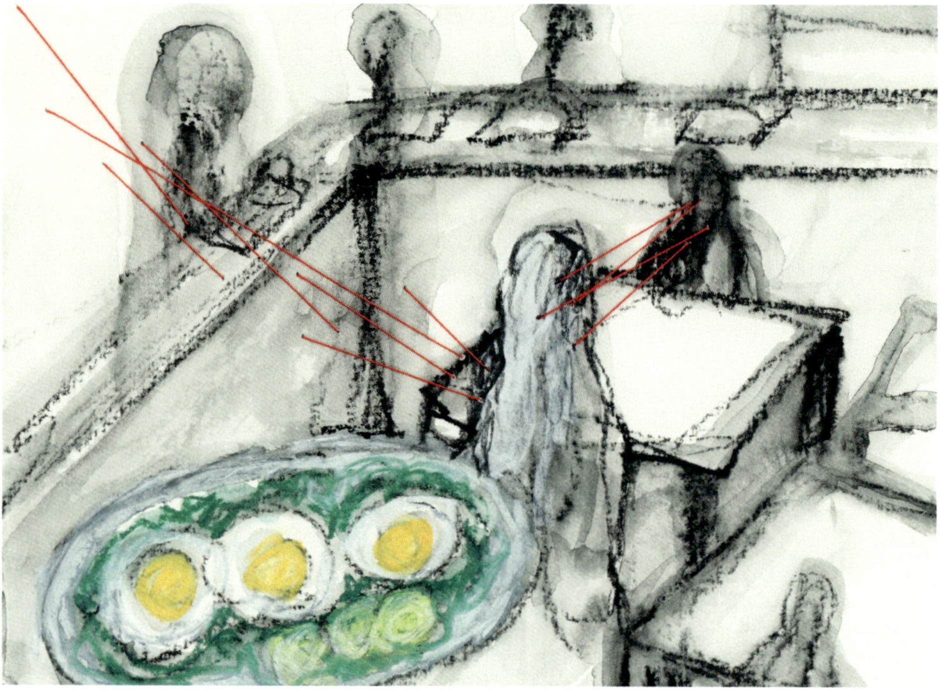

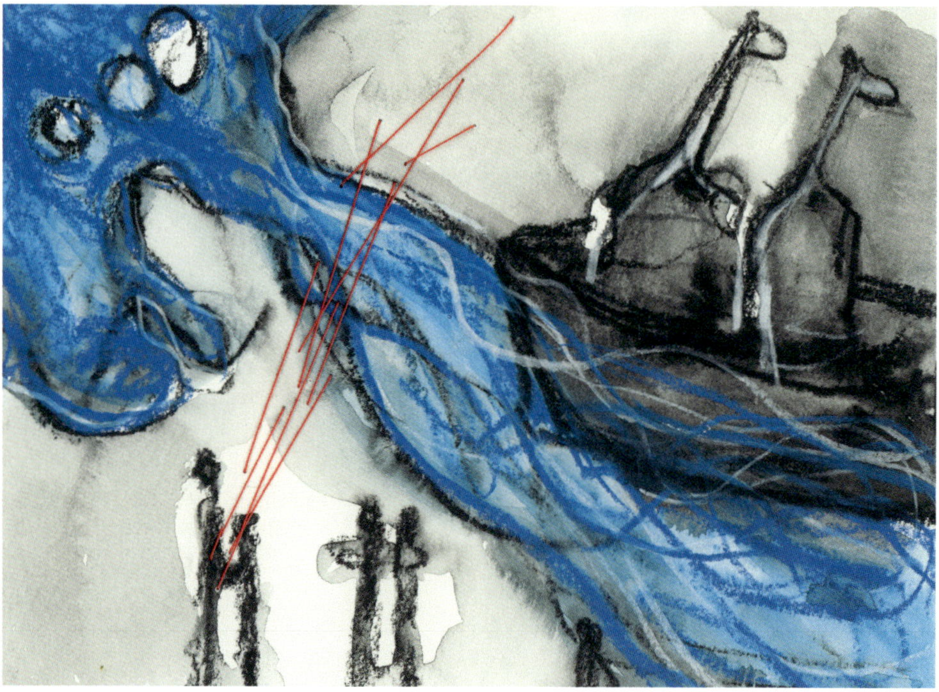

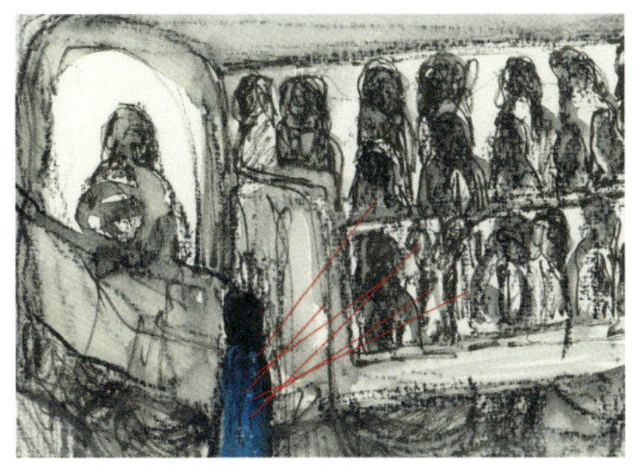
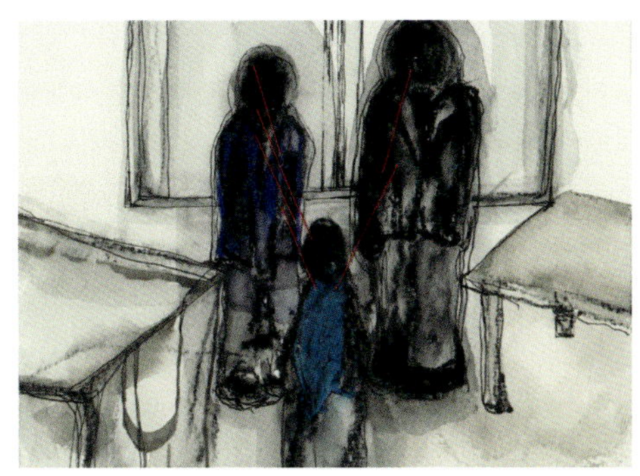
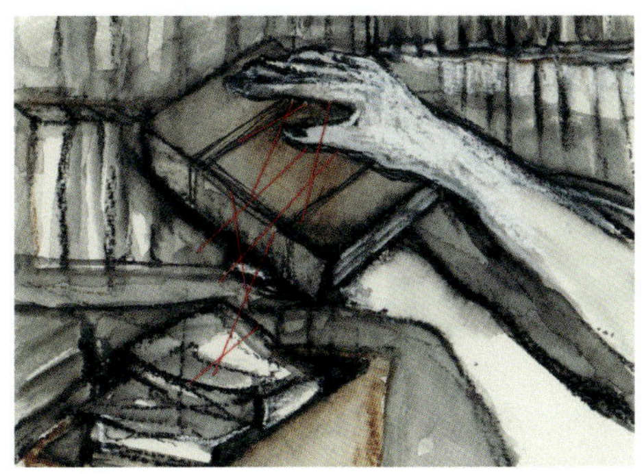
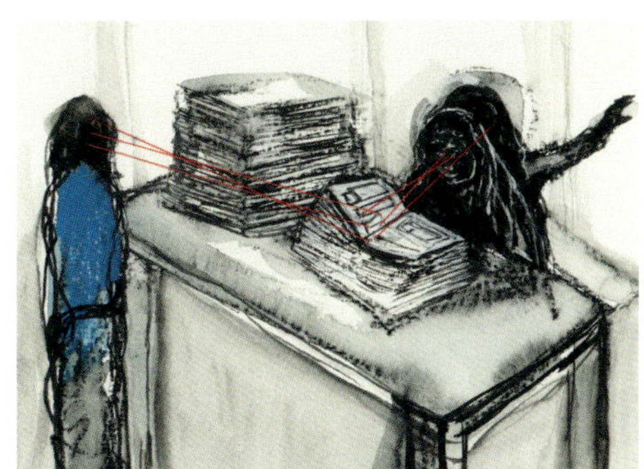
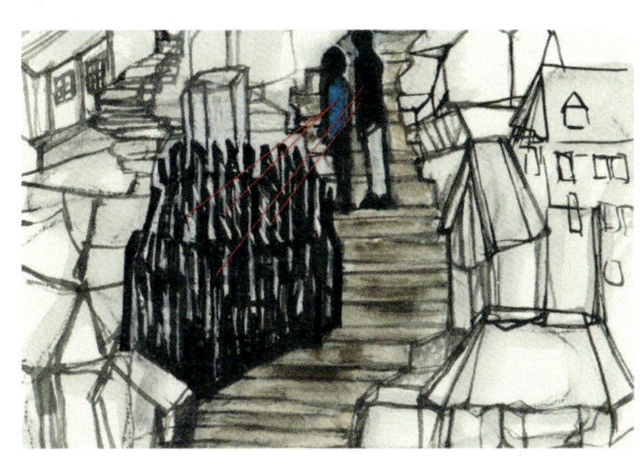
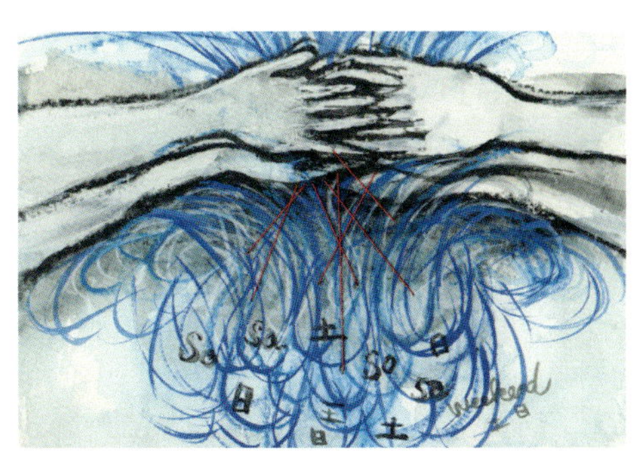
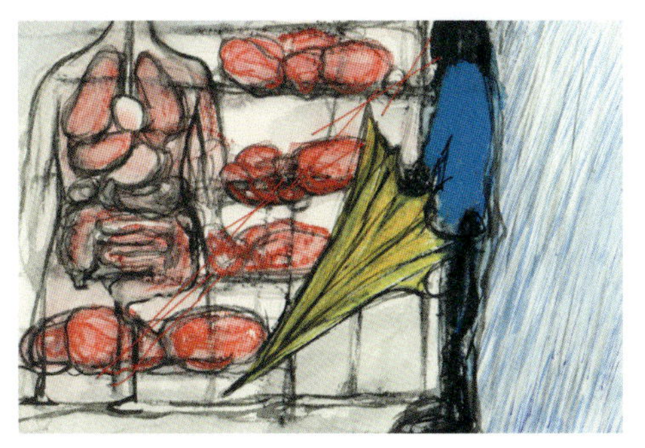
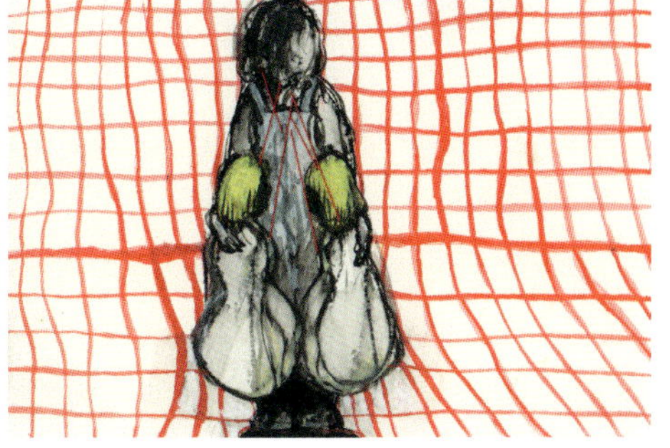

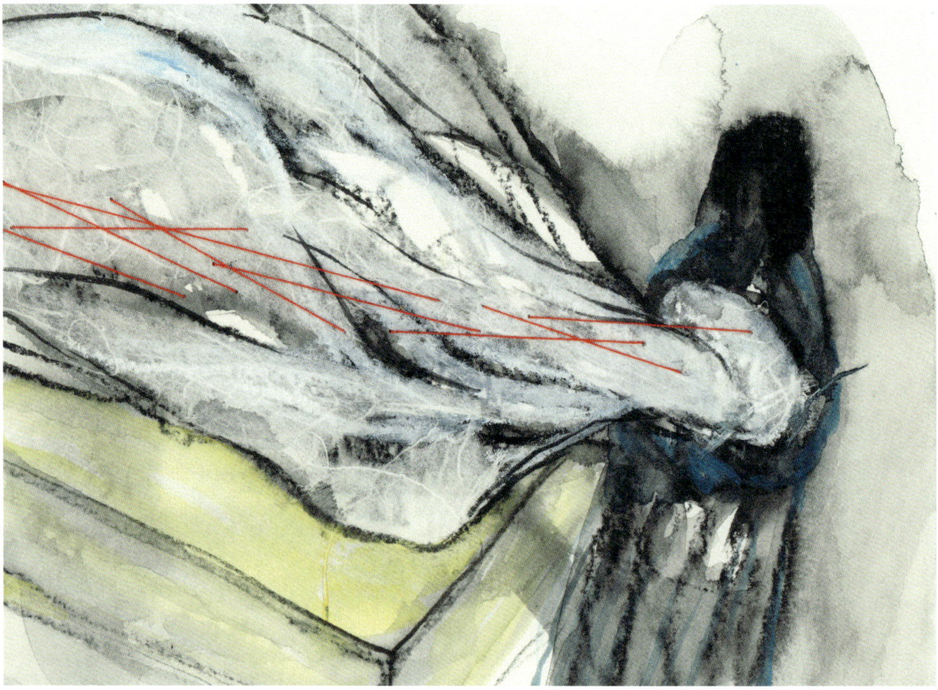

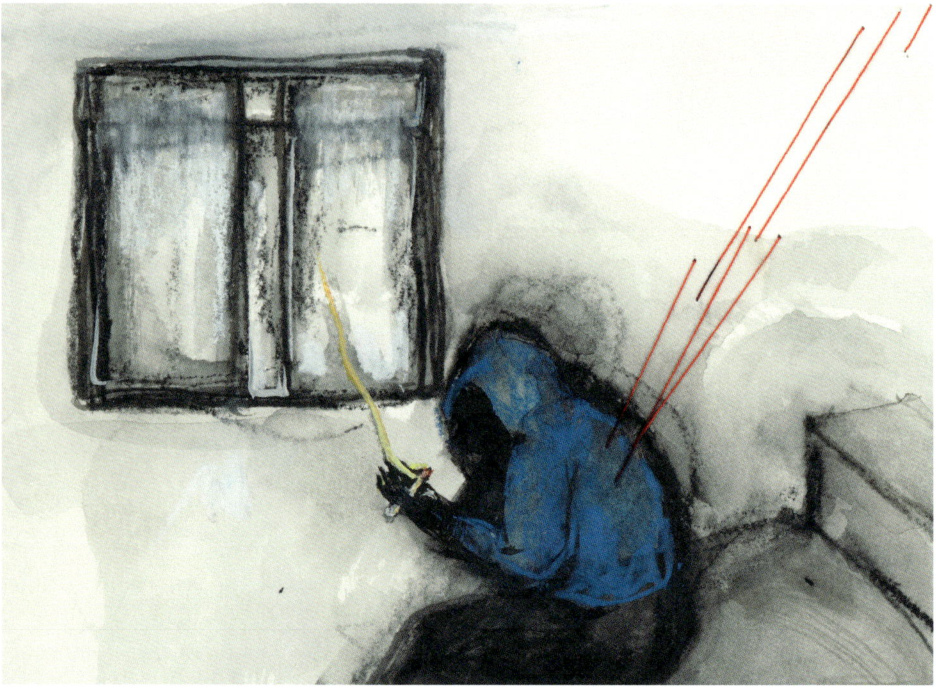

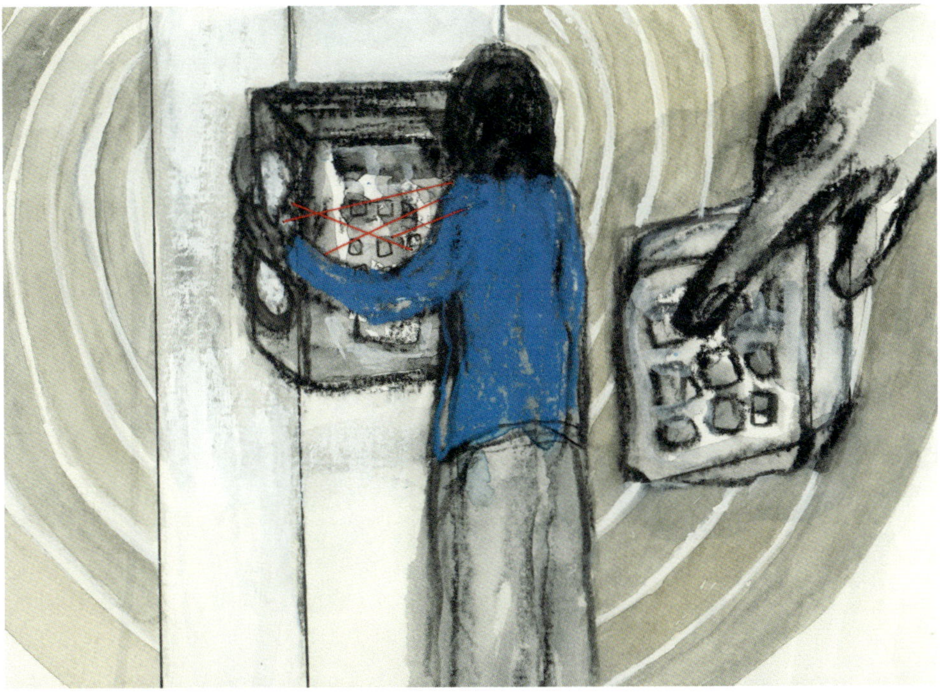

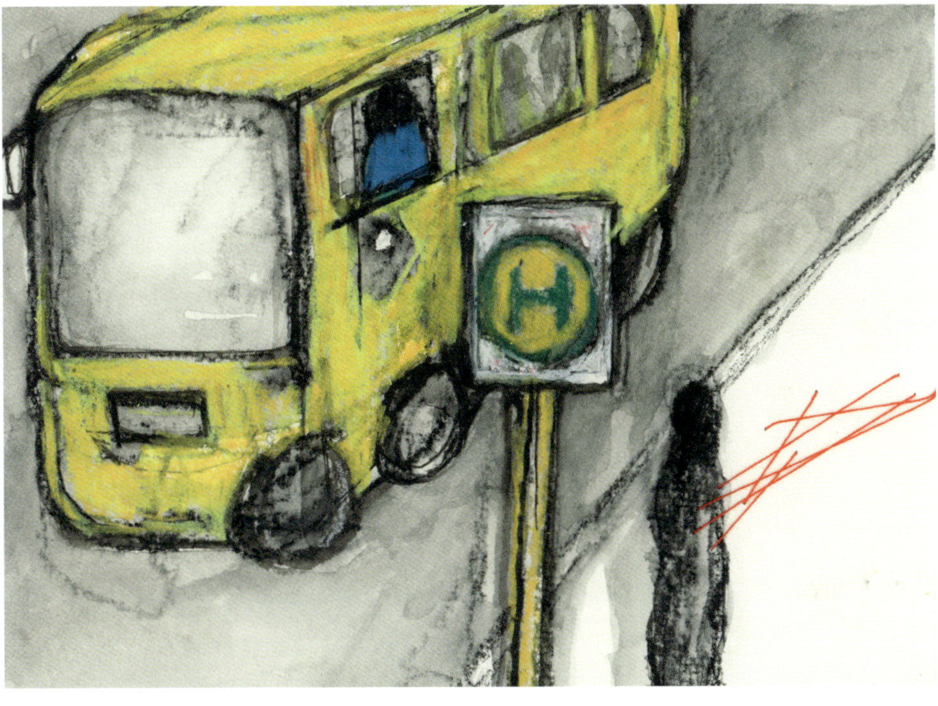

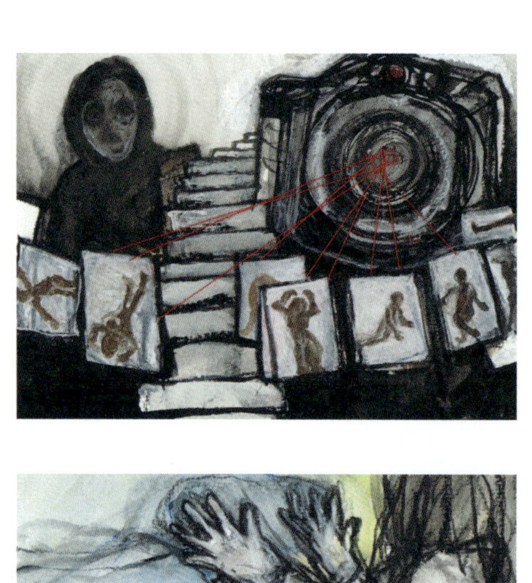
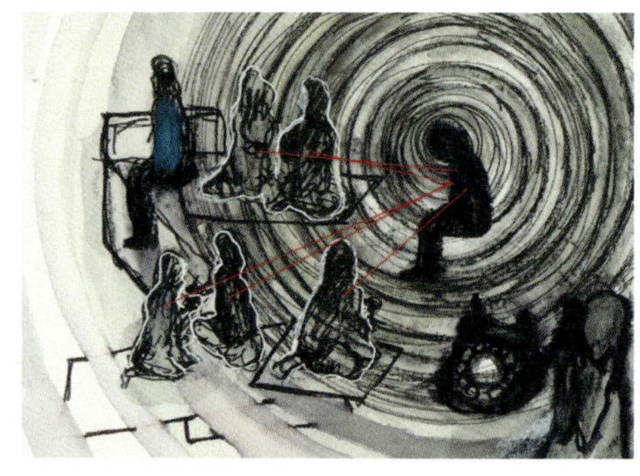
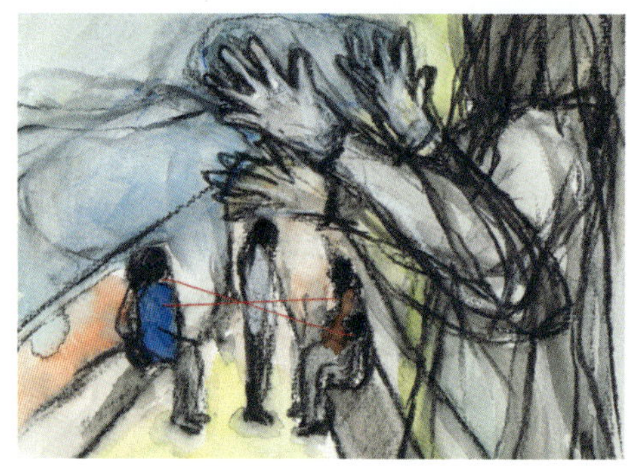
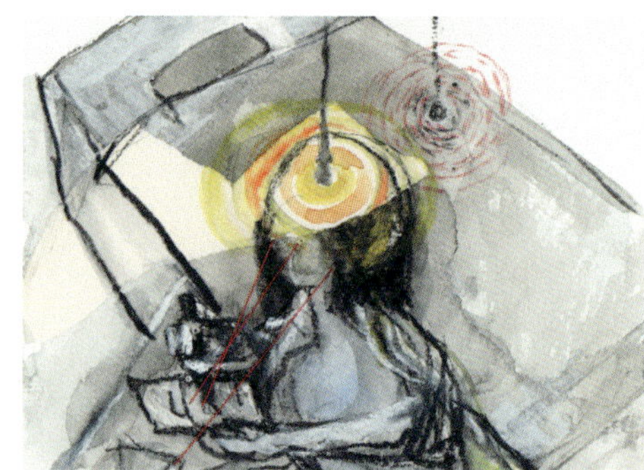
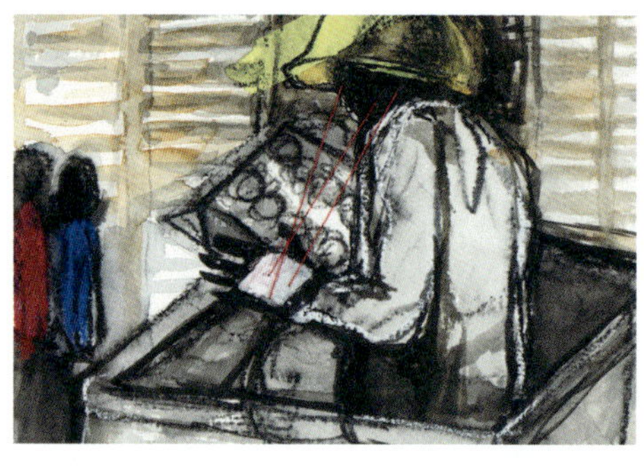
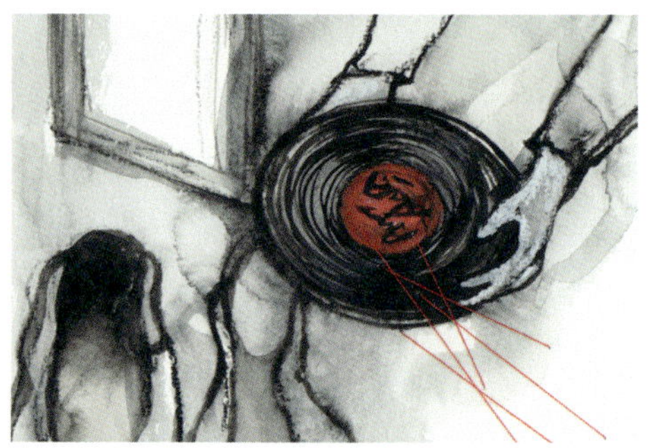
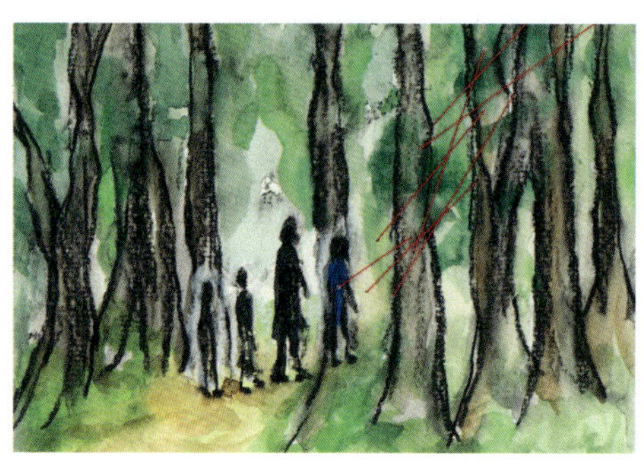
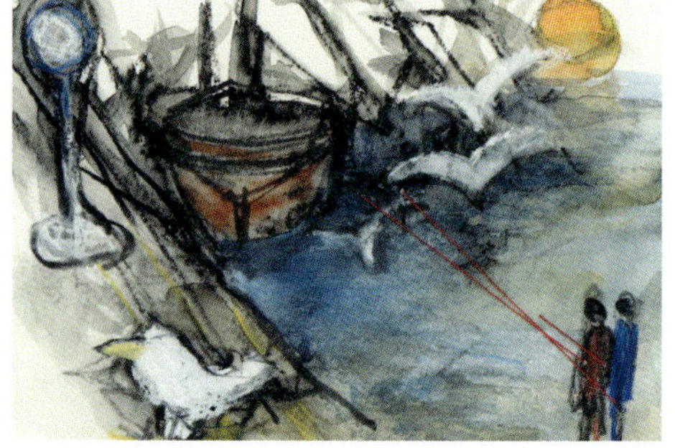

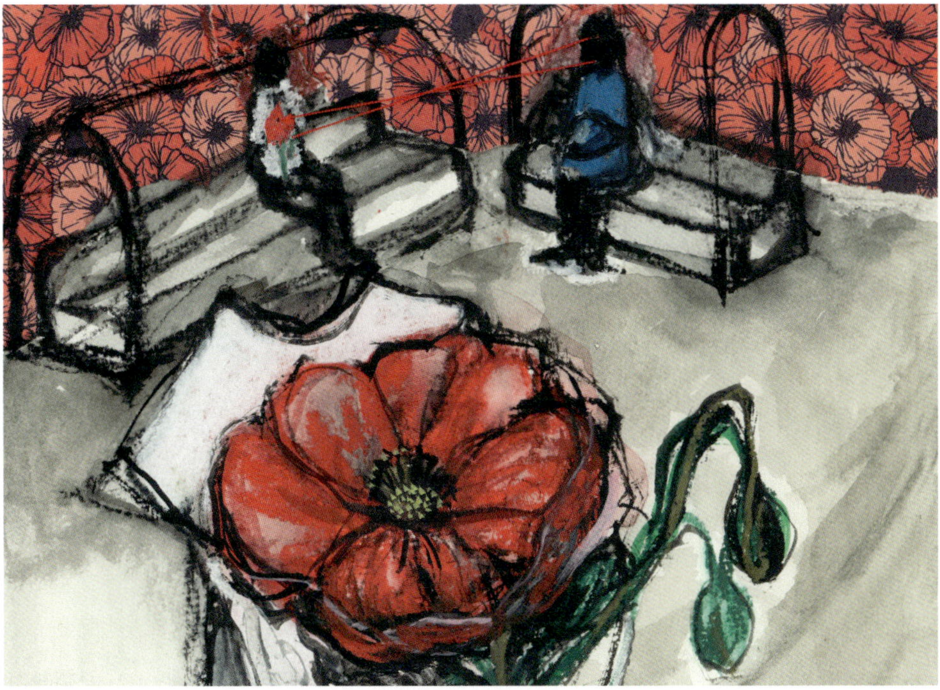

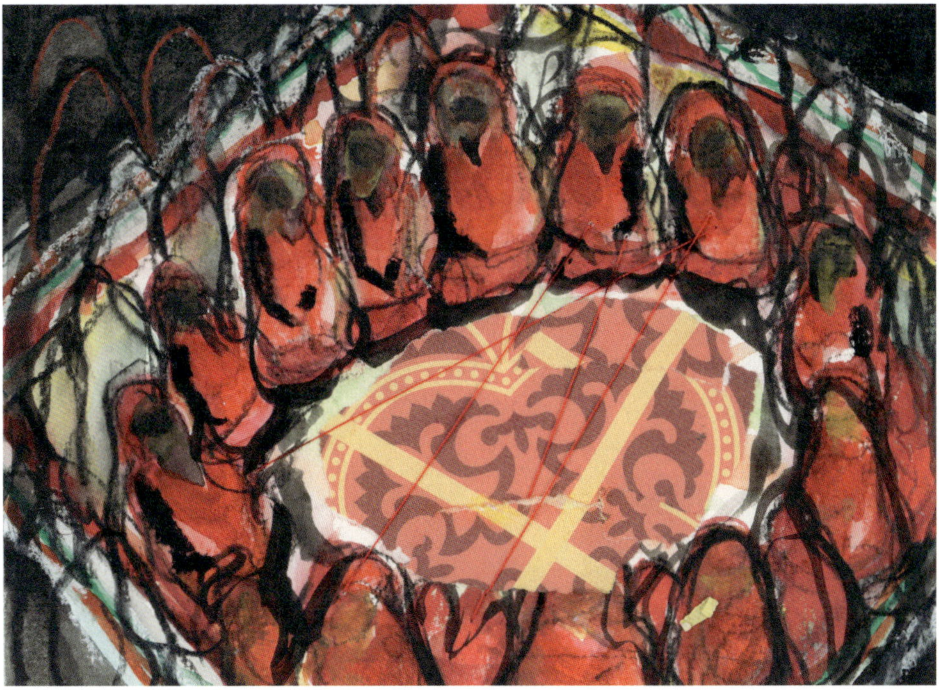

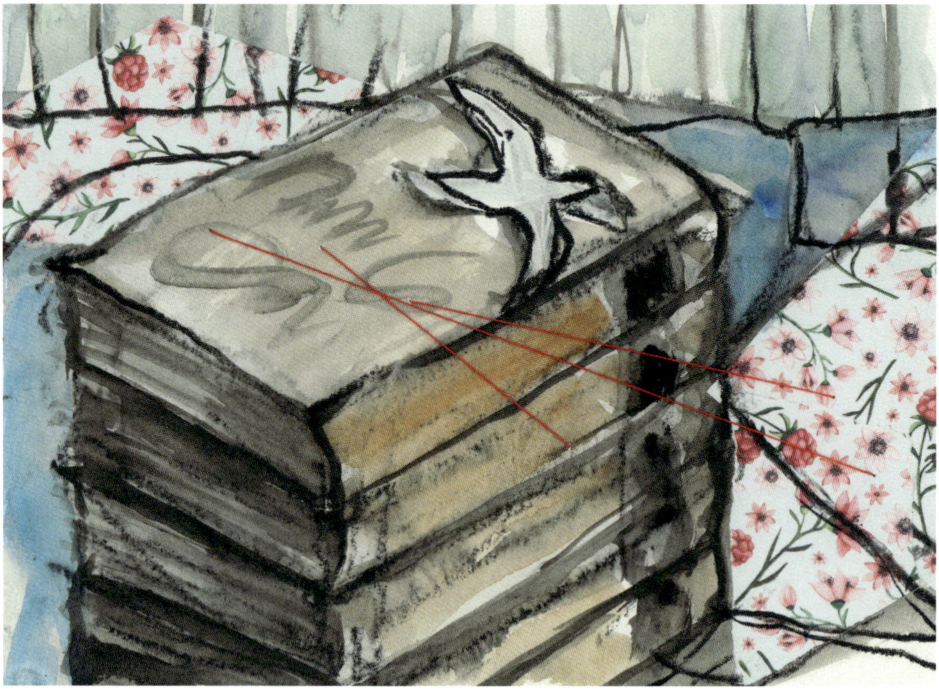

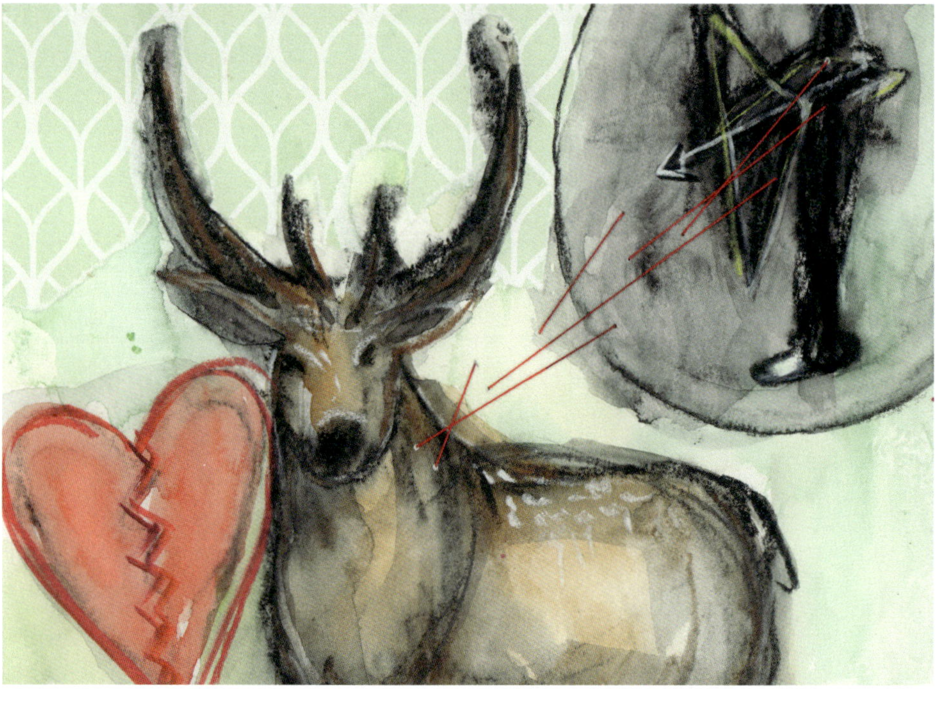

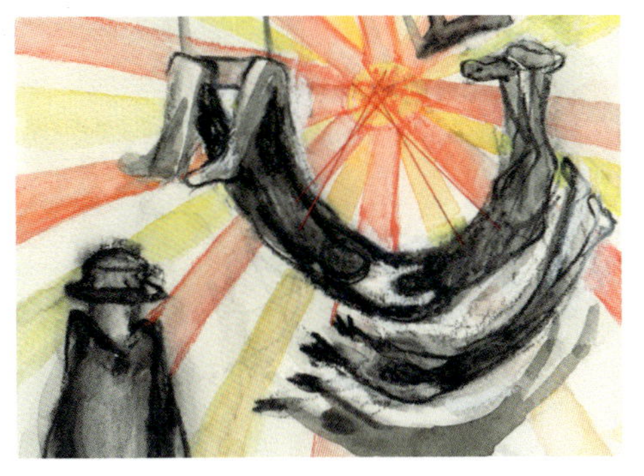
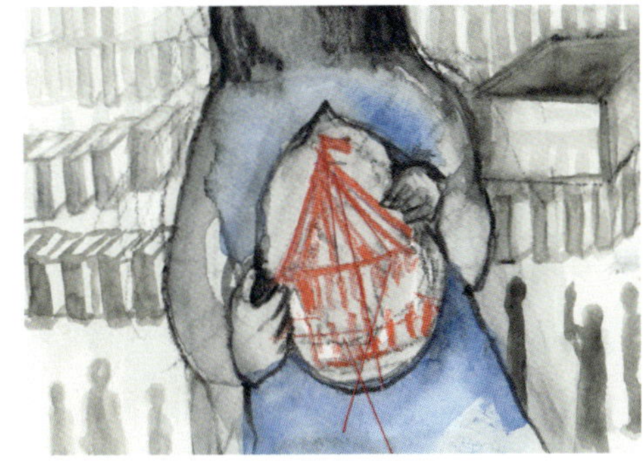
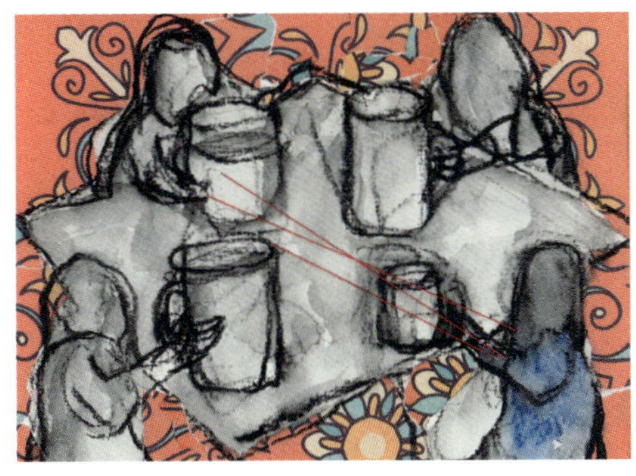
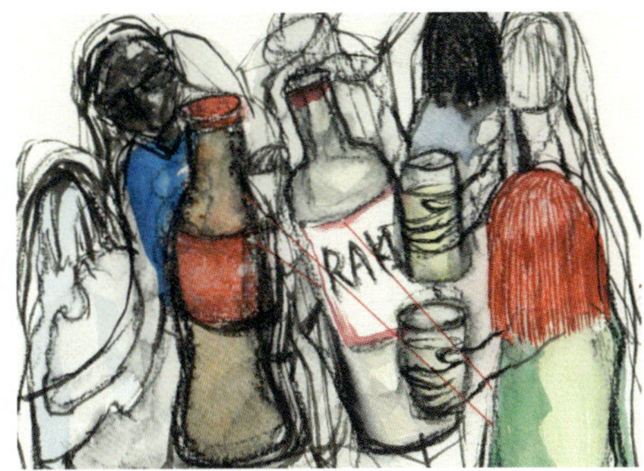
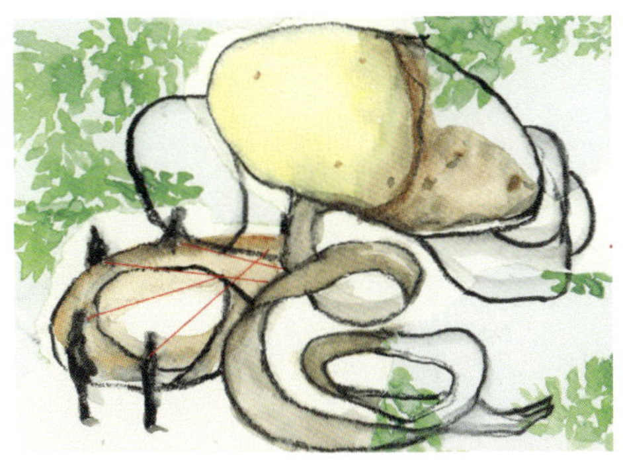
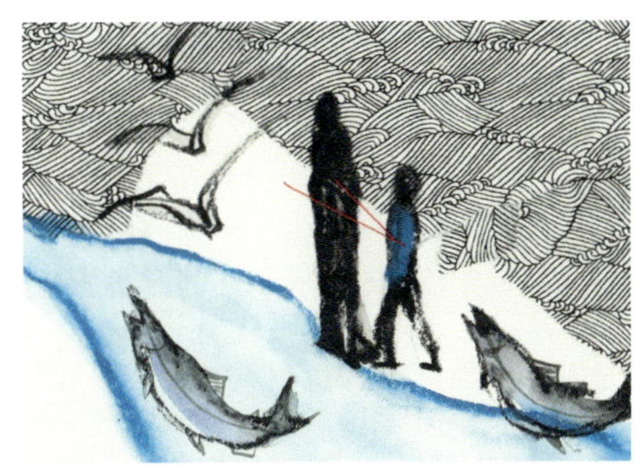
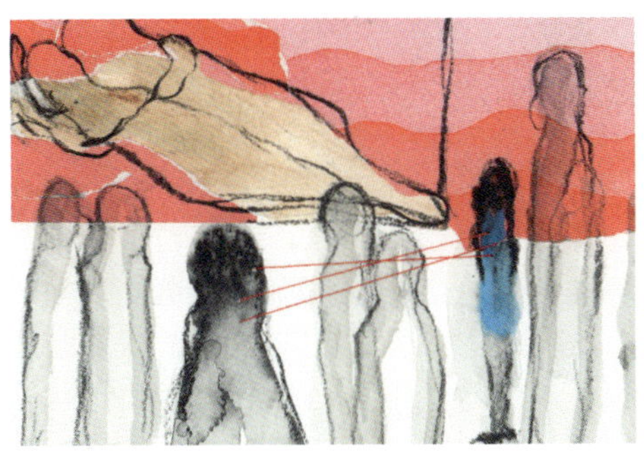
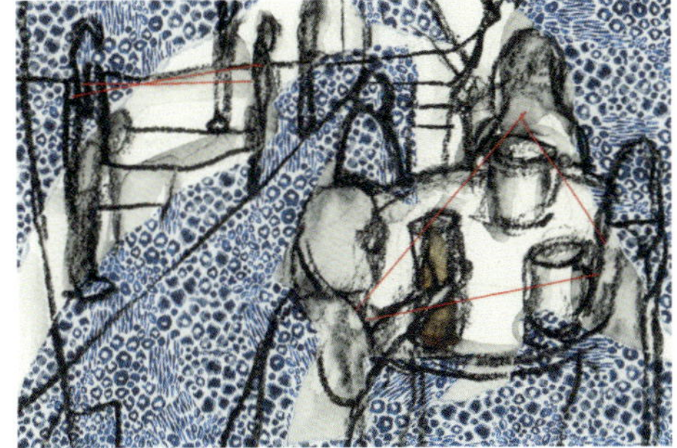

RAK

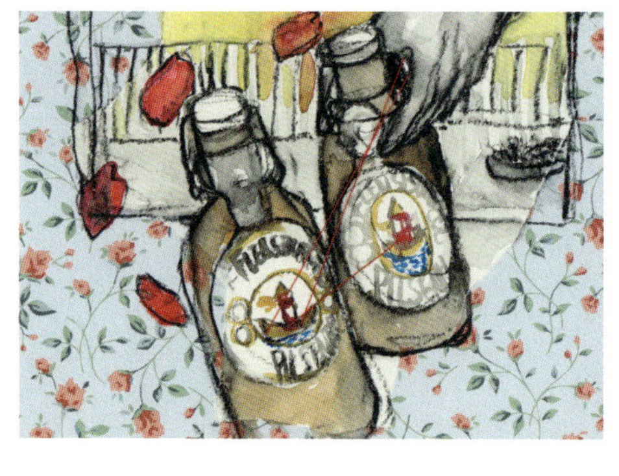
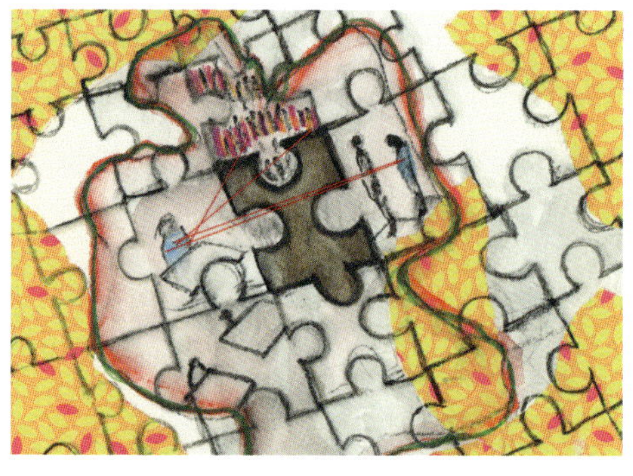
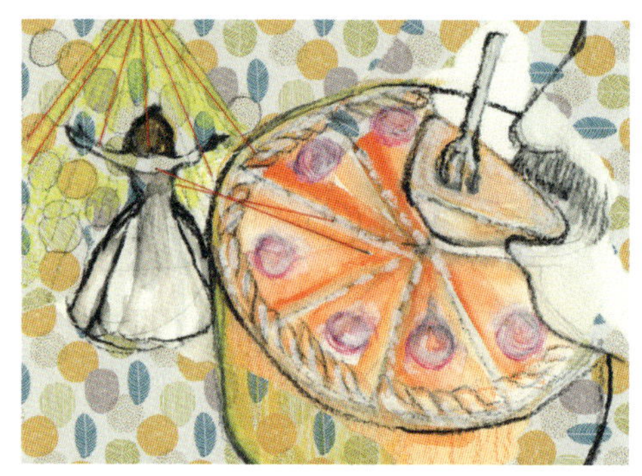
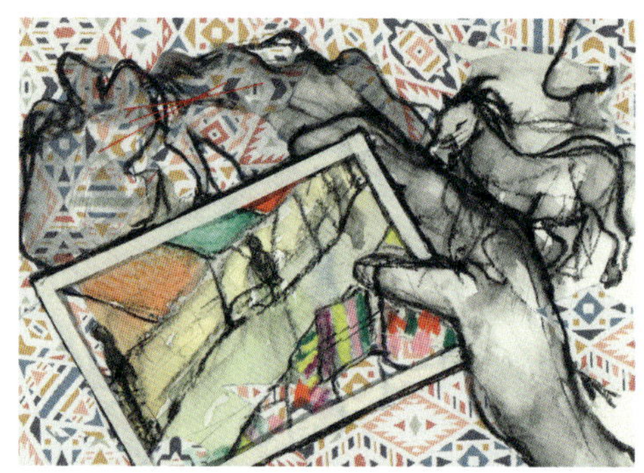
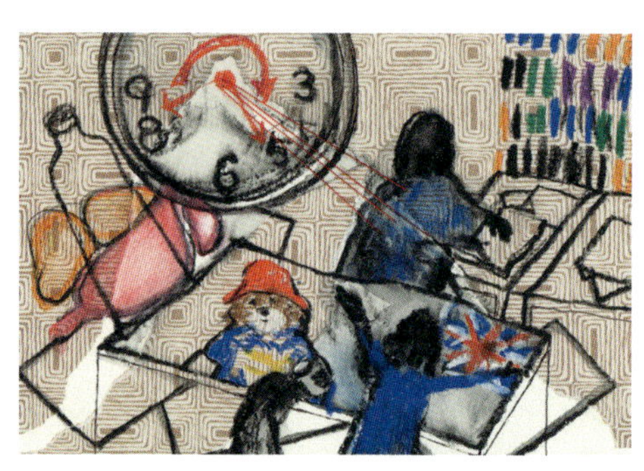
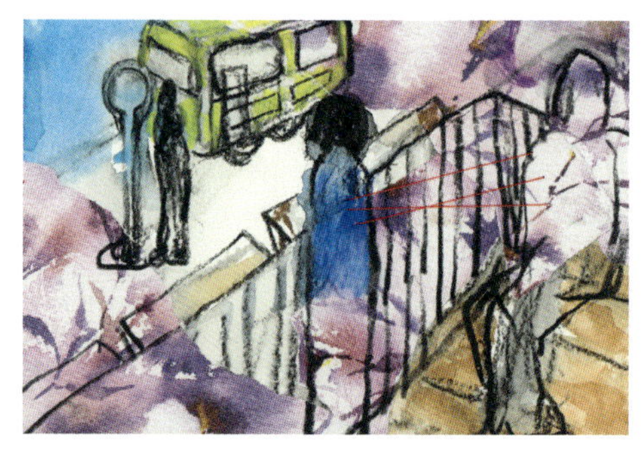
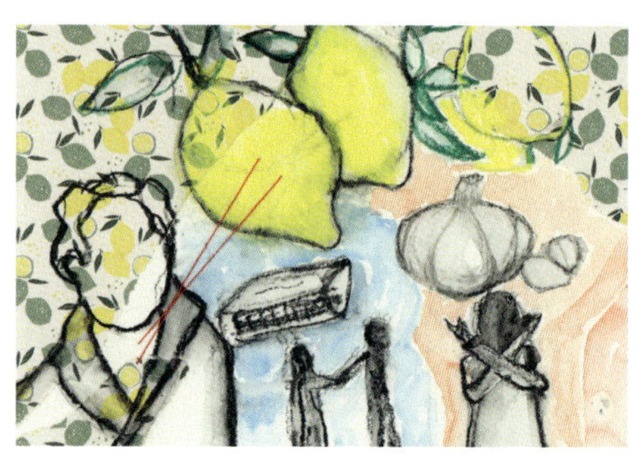
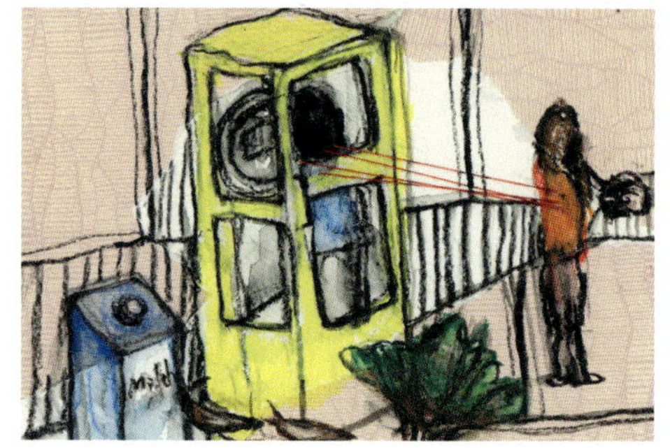

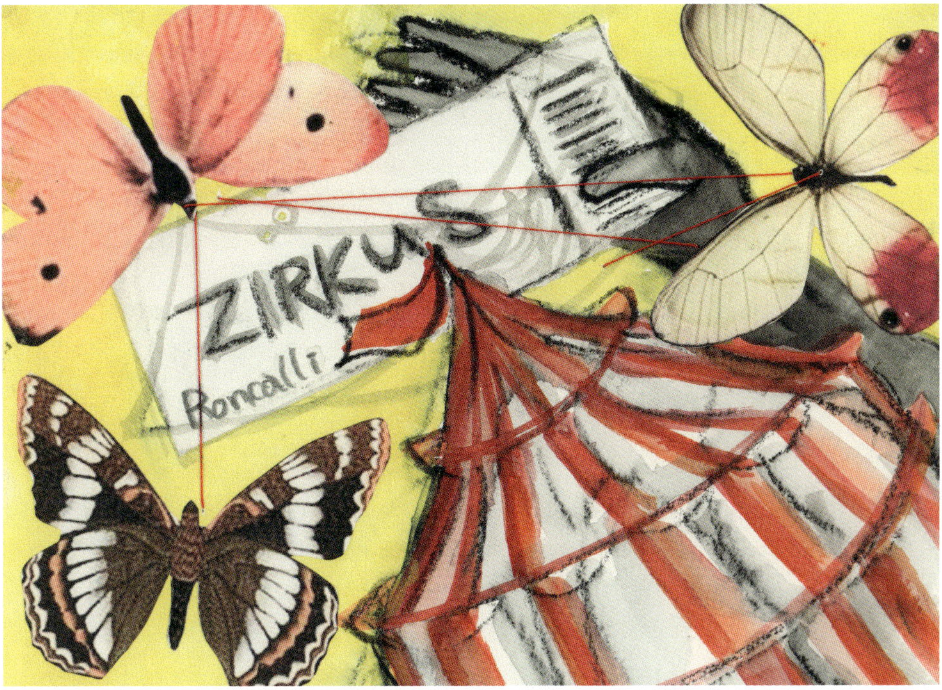

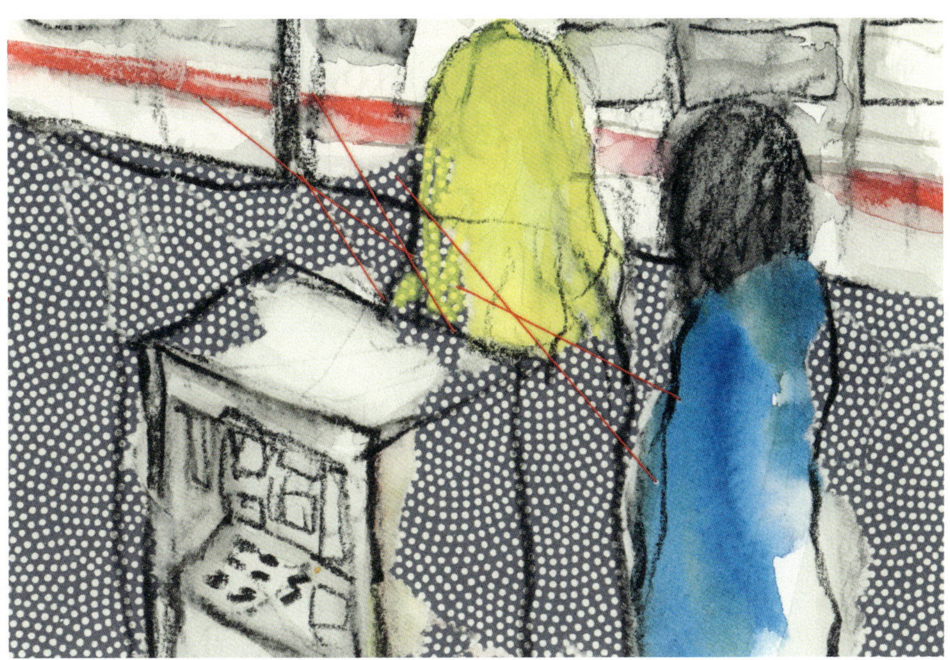
ZIRKUS
Roncalli

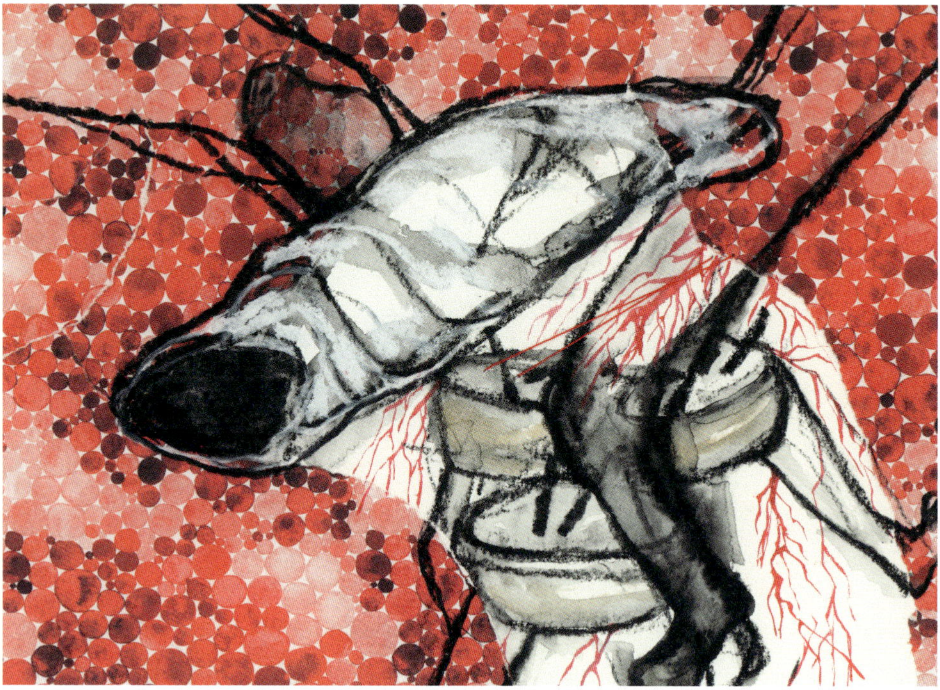

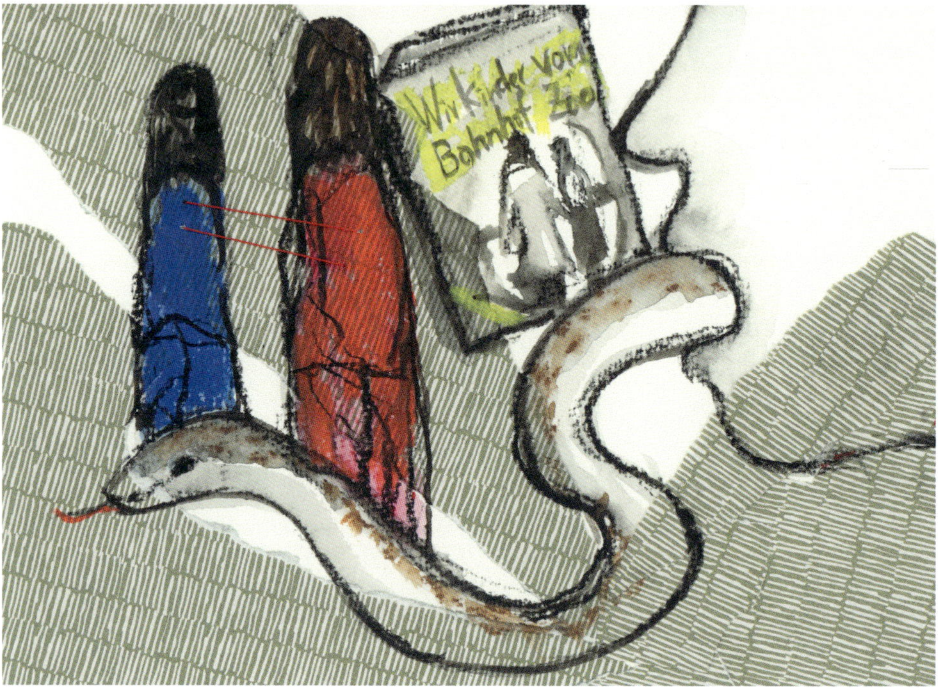

Wir Kinder vom
Bahnhof Zoo

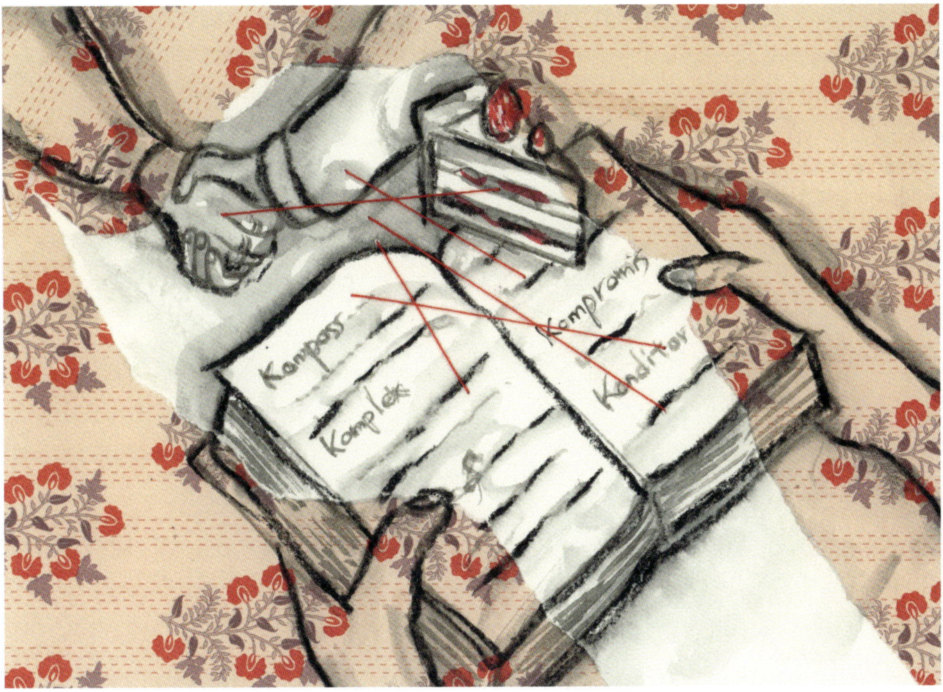

Kompass

Komplex

Kompromiss

Konditor

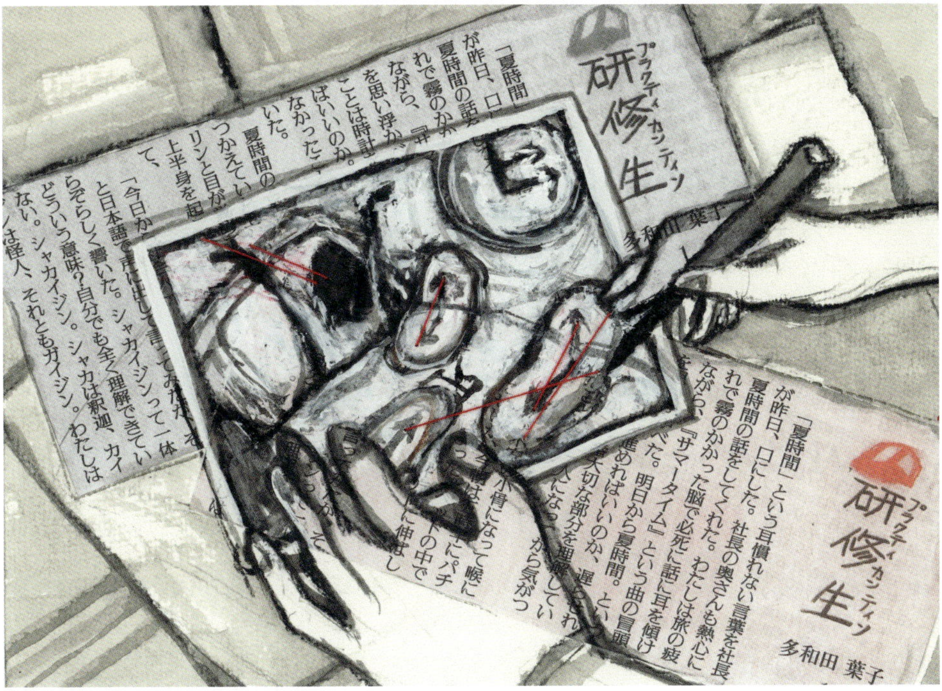

研修生

多和田 葉子

「夏時間」という耳慣れない言葉を社長
が昨日、口にした。夏時間の話をしてく
れで霧のかかった脳で必死に話に耳を傾け
ながら、『サマータイム』という曲の冒頭
を思い浮かべた。明日から夏時間。とい
ことは時計を進めればいいのか、遅らせ
ばいいのか。大切な部分を理解してい
なかった。

夏時間の
つかえてい
リンと目が
上半身を起
て、
「今日から夏時間」と日本語で声に出して言ってみたが
と日本語で声に出して書いた。シャカイジンって一体
どういう意味？自分でも全く理解できてい
らそらしく響いた。シャカイジン。カイ
ない。シャカイジン。シャカは釈迦、カイ
は怪人、それともガイジン。わたしは

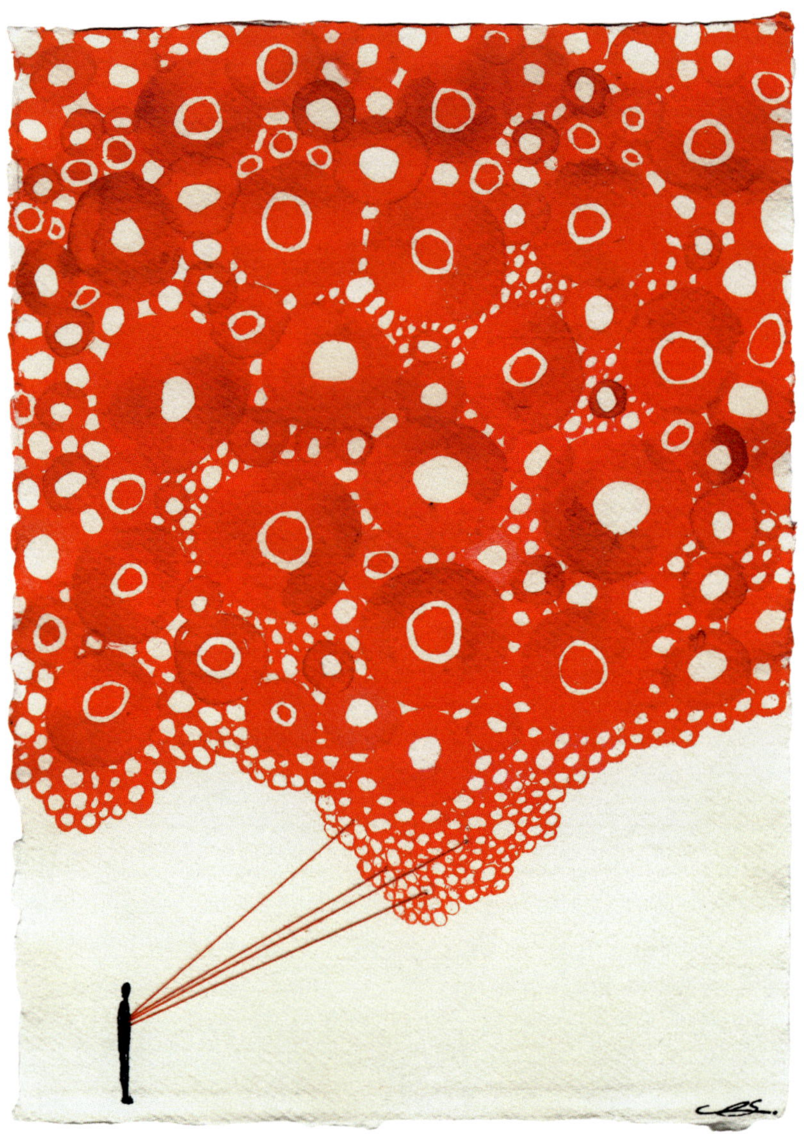

Connected to the Universe,
2023

1972 — Born in Osaka and raised in Kishiwada City, youngest child and only daughter. Her parents, originally from Kochi, ran a wooden fish-box manufacturing company in Osaka.

1991 — Visits *Magdalena Abakanowicz: Confession* at the Shiga Museum of Modern Art, Japan, aged 19, and is deeply moved by the work of the Polish artist:

'I felt as if I was being overwhelmed by a living power, something elemental. I was ecstatic to have seen work imbued with such a powerful life force encompassing all humans, regardless of gender.'

| 1992 | – Enrols at Kyoto Seika University, studying under Saburo Muraoka in the Painting Department, but struggles with the limitations of what painting can express. |

| 1993–94 | – Attends the Australian National University (ANU) Institute of the Arts, Canberra, as part of the student exchange program between 1993 and 1994. Explores her interest in three-dimensionality, creating installations and performances that allow her to use the entire space to express herself. |

– Performs *Becoming Painting* at ANU Institute of the Arts, Canberra.

'I dreamed that I had become a painting. I found myself thinking, how should I move inside the pictorial surface so that this will turn out to be a good painting? Totally covered under all this oil paint on the surface, I found it hard to breathe. That night, I had become part of an artwork.'

– Presents *From DNA to DNA* (p. 8), her first installation using yarn, in her Kyoto Seika University graduation show at the Kyoto Municipal Museum of Art.

| 1996 | – Moves to Germany to study at the Hamburg University of Fine Arts with Marina Abramović (whom she initially mistakes for Magdalena Abakanowicz). |

– Creates performance *Try and Go Home* (pp. 36–37) as part of five-day workshop led by Abramović at Domaine de Kerguéhennec, Bignan, France.

'After this class, I feel that
my sensation of the passage of time
and perception itself have changed.'

| 1999 | – Moves to Berlin and starts studying under Rebecca Horn at University of the Arts Berlin. Establishes an atelier in the city and starts working as an artist full-time. Creates *Bathroom*, her first work involving a video version of a performance. |
| 2000 | – First time using dresses in her artwork, in *After That* (later retitled *Memory of Skin*, pp. 38–39) at E-Werk, Weimar, Germany. *Breathing from Earth*, Maximiliansforum, Munich, Germany: first installation created with beds. Later retitled *During Sleep* (see pp. 70–73). |

'I believe sleeping and dreaming are
connected to humans in their
everyday life and it is an important
foundation for our sense of reality.'

| 2001 | – Receives international recognition after exhibiting *Memory of Skin* at first Yokohama Triennial, curated by Akira Tatehata. It is her first large-scale installation in Japan. |
| 2003 | – First solo exhibition at a public institution, *The Way into Silence*, Württembergischer Kunstverein Stuttgart, Germany, curated by Andrea Jahn. Publication of her first catalogue.
– Expands her activities into theatre and set design, collaborating with Japanese dancer Yuko Kaseki for *all A lone*, Ujazdowski Castle Centre for Contemporary Art, Warsaw, Poland. Creates stage design for Alex Novak's *Solitude* at the Akademie Schloss Solitude, Stuttgart, Germany. |

| 2004 | – Presents the installation *From-Into*, created from old windows found around Berlin, at *The Joy of My Dreams*, first International Biennial of Contemporary Art of Seville, Spain, curated by Harald Szeemann. |

| 2007 | – *From in Silence* at Kanagawa Prefectural Hall Gallery, Yokohama, Japan awarded a prize by the Minister of Education, Culture, Sports, Science and Technology. |

2009	– Exhibits *Flowing Water* (p. 75) at Nizayama Forest Art Museum, Toyama, Japan. The work reflects her recurring use of beds, symbols of both life and death in her work.
	– First time exhibiting in London: *After the Dream* (pp. 48–49), part of group exhibition *Walking In My Mind* at the Hayward Gallery, London, UK, curated by Stephanie Rosenthal and Mami Kataoka.
	– Creates stage designs for *Oedipus Rex*, performed by Berlin-based dance company Constanza Macras	Dorky Park, and *Tattoo*, directed by Toshiki Okada, premiering at the New National Theatre, Tokyo.

| 2010 | – Designs stage for *Matsukaze*, choreographed by Sasha Waltz and composed by Toshio Hosokawa in collaboration with Pia Maier Schriever, which tours across Europe. |
| | – Completes video performance *Wall* (pp. 40–41), exhibited at Kenji Taki Gallery, Nagoya, Japan. |

| 2012 | – Named Japan Cultural Envoy by the Agency for Cultural Affairs, visiting Australia as part of the Cultural Envoy programme. |

| 2013 | – *Letters of Thanks* at The Museum of Art, Kochi, Japan, her first show in her parents' hometown. |

'In truth, I wanted to convey
my gratitude to my father, who had
worked so hard for his family
and waited so long for his daughter
to return.'

2015   – Represents Japan at the 56th Venice
                 Biennale, Italy with *The Key in the Hand*
                 (pp. 52–57) at the Japan Pavilion.

2016   – *The Locked Room* (pp. 59–65) exhibited
                 at Kanagawa Arts Theatre, Yokohama,
                 Japan.

2017   – Receives invitation to exhibit at Mori Art
                 Museum, Tokyo, but is informed the
                 next day that her cancer has returned after
                 12 years.
                 – *Absence Embodied*, Art Gallery of South
                 Australia, Adelaide, inspired by her
                 experience, during her cancer treatment,
                 of a feeling of separation between body
                 and mind.

'Death is part of my work, and I see
it more as a new beginning, not
an end. It belongs to the cycle of life
as a new state of being. It is like
moving to a bigger Universe.'

2019   – Extensive mid-career survey *The Soul
                 Trembles,* Mori Art Museum, Tokyo, curated
                 by Mami Kataoka, attracts 660,000
                 visitors, becoming the most visited exhibi-
                 tion by a solo artist in the museum's history.
                 Tours to Busan Museum of Art, South
                 Korea (2019); Taipei Fine Arts Museum,
                 Taiwan and Long Museum, Shanghai,
                 China (both 2021); Queensland Art Gallery
                 of Modern Art (QAGOMA), Brisbane,
                 Australia (2022); Museum MACAN,
                 Jakarta, Indonesia (2022–23), Shenzhen

Art Museum, Shenzhen, China (2023–24);
Le Grand Palais, Paris France (2024–25),
and MAO Museum of Oriental Art,
Turin, Italy (2025).
– Receives the 61st Mainichi Art Award,
hosted by newspaper *Mainichi Shimbun*.

2022   – Participates in major international
exhibitions including *Manifesta 14*
in Pristina, Kosovo; Aichi Triennial,
Japan; Bangkok Art Biennale, Thailand.
– *Invisible Line*, ARoS, Aarhus, Denmark.
– *Letters of Love*, MOCA Jacksonville,
Florida, USA.

2023   – Inaugural artist in newly designed lobby
of the Hammer Museum, Los Angeles,
California, USA.
– *Song Dong x Shiota Chiharu*, Yuelai Art
Museum, Chongqing, China.
– Provides illustrations to accompany
daily serialisation of Yoko Tawada's novel
Praktikantin (The Trainee) in newspaper
Tomiuri Shimbun (see pp. 115–27).

2024   – First large-scale solo exhibition in
her hometown in 16 years, *I to Eye* at
Nakanoshima Museum of Art, Osaka,
Japan, reflects on her experiences
during the global pandemic.

2025   – Awarded the Officer of the Order of Arts
and Letters by the French Ministry
of Culture.
– *Home Less Home*, Institute
of Contemporary Arts, Boston,
Massachusetts, USA.
– *Silent Emptiness*, Red Brick
Art Museum, Beijing, China.

2026   – *Threads of Life*, Hayward Gallery,
London.

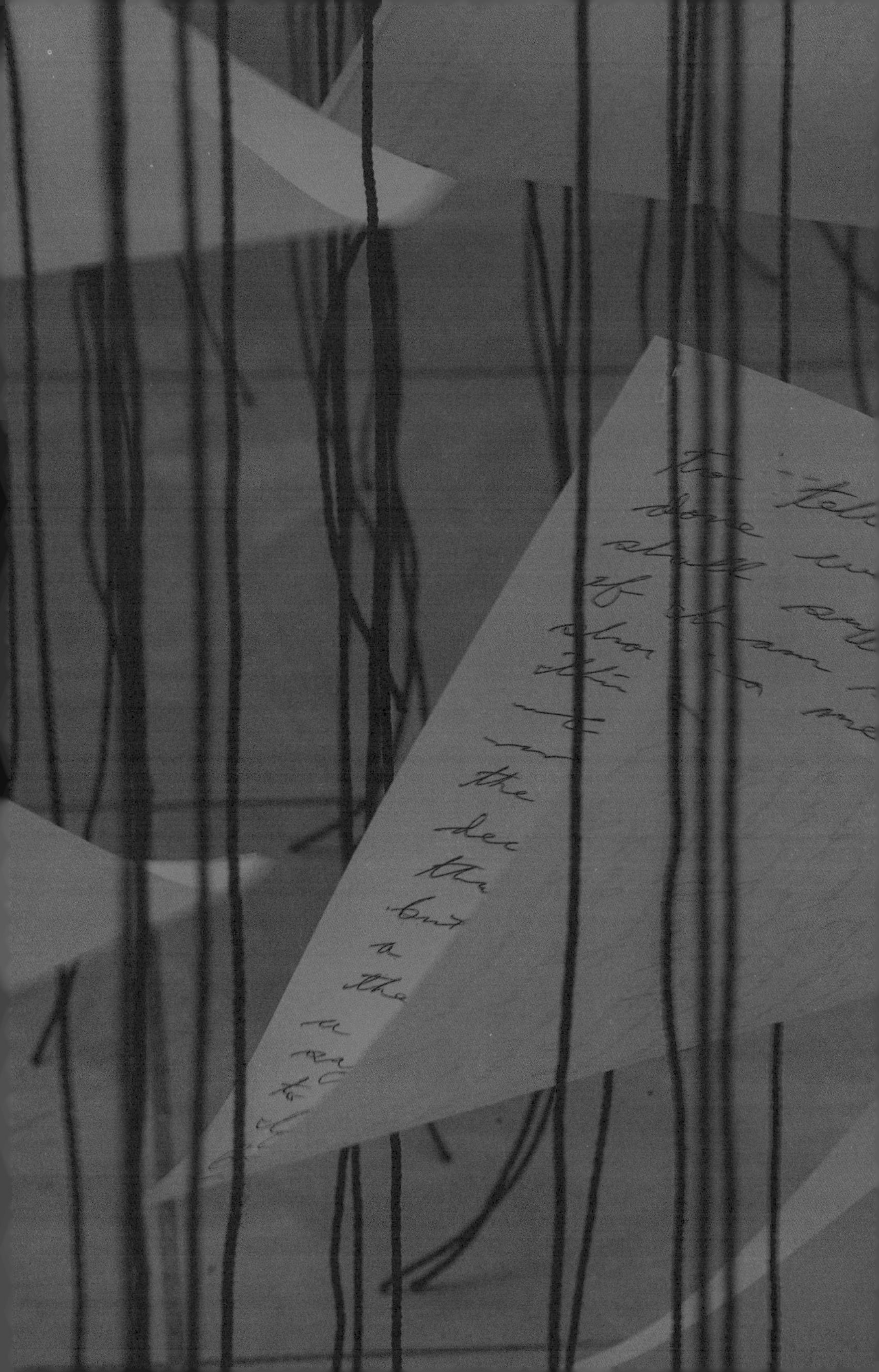

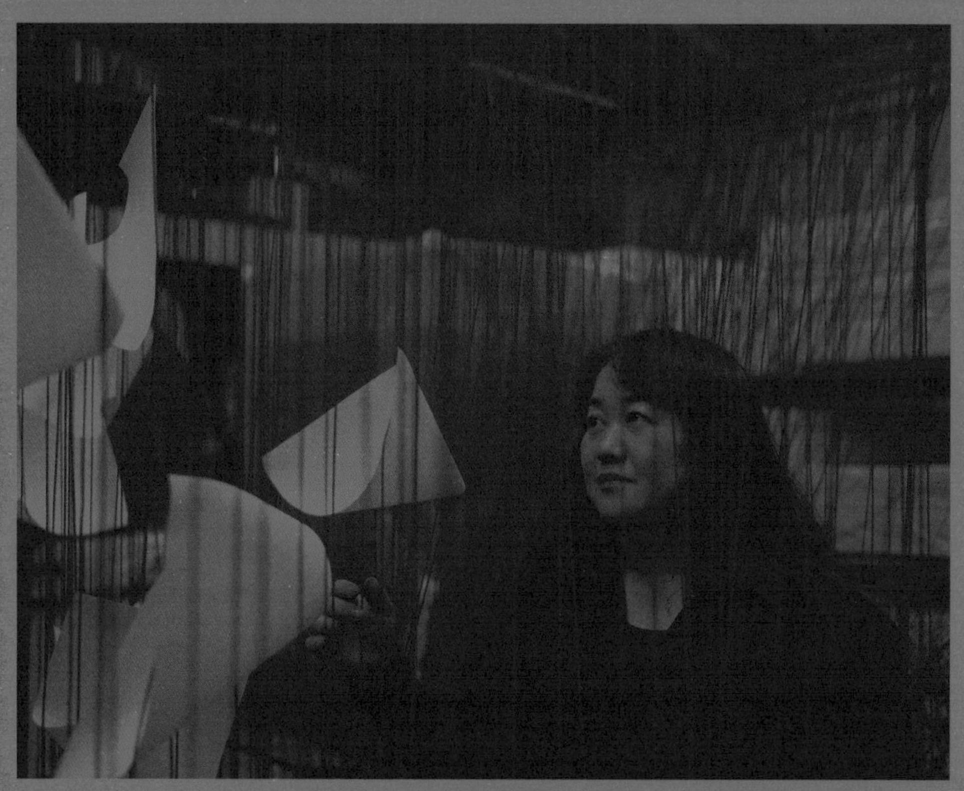

LIST OF WORKS

All works are courtesy of the artist. Dimensions are in centimetres, height before width, unless otherwise stated.

EXHIBITED WORKS

Try and Go Home, 1997
Performance documentation
· pp. 36–37

Wall, 2010
Performance video: colour, sound 16:9
3'39"
· pp. 40–41

Threads of Life, 2025
Wool, door, keys
Dimensions variable

State of Being (Dress), 2025
Metal frame, dress, thread
230 × 180 × 83
· p. 51

Letters of Thanks, 2025
Rope, paper
Dimensions variable

*Drawings for Yoko Tawada's Praktikantin
(The Trainee)*, 2023–24
Water-soluble wax pastel, ink,
thread and collage on paper
460 drawings, each 15 × 19.9
· pp. 115–27

During Sleep, 2025
Wool, beds
Dimensions variable

ILLUSTRATED WORKS

Becoming Painting, 1994
Performance, installation: red enamel paint
The Australian National University School
of Art, Canberra, Australia
· pp. 13, 33, 35

From DNA to DNA, 1994
Mixed media
Graduation exhibition: Kyoto Seika University
Kyoto City Museum of Art, Kyoto Japan
· p. 8

Memory of Skin, 2001
Installation: dresses, dirt, water, showers
Yokohama 2001 – International Triennale of
Contemporary Art
· pp. 38–39

In the Bathroom, 2002
Video stills, series of 4
Solo exhibition, *The Unsettled Soul*
Kunsthalle Praha, Prague,
Czech Republic
· pp. 68–69

During Sleep, 2002
Performance, installation: metal bed,
bedding, black wool
Ujazdowski Castle Centre
for Contemporary Art,
Warsaw, Poland
· p. 70

During Sleep, 2002
Performance, installation:
metal bed, bedding, black wool
Group exhibition: *Another World –
Twelve Bedroom Stories*
Kunstmuseum Luzern, Lucerne,
Switzerland
· pp. 69, 72–73

In Silence, 2007
Installation: burnt grand piano,
burnt chairs, black wool
Kanagawa Prefectural Gallery,
Yokohama, Japan
· p. 29

In Silence, 2008
Performance, installation:
burnt grand piano, burnt chair,
black wool
Solo exhibition: *State of Being*
Kunsthaus Centre d'art Pasquart,
Biel / Bienne, Switzerland
· pp. 80–81

After the Dream, 2009
Installation: dresses, wool
Group exhibition: *Walking in My Mind*
Hayward Gallery, London
· pp. 48–49, 141

Diary, 2025
Installation: mixed media
Solo exhibition: *Two Home Countries*
Japan Society, New York
·   p. 25

Living Inside, 2025
Installation: mixed media
Azkuna Zentroa, Bilbao, Spain
·   p. 101

PHOTOGRAPHIC CREDITS

All works of art by Chiharu Shiota
© 2026 DACS.
All images are courtesy of the artist.

·   Isabella Arthurs and José Huedo:
       pp. 75–76
·   Deim Balázs: pp. 66–67
·   Atelier Chiharu Shiota: pp. 68, 110–11
·   Jeff Eden: pp. 88–91
·   Doug Eng: pp. 93–97
·   Tetsuo Ito: pp. 38–39
·   Fotoagentur Nordlich: pp. 83–86
·   Hayward Gallery, London: pp. 48–49, 141

·   Sunhi Mang: pp. 29, 43, 44, 45,
       47, 52, 54, 55–57, 66–67, 69, 72–73,
       75, 80–81, 99–100, 107–08
·   Roman März: p. 18
·   Kayoko Matsunaga: p. 8
·   Paul Green and Anna Schwartz: p. 79
·   Jonathan Shaw: p. 113
·   Chiharu Shiota: pp. 38–39
·   Ben Stone: pp. 13, 33, 35
·   Go Sugimoto: p. 25
·   Anders Sune Berg: pp. 103–05
·   Roger Wooldridge: pp. 48–49, 141

SOURCES OF QUOTATIONS

Quotations by the artist in the Chronology
are taken from the following sources:

·   Omori, Toshikatsu, 'Contemporary Fine
       Art vol. 12: Correspondence with Shiota
       Chiharu', *Bijustu Techo*, Vol. 66, No. 998,
       Jan. 2014, p. 125 (Japanese)

·   *Chiharu Shiota: The Soul Trembles*
       (Tokyo: Mori Art Museum / Bijutsu
       Shuppan-Sha Co., Ltd.), 2019,
       pp. 278, 282

·   *An Interview with Chiharu Shiota*
       by Andrea Jahn, Kerber Verlag, 2016
       https://www.kerberverlag.com/en
       /buecher/an-interview-with-chiharu
       -shiota-by-andrea-jahn

·   *Chiharu Shiota: Beyond Consciousness*
       (Aix-en-Provence: Edition
       Ville d'Aix-en-Provence), 2024, p. 5

·   *Chiharu Shiota – Milestones: At The Heart*
       of Creations (Paris: Éditions Skira),
       2024, p. 116

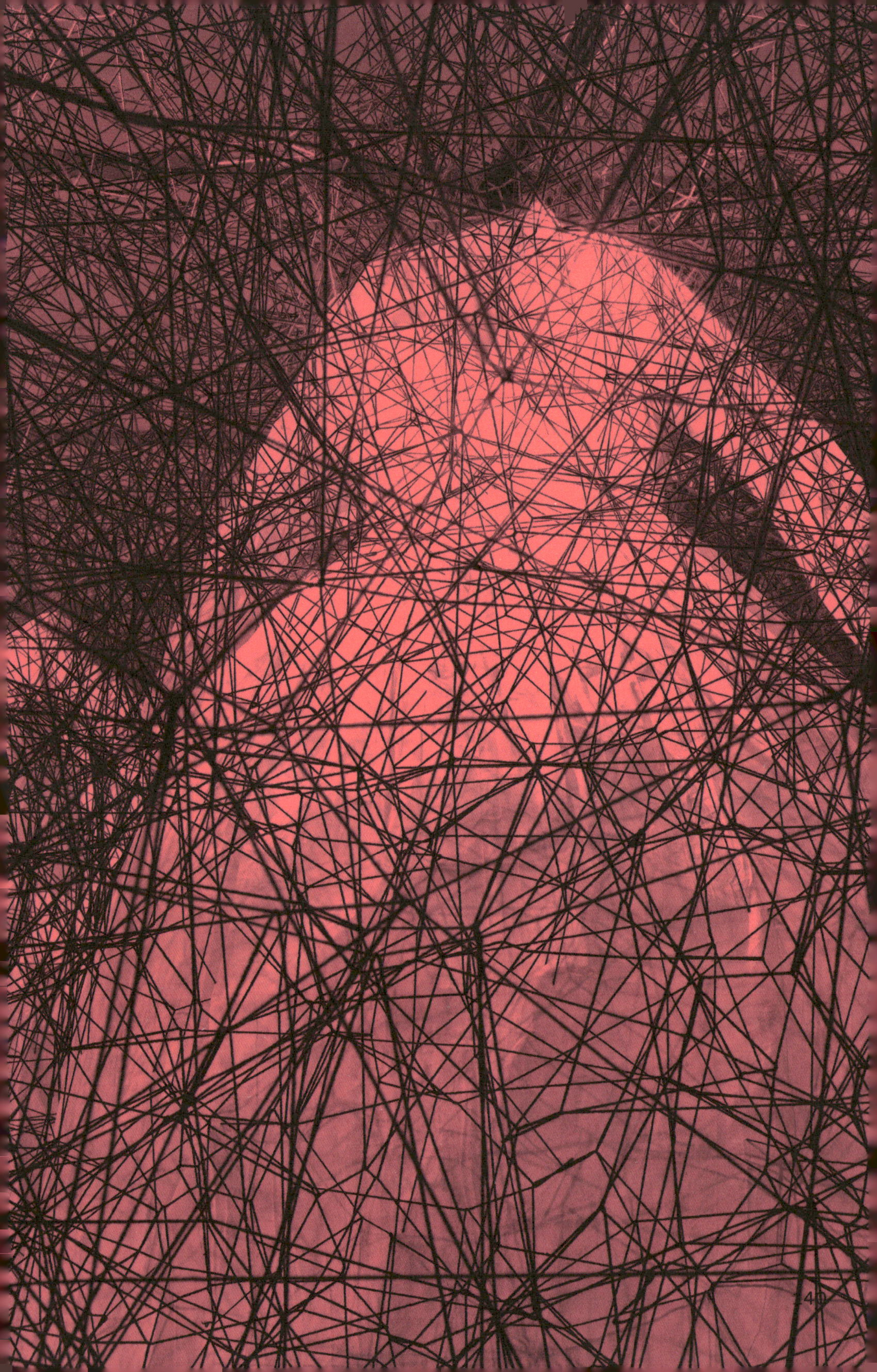

ACKNOWLEDGEMENTS

This exhibition woud not have been possible without the artist and Atelier Chiharu Shiota: Julia Strebelow, Rosalie Pfleger, Tomoko Fujimura, Dahye Jong, Yeosong Kim and Tetsuhiro Uozumi.

Chiharu Shiota: Threads of Life was realised with generous support provided by the Huo Family Foundation and Hiroyuki Maki. We are also grateful for key support from Max and Monique Burger and the TOY family, and Nicola Chu.

EXHIBITION CREDITS

- Yung Ma,
  Senior Curator
- Suzanna Petot and Katie Guggenheim,
  Assistant Curators
- Ananya Jain,
  Curatorial Assistant
- Chris Spear,
  Installation Manager
- Sophie Risdale-Smith,
  Registrar
- Mary Richards,
  Publisher
- Juliane Heynert,
  Senior Installation Manager
- Matt Arthurs, Phil Gardner and Konstantinos Pettas,
  Hayward Installation Technicians
- Kate Sullivan,
  Deputy Director, Visual Arts
- Alison Maun,
  Indemnity Coordinator
- Ellen Duffy,
  Administration and Events Coordinator
- Maria Pena,
  Visual Arts Administrator
- Marcia Ceppo,
  Operations and Logistics Manager
- Jules Denton,
  Operations Administrator
- Nancy Bryan,
  Librarian
- Leonie Warner,
  Senior Visitor Experience Manager
- Kate Ford, Jack Rooney and Malini Stevenson,
  Duty Managers
- Jennifer Ubenyi,
  Curatorial Intern
- Fatima Sheriff,
  Bring Out Potential Placement

We are grateful to all our collaborators across Southbank Centre, without whom this exhibition would not have been possible. In particular, we would like to acknowledge the contributions of our colleagues in Southbank Centre's Creative Learning, Design, Development, Digital, Health and Safety, Marketing, Press and Retail teams.

After the Dream, 2009

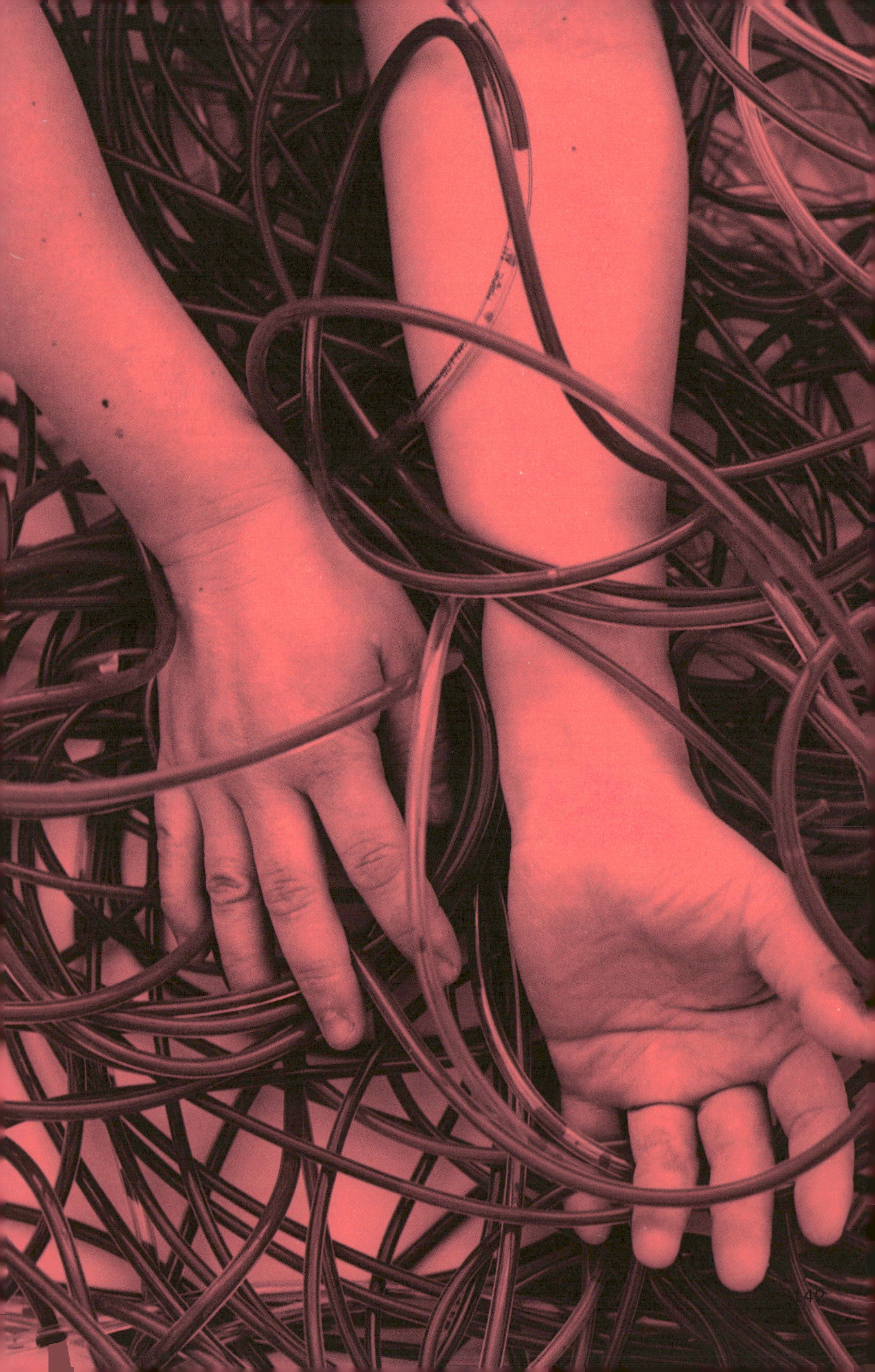

Published on the occasion of the exhibition
Chiharu Shiota: Threads of Life
Hayward Gallery, London
17 February – 3 May 2026

Curated by
Yung Ma
Assistant Curators:
Suzanna Petot and Katie Guggenheim
Curatorial Assistant:
Ananya Jain

Chiharu Shiota: Threads of Life was realised
with generous support provided by the
Huo Family Foundation and Hiroyuki Maki.
We are also grateful for key support from
Max and Monique Burger and the TOY family,
and Nicola Chu.

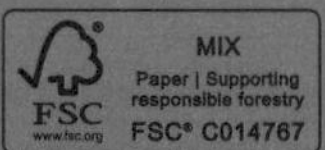

Published in 2026 by
Hayward Gallery Publishing
Southbank Centre
Belvedere Road
London SE1 8XX
www.southbankcentre.co.uk

Hayward Publisher:
Mary Richards
Catalogue designed by
In the shade of a tree
Typefaces
Attila Sans (Kometa Type)
Söhne (Klim Type)
Papers
Arena Bulk Natural 100 gsm
Magno Volume 135 gsm
Wibalin Natural White 120 gsm
Toile du Marais Corail

Printed in Belgium on paper
from sustainable forests

A catalogue record for this book is available
from the British Library

ISBN 978-1-85332-385-0

This catalogue is not intended to be used
for authentication or related purposes.
The Southbank Board Limited accepts
no liability for any errors or omissions
that the catalogue may inadvertently contain.

Distributed in North,
Central and South America by
ARTBOOK | D.A.P.
75 Broad Street, Suite 630
New York, NY 10004
tel: +1 212 627 1999
www.artbook.com

Distributed in the rest of the world by
Thames & Hudson Ltd
6–24 Britannia St
London WC1X 9JD
www.thamesandhudson.com

INTERART S.A.R.L. (GPSR)
19 rue Charles Auray
93 500 Pantin
Paris, France
http://www.interart.fr/
productsafety@thameshudson.co.uk

Cover: *Rain of Memories*, 2016 (detail)
Page 144: *The Key in the Hand*, 2015 (detail)

Notes on Contributors
Yoko Tawada is a Japanese novelist and
poet. For her novel *The Trainee*
(2023–24), serialised in Japan's *Yomiuri*
newspaper, Chiharu Shiota created over
400 watercolour and charcoal drawings,
each stitched with her signature red
thread.

Yung Ma is Senior Curator at the Hayward
Gallery, London. Before joining the
Hayward, he held key curatorial positions
at institutions including the Centre
Pompidou in Paris, where he was Curator
in the Contemporary and Prospective
Creation Department, and the M+
Museum in Hong Kong, where he was
Curator of Visual Art.

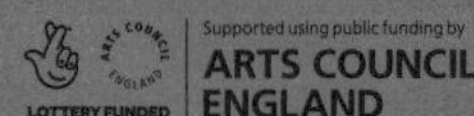

Wall, 2010

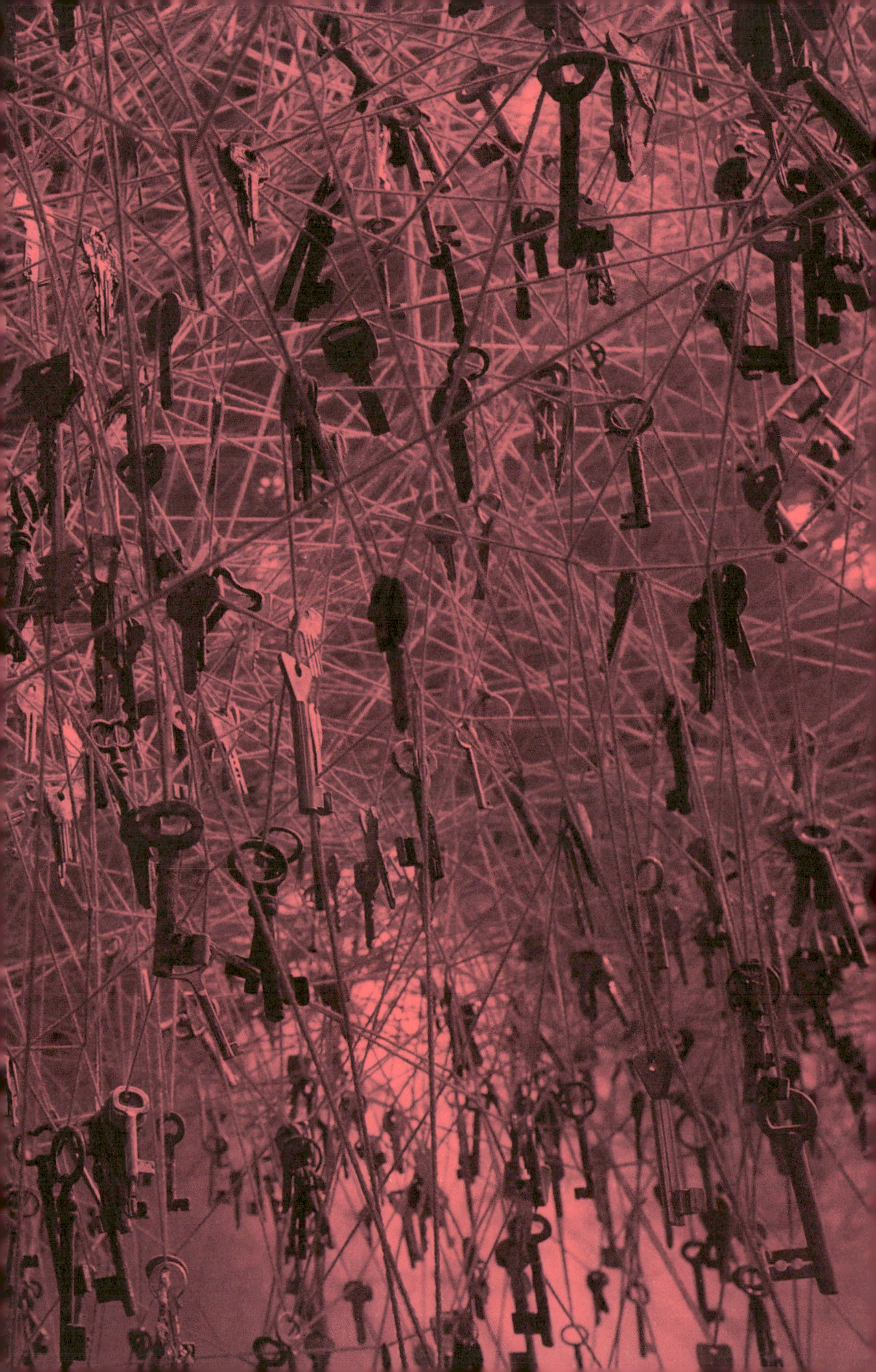